T0339307

The New Despotism

JOHN KEANE

The New Despotism

HARVARD UNIVERSITY PRESS

Cambridge, Massachusetts

London, England

2020

First printing

Library of Congress Cataloging-in-Publication Data

Names: Keane, John, 1949– author.

Title: The new despotism / John Keane.

Description: Cambridge, Massachusetts : Harvard University Press, 2020. |
    Includes bibliographical references and index.

Identifiers: LCCN 2019056411 | ISBN 9780674660069 (cloth)

Subjects: LCSH: Authoritarianism. | Democracy. | Democratic centralism.

Classification: LCC JC480 .K43 2020 | DDC 320.53—dc23

LC record available at https://lccn.loc.gov/2019056411

For George and Alice, always

Contents

The New Despotism

Someone must watch, it is said.
Someone must be there.

—FRANZ KAFKA

Dark Times, Again

Desolation Row

Each age suffers moments of bitter disappointment, and so it was at the beginning of the new century, when hopes faded for that thing everybody called democracy. Citizens with a taste for public affairs had grown gloomy. Opinions differed about why the democracy they had lived and loved for a generation now sleepwalked and stumbled into confusion, toward impotence, or outright irrelevance. The disappointed pinned blame on out-of-touch governments, corrupt politicians, sluggish economies, greedy banks, predatory corporations, and the spread of hate crimes and contempt for the rule of law. Those who stayed optimistic, hoping against hope, supposed the demise of democracy could be reversed and that at some point, helped by a change of government, things would improve. Global surveys showed they were in the minority.[1]

Many more citizens felt dragged down by economic dissatisfaction and anger at political elites, broken promises, social injustices, disorder and decline. As if to prove old Machiavelli's observation that the road to hell is easy, since it is downhill and followed with eyes shut, just as many people simply didn't care. With a shrug of shoulders and wave of hand, they cursed under their breath. Yet amid all the anger, despondency, and muddle during those years, there was one general point of agreement: within states that had been known as democracies, rot and decay had the upper hand. Things were going badly—much worse than anybody had expected.

A measure of the gloom of those years was the way American political scientists—once the trumpeters of good news about the global triumph of democracy, as if it was human destiny—spoke in mournful tones about the fading of the democratic dream. Communism was dead and postcolonial dictators had fallen like flies. Yet the grand march of history no longer appeared to favor democracy. The world in fact faced "more authoritarian momentum and greater democratic instability than at any time in the last several decades," wrote a respected leader in the field.[2] Others talked cheerlessly of an existential crisis of liberal democracy or warned that its slow-motion death caused by extreme wealth inequality, poor health care, mass shootings, and opioid addiction was on the horizon.

Once upon a time, ran the lament, the most powerful democracy, the United States of America, functioned as a "shining city upon a hill" (those were President Ronald Reagan's parting words upon leaving the Oval Office in January 1989). Liberal democracy had done "more to spread peace and prosperity than any other [political system] in the history of humanity." During the 1980s and 1990s, "freedom flourished, markets expanded, civil societies grew, representative institutions strengthened, and democracy became, for the first time in human history, the most common form of government."

But in the United States, as elsewhere in the democratic world, the ideals of popular self-government faced a "gathering global crisis." Democracy found itself on desolation row. There were chal-

THE NEW DESPOTISM

lenges such as "economic stagnation, income inequality, immigration." Disappointment with democracy had become palpable, spearheaded by "working class white voters with limited skills and education, who feel culturally displaced and economically threatened by immigration, globalization, and racial and cultural diversity." More than a few middle-class voters felt the same. The whole dynamic fed support for a new wave of nasty "populism and illiberalism."[3]

Understandably, these trends spooked more than a few people living in the United States, a global empire gripped by a sense of national decline. When peering into the future, a clear majority of its citizens, often more than seven in ten, predicted that the gap between rich and poor in their society would widen, their leaders would fail to solve the country's biggest problems, and their country's global influence would continue to shrink.[4] The trend was not confined to the United States. Practically all political orders called democracy were plagued by institutional dysfunctions, growing social inequality, and public disillusionment. Most were no longer regarded as paragons of probity, fairness, and stability.

It is true that public disaffection with democracy wasn't the whole story. Positive things had happened: they ranged from whistle-blowing and public exposure of corruption by civil society watchdogs to local efforts to build basic-income schemes and protect refugees, migrants, and homeless people. Feminists everywhere contested male-dominated institutions and everyday practices damaged by misogynist double standards. In the name of democracy, a word whose semantic fuzziness kept alive its public appeal, several long-term countertrends managed to survive, including self-government experiments among indigenous peoples, the extension of citizenship rights to children, Finland-style parliamentary scrutiny of the impact of legislation on future generations, and the political enfranchisement of the biosphere. The advances served as reminders that time's arrow does not fly in a straight line and that democracy is marked by braided tempos and multiple rhythms. The countertrends contradicted the prevailing *fracasomania:* the dogmatic belief that the decomposition of democracy was unstoppable and that everything therefore had to be changed because nothing worked any more. The democratic advances certainly handed cheer to sullen observers. Some even used questionable biological metaphors to claim that although democracies have a beginning and an end, it was too early to announce their death. They were only "going through a mid-life crisis."[5]

Despite such reassurances, the sad fact was that in those years of the new century, in a wide range of countries, multiple forces pushed the spirit and substance of democracy toward the cliff's edge. This was certainly true in the field of international relations, where US officials dropped talk of democracy promotion and sided openly with scoundrels worldwide. The cluster of nominally democratic states known as the European Union did much the same by choosing—for instance, at the February 2019 EU–Arab League summit—to suck up to their opponents. "Sometimes you have to dance with whoever's on the dance floor," said the cold-sober Dutch prime minister, Mark Rutte, at another event. His defense of Europe as the "bedrock of freedom, democracy and the rule of law" and his simultaneous call for it to be "streetwise" and "less naive and more realistic" revealed the extent to which Europe had lost both the confidence and the ability to spread the spirit and institutions of power-sharing democracy beyond its borders.[6]

Double standards flourished at home too, as a wide range of democracies failed to deliver on their promises of social equality and good government. Surveys showed that less than a quarter (24 percent) of Latin America's citizens were happy with the way democracy worked in their countries, the lowest figure since polling began. The reasons were not hard to find. More than a third of Argentina's 44 million people lived in shantytown poverty. After 2000, when the shift to multiparty democracy in Mexico had begun, the number of people officially living beneath the poverty line increased to over 50 percent of the population. Fed by a criminal reserve army of the poor, mafia violence grew by alarming proportions. Scores of elected city mayors were assassinated, several hundred journalists were murdered or disappeared, and more than a quarter of a million citizens were robbed of their lives.[7] Indian democracy was similarly gripped by morbid symptoms. It hosted fourteen of the world's most polluted cities. There were more poor people in eight Indian states than in the twenty-six countries of sub-Saharan Africa. India's public hospitals were often death traps. Violence was everywhere: knives, guns, and bombs, wielded by cavalcades of men in cars and on bikes, were often weapons of choice in political turf wars. Studies ranked India as the most dangerous country for women. A high court judge estimated that it would take the Indian judiciary 320 years to clear the backlog of more than 32 million cases.[8]

The citizens of India and other democracies, meanwhile, found themselves confronted by the political dangers and antisocial effects of giant digital media platforms designed to harvest personal data for sale to advertisers and to hook users by spreading hate speech, conspiracy theories, revenge porn, and other pernicious content.[9] The decadence had additional sources.

Almost every democracy felt the truth of the old observation that there are historical moments when "democratic sovereignty" is converted into "a cloak to cover the nakedness of a government that does business for the kept classes."[10] Daily life was scarred by widening gaps between rich and poor and by the emergence of a substantial "precariat" of part-timers and underemployed people in gloomy gig-economy jobs that paid poorly and offered no long-term security.

The toxic trends were fed by deepening public disaffection with the poor leadership skills and mainstream narratives of politicians, the hollowing out of mass-membership political parties, and the poisoning of elections by dark money. Everywhere were signs of the collapse of the cartel party systems that once had served as in-struments for integrating and reconciling social differences. Complaints about empty-headed voters and claims that election rituals were "killing democracy" flourished.[11] The public service bureaucracies of many democracies meanwhile found themselves battered by a "permanent revolution": downsized and damaged by spending cuts, performance-management imperatives, and pres-sures to become unaccountably partisan during the permanent campaigns waged by governments of the day.[12] And there was a growing sense that democracies were becoming less open, more fearful, and more repressive.

Democracies everywhere were gripped by dragnet surveillance, militarized policing, rising rates of incarceration, and state clamp-downs on public assembly. The unending war on terrorism com-pounded the pressures on civil liberties by strengthening the hand of the garrison state. Dawn police raids, red alerts, tear gas and pepper spray, and security checks were bad for democracy. So were drones and helicopters hovering overhead, troops on the streets, gun battles, and the "antiterrorist" siege mentality that settled on civil society.

For many observers, the worldwide resurgence of populism was the knockout blow against democracy. The new populism brought to power elected demagogues spinning webs of confusion, lies, and unhinged talk of conspiracies. Mainstream politics was plagued by "post-truth" carnivals, curbs on media freedom, and disrespect for expertise and public service institutions. There were bitter cultural clashes over racial and religious identity, environmental standards, norms of sexual preference, and the future of family life. And with populism came much talk of "us" and "them," delight at humiliating others, and moves to restore borders and build walls, all backed by a sharpening sense that local institutions, such as parliaments, were being swallowed by cross-border chains of corporate and governmental power wholly unaccountable to citizens and their elected representatives.[13]

Jeremiads

While the forces serving the devils of discontent were many, with plenty lurking deep inside existing democracies, the point gradually dawned on people in those years of the new century that something bigger and more sinister was happening on a global scale. Collective feelings about the larger global picture spawned gloom, oiled by rising concerns about the kind of world order that was now emerging from the collapse of the Soviet Union, European stagnation, disorder in the Arab world, and the return of a belligerent Russia and a self-confident and ambitious China to the global stage.

Today global trends are more transparent. Anxiety about the new global order is replacing haughty talk of the end of history, the once-popular presumption that democracy would indefinitely enjoy a global triumph. Growing numbers of observers now see that this vision, championed by Francis Fukuyama and his supporters, was a fable, a confabulation that misled many people into thinking that the world would become a better place thanks to the spread of American-style liberal democracy. The dying fable is now the target of the longtime critics and outright enemies of democracy. Like vultures pecking at rotting flesh, they are enjoying once-in-a-lifetime feasts of cynicism and outright rejection of power-sharing democracy. "We are being lectured on democracy by everyone," comments Russian president Vladimir Putin bitingly, before adding that "we are seeing the degradation of the idea of democracy in Western society in the political sense of the word."[14]

Turkey's strongman Recep Tayyip Erdoğan speaks in similar prose. "No one can lecture our country about democracy, human rights and freedom," he says. "No Turkish citizen receives ill-treatment due to their ethnic background, the way they dress or their opinion." He adds, "Those who spoke out against Turkey's democracy at every chance possible are now facing their own trials. Now, nobody has the guts to lecture Turkey about democracy." The same self-confident spirit of defiance flows through the speeches of Sheikh Mohammed bin Rashid Al Maktoum, ruler of Dubai and vice president and prime minister of the United Arab Emirates (UAE). Government should be "closer to its people, faster, better, and more responsive," says Al Maktoum, a military man, champion horseman, and poet. Luckily, local forms of nonliberal democracy have been part of the UAE's heritage "since the time of our fathers and forefathers," inherited "with pride and belief in our social, cultural and religious legacy without compromising the rich Arab-Islamic culture."[15]

Minus the religion, the prominent Chinese scholar Su Changhe chips in with similar words. "Western democracy is already showing signs of decay," he writes. "This should put on guard those developing countries still searching for a path to building a political system." Su adds, "We must pull apart the language of Western democracy. To have a truly free spirit and an independent national character, we must first take the idea of democracy promoted by a minority of Western countries and demote it from universal to local." The priority is to steer well clear of the "democracy trap" that produces "social divisions, ethnic antagonism, political strife, endless political instability and weak and feeble governments."[16] China's leading sci-fi writer, Liu Cixin, is more categorical. "If China were to transform into a democracy, it would be hell on earth," he says. The sentiment is repeated in a final part of his best-seller trilogy *Remembrance of Earth's Past*. It describes the catastrophic effects of an invasion of earth by peoples from a distant planet who forcibly intern most of humanity on the Australian continent. "The society of resettled populations transformed in profound ways," he writes. "People realized that, on this crowded, hungry continent, democracy was more terrifying than despotism. Everyone yearned for order and a strong government."[17]

The Specter of Despotism

The jeremiads may well prove to be writing on history's democracy wall, a warning to democrats in the "minority of Western countries" and elsewhere that in these years of the dawning century, the world is gradually being shaped by self-confidently alternative methods of governing people—methods that defy existing politics and government textbooks and represent a fundamental challenge to power-sharing democracy as we have known and experienced it during recent decades. Not since the 1920s and early 1930s, when parliamentary democracy found itself confronted by military dictatorships and aggressive totalitarianism, has a similar convergence of trends happened. Driven by the sudden rise and fall of empires and great powers, the convulsions during that period were often frighteningly dramatic.[18] Today's most obvious threats to democracy—the inner decay and corruption of a declining American empire and the growing global ascendancy of a powerful

China—seem for the moment to be more funereally paced. Or so this book contends.

It aims to do more than make general sense of a major political trend shaping our world. Written in the style of Niccolò Machiavelli's tough-minded classic *The Prince* (1532), this book dives deep into the murky dynamics of power in countries such as Russia, Vietnam, Iran, Tajikistan, China, Brunei, Saudi Arabia, Hungary, and the United Arab Emirates—countries that, though different from each other in all sorts of ways, display common political qualities. The pages that follow may embolden and delight their powerful rulers, who will find more than a few tips about how more effectively to rein in their subjects and win their loyalty.[19] By contrast, the friends of democracy should feel trepidation at what these pages reveal about the cunning and capability of these rulers. For readers who have not visited these countries or know little about them, this book should fascinate, jolt, and disturb, if only because it reveals how many key features of these systems of government are alive and well *inside* our democracies.

The big idea is that the principles and practices of constitutional power-sharing democracies as we have known them for a generation are not threatened only by their outside political rivals. The arrangements of power-sharing democracy can be snuffed out at home, bit by bit, by means of the quiet seductiveness of new forms of power and methods of government found in China, Russia, Saudi Arabia, Singapore, and elsewhere. Amid the present-day confusion and disagreement about global trends, the book proposes that everywhere something sinister is being born of our darkening times: a kind of despotism the world has never before known.

The word "despotism" may be unfamiliar, or it may grind on our senses, causing them to clang shut. But it is the word we need to understand how power-sharing democracies can be choked and killed not just by social disorder, economic breakdown, political conspiracy, and military violence but also by twenty-first-century forms of power that exude a definite fatal attractiveness. Although later pages reveal how this ancient term—despotism—has a complicated and checkered history, and why it has long been out of fashion, it now has a raw and biting pertinence. Past thinkers dismissed "despotism" as an "emotionally charged" word laden with Orientalist prejudice and without "precise meaning."[20] Yet when suitably revised and carefully applied, "despotism" is an indispensable keyword for making sense of the threats to democracy posed by a new type of power with thoroughly twenty-first-century characteristics.

The keyword "despotism" used in this book draws together quite different cases, carefully abstracts from their messy and fluid realities, and knowingly simplifies matters in order to foreground and render intelligible their common features. The word aims to unsettle orthodox taxonomies, old-fashioned ways of ordering things. It urges readers to think in fresh ways, to see the world with new eyes, to arouse different feelings, to pry open unfamiliar horizons of action. It draws attention to the family resemblances of the new despotisms, despite their incongruities.

Yes, Singapore is an older and much more sophisticated species of despotism than Hungary, Belarus, and Vietnam. In Saudi Arabia, consuming, importing, brewing, and selling alcohol are forbidden, whereas for millions of Russians liquor is the fragrant elixir of everyday life. China is a global imperial power in the making; its business, political, and military friends in Pakistan, Laos, and Kazakhstan are happy to tag along. The term "despotism" most definitely has blurred edges. But when used in this book, the word privileges the propinquity rather than the incongruity of things. It concentrates on the urgent problem of making sense of the genus of despotism rather than the lesser task of providing a detailed taxonomy of its many species. The word does not suppose that our planet is square, or that all dogs are Dalmatians. But it does draw a thick red line under states that not only exhibit many features in common but also gang up against their enemies and cooperate with their allies in such matters as trade and investment, diplomacy, intelligence gathering and propaganda, and sales of military equipment.

Using a first-cut definition, we could say that today's despotism is a new type of pseudo-democratic government led by rulers skilled in the arts of manipulating and meddling with people's lives, marshaling their support, and winning their conformity. Despotisms craft top-to-bottom relations of dependency oiled by wealth, money, law, elections, and much media talk of defending "the people" and "the nation" against "domestic subversives" and "foreign enemies." Despotisms are top-down pyramids of power that defy political gravity by nurturing the willing subservience and docility of their subjects.

Those who think the word "despotism" is a synonym for repression and raw force are mistaken. In practice, the rulers of the new despotisms are masters of deception and seduction. They manage— using a combination of slick means, including election victories— to win the loyalty of the ruled, including important sections of the middle classes, skilled and unskilled workers, and the poor. Voluntary servitude is their thing. They even win admirers and friends well beyond the borders of the states they rule.

The new despots of our century have no love of power-sharing democracy. Their passion is power for the sake of power, exercised arbitrarily over others. They are relentless and can be ruthless and vengeful in its pursuit. Yet they are not blindly reckless. They often pay meticulous attention to details, cleverly interfere with people's lives, stand over them, and sometimes bully them into submission. The public support the rulers enjoy is thus surprising, especially when it is considered that despotisms are dominated by "poligarchs": rich government officials and businesspeople who work together to stuff staggering amounts of wealth in their own pockets and inside the family dynasties they control and protect.

These poligarchs are state-protected crony capitalists who practice the dark arts of corruption. They are contemptuous of independent courts—what Erdoğan calls the "juristocracy"—yet they are skilled at using courts to rule to their advantage.[21] Despots know how to employ law to defeat the rule of law. Law is their double-edged weapon, a gentle wand waved in favor of supporters and a sharp sword used against opponents. Despots bolster their rule by using television, radio, newspapers, and social media platforms to spread rumors and fake news, to target their opponents using media-savvy smears (a technique Russians call black public relations, *chernyi piar*). Despots regularly administer doses of fear and targeted violence against dissenters. There are moments when they forcibly disappear their critics. They pick fights with civil society groups they consider to be troublemakers and disturbers of order. Yet their methods are sneaky. Their violence is stocking-masked. The new despotisms are police states with a difference. They use "a less abrasive way of exercising control than actually killing people who disagree."[22]

This doesn't mean that violence has become an outdated weapon in the arsenal of despotic rule. The despots of our age know it still matters. They take to heart Machiavelli's advice that princes must never let their thoughts wander from weapons and war.[23] Military actions by the rulers of Saudi Arabia, the UAE, Turkey, and Russia suggest that the new despotisms—for the sake of their own domestic legitimacy and geopolitical survival—are prone to picking fights, launching wars in their neighborhoods and well beyond. Their war zones are spaces of killing and wounding innocent civilians, arbitrary detention, disappearances, and torture. At home, things are different. These despotisms are much more than old-fashioned military dictatorships, or *piramida* of power with iron fists, as Russians say. So long as they are not openly disobedient, people are left alone by the new despotisms. These are not fascist or pre-fascist regimes based on terror, mass rallies, and torchlight parades. Things generally seem relaxed in their towns and cities. Lovers stroll hand in hand along tree-lined boulevards. Bustling cafes and restaurants prove that pleasure can be innocently naive. Everyone seems constantly to be online. The shopping malls resemble temples packed with stylishly dressed consumers. Tourists sporting cameras and maps gawp at arched porticos, columns, domes, and minarets. They marvel at ornate public squares, lose themselves in narrow alleys, watch pigeons courting in cobbled yards, linger in street markets, and sip local wines in restaurants. Unlike the austere "socialist despotism" of the Soviet era, the new despotisms thrive on hedonism.[24]

In some little-known prescient writings, the eighteenth-century French aristocrat and political thinker Montesquieu warned that modern despotism could grow plump on the bourgeois culture of luxury, egoism, and avarice associated with unregulated market commerce.[25] The new despotisms confirm his warning. They strive to be provident. They draw people in, invite them to submit, offer them the chance to enjoy their own powerlessness. They cajole, engage, and persuade. Nearly 150 years after Friedrich Engels, their aim is to convince subjects to obey necessity and call it freedom. They want their subjects to suppose that things are getting better and bigger. The new despotisms cultivate submission. They produce cowardice. They pose as the frenemy of the people. They have no great need of paramilitaries, street violence, bricks tossed through windows, or early morning visits by the secret police. Seduction, not repression, is their defining quality. In this sense, the despotisms of our time are state-of-the-art forms of tutelary power, a new type of media-saturated political rule that manages to do something many observers thought impossible: they dominate their subjects by winning their calculated support and affection by means of top-down, people-friendly techniques of government.

Here we encounter the new despotisms' strangest and most surprising quality, a feature that is often ignored. Professors mislead us when they say these new despotisms are "non-democratic" systems of "pragmatic authoritarianism" propped up by the material benefits they deliver to their sycophantic subjects.[26] Too many scholars follow Samuel P. Huntington's famous and influential definition: that "authoritarian systems are non-democratic," while in liberal democracies "the principal leaders are chosen at regular intervals through competitive elections in which the bulk of the adult population has the opportunity to participate."[27] In fact, the new despotisms experiment with locally made democratic procedures such as elections, public forums, and anticorruption agencies. They are phantom democracies.[28]

It is wrong to describe the new despotisms as autocracies or as systems of authoritarianism, the supposed opposite of liberal democracy. The new despotisms do all within their power to portray themselves as incarnations of the people. These phantom democracies have a definite effectiveness. That they manage to win the support of those they dominate is striking, and that is why they are a serious alternative to the power-restraining, power-sharing democratic arrangements of the past generation. Although nobody can know this in advance, it is even possible that the new despotisms will carve their legacy on the hearts of their subjects, so that sometime in the future, when despotic regimes are politically defeated and disappear from our planet, their subjects will wallow in admiration for their deceased masters and yearn for times remembered as their most glorious years.

Misconceptions

Described in this shorthand way, the new despotisms of our century are more stable and more attractive than many outsiders suppose. In practice, as the following pages show in detail, the new despotisms show signs of skill and efficiency at governing people. Their resilience stems in part from their recombinant qualities. Recombination breeds strength. By drawing together seeming opposites—plutocracy with talk of "the people," periodic elections with lawlessness and targeted violence, tough media censorship with toleration of digital publics—the new despotisms become earthquake-resistant polities. They fare better than most polities during seismic upheavals.

Their resilience stems from the fact that they learn the arts of ruling under duress. Trial-and-error perfection of the techniques of exercising power over their subjects is their specialty, and a key explanation of their tightening political grip in world affairs. This book offers no grand theory of the forces supporting the new despotism. Why? Simply put, its working precept, supported by many examples, is that the new despotism is the product of multiple overlapping forces that operate in different combinations, in different contexts. The new despotism is not the straightforward result of, say, general historical laws of politics that favor the strong at the expense of the gullible weak, or the political expression of modern capitalism. Monocausal explanations may be "soothing, gratifying" because they offer the explainer a "feeling of power," as Friedrich

Nietzsche said in *Götzen-Dämmerung* (1889).[29] But they hinder awareness of the many drivers of the new despotism, which include historical traditions, economic forces, state power, and the unfinished digital communications revolution. Special emphasis throughout this book is given to what can be called the pragmatics of the new despotism—that is, the ways in which its rise and consolidation are the effect of clever and cunning rulers who learn the skills of managing economic, governmental, and communications resources in order better to win the loyalty of their subordinates.

The big general point here is that the new despotisms are learning how to make the best of power resources ranging from capital markets and technology start-ups to media and public relations services, secret intelligence agencies, and armed force. Despite their vulnerability to internal dysfunctions, external shocks, and chronic public resistance, they display strong signs of long-term durability and metastasis. In a wide range of global settings, these despotisms and their methods are proving to be both effective and attractive. It is a key reason their whip-smart ruling methods are going viral.

Little wonder that journalists and scholars have been flung into confusion about how to name and describe these new structures of power. More than a few observers postpone the task of careful categorization by labeling them "hybrid regimes." This fuzzy phrase means little yet supposes that they are somehow stuck in transition between democracy and nondemocracy. Hence they can be described as unstable mash-ups of power that measure up badly against the only-game-in-town principles of what is usually called liberal democracy.[30] Truth is, though, the new despotisms are not halfway houses to democracy of the kind globally known and valued during the past generation. These despotisms cannot be understood by adding a qualifying prefix or suffix to the word "democracy." They are not quasi- or controlled or partial or restricted democracies. Nor are they defective democracies marked by a shortage of checks and balances. They aren't delegative democracies or illiberal democracies that fail to uphold the liberal ideal of rule of law. Similarly, they aren't semi-authoritarian regimes, semi-dictatorships, or competitive authoritarian regimes in which electoral competition for high office is "real but unfair." As we are going to see, these despotisms are certainly not to be interpreted as the inferior polar opposites of American-style liberal democracy.[31]

The jargon may be crushing, but it is mentioned here to throw into doubt the widespread presumption that the new despotisms are stuck, stalled, or adrift in a twilight zone between democracy and nondemocracy. The presumption makes no sense. It is a big mistake to describe these regimes as in transition to or from democracy. The new despotisms are in fact reactions against the ideals and practical mistakes and failures of power-sharing democracy. They are like parasites, feeding upon democracy's present dysfunctions. As such, they are not to be judged as cases of failed transition.

Nor, for that matter, should they be likened to twentieth-century African and Latin American dictatorships, or seen as the equivalent of past European and Asian totalitarian regimes that geared "the whole of society and the private life of the citizen to the system of political domination."[32] The new despotisms are most definitely not to be categorized, as more than a few observers unfortunately do, using dog-tired words such as "autocracy" and "tyranny." Autocracy, a political system in the hands of a sole ruler with absolute power, does not apply. Nor does tyranny, which according to Socrates is a dangerously unjust type of rule by a strongman consumed by lawless desires directed at the confiscation of others' property "by fraud and force."[33]

The problem with all this language is that it blinds us from seeing with clear eyes that what is happening today—and what might come to be—is not the same as what has passed. The despotisms of our time are something new under the sun. They certainly have roots in the past. But they are something other, something defiantly different from anything our forebears knew.

Let's pause for a moment to gather our thoughts, to prepare for some surprises by focusing on their sources of novelty. Once upon a time, the word "despotism" referred to a confused, half-crazed form of power prone to self-destruction and implosion. Despotism was said to resemble a madhouse built of stacked cards. Montesquieu, whom we'll meet often in these pages, usually thought in this way. Under despotism, he famously remarked in his classic *De l'esprit des lois* (1748), those who rule are reckless: "When the savages of Louisiana want fruit, they cut down the tree and gather the fruit. There you have despotic government." Mutual suspicion and fear among the subject population flourish. Nobody is safe. The lives, liberties, and properties of subjects are always up in the air. They are at the mercy of the frightful maxim that in a despotism "a single person should rule according to his own will and caprice."[34]

In his earlier *Lettres persanes* (1721), Montesquieu expressed similar thoughts. The epistolary work relates the allegory of Persian travelers in France describing life in a Persian seraglio gripped by "horror, darkness, and terror." Despotism—Montesquieu had in mind the monarchy of Louis XIV and Louis XV—is a synonym for cruel, arbitrary power. Its odious laws excuse perfidies and injustices and nurture hunger for unlimited wealth. Its princes love "trophies and victories" and drink to their "sovereign grandeur." They heap favors on "some men without inquiring after their real merit," while "putting to death all who displease them." Despotisms are ruled by scoundrels who are so drunk on power that their singular idea of political harmony is "not citizens who are united but dead bodies buried one next to the other."[35]

The despotisms of our time are not describable in these twisted terms. They are different in that they are certainly not repeats of the totalitarianism of, say, Kim Il-sung's North Korea, or that of 1970s Cambodia, where the mostly invisible, all-powerful ruling clique known as Angkar perfected homicidal radicalism, resulting in the deaths of an estimated 1.7 million people by execution, hunger, disease, and broken hearts. Strictly speaking, despotisms are not barbarous totalitarian regimes in constant motion, forms of single-ruler domination in which nobody is safe, not even the dead.[36]

The new despotisms also aren't to be compared with tin-pot garrison states—for instance, corrupt military-bureaucratic regimes of the kind that plagued the African continent following independence from Europe's colonial powers. Robert Mugabe's Zimbabwe was among the most talked-about examples. His brutal military-bureaucratic regime grew like a bulbous cancer from the armed struggles against British colonialism, encirclement by South African apartheid, and other foreign pressures.[37] With formal independence in 1980 came elections, power scrambles, dirty tactics, and outbreaks of terrible violence, a resource used by the budding dictator to build a state ruled by him alone. Zimbabwe was turned into a dictatorship: a military-bureaucratic state shaped by periodic elections, heavy-handed policing, conscription, and appeals by the leader for sacrifice in defense of the nation against its enemies at home and abroad.

Like most other postcolonial men intoxicated by the liquor of power, Mugabe was a dictator with diction. He spoke the language of democracy, but he always complained that in practice democracy—he meant elections—deludes the opposition into demanding "more than it deserves." And so the well-educated man who spent nearly a dozen years behind bars, who was knighted by Queen Elizabeth, who displayed impeccable English table manners, who loved the music of Cliff Richard, and who detested his former British masters set out to prove that government minus opposition was in practice a good and desirable thing.

Mugabe abolished the position of prime minister and assumed the new office of executive president of Zimbabwe, gaining extra powers in the process. Cocooned in his signature five-ton bulletproof Mercedes and coddled by political friends whom he rewarded with licenses to loot, Mugabe mobilized propaganda and disinformation, kickbacks and dirty tricks, land grabs and gun-backed terror. More than a few of the several million people who voted against him in a heavily disputed election were rewarded with forcible displacement from their homes through Operation Murambatsvina (Drive Out Rubbish). Mugabe's North Korean–trained security force, the Fifth Brigade, supposedly built to "reorient the people," treated dissidents as cockroaches to be crushed. There were mysterious deaths, abductions, and sadistic assassinations of opponents, as well as more than a few episodes of grotesque violence directed against citizens. Zimbabweans were burned alive in buildings and forced to dig their own graves in public executions. The transition to dictatorship also had ruinous effects on the economy. Amid hyperinflation, the size of the economy shrank by nearly half, pushing many citizens toward destitution and reducing life expectancy to the lowest of any country on earth.

All this happened within a bankrupted police state marked by moments of lunacy. The president for life was frighteningly unpredictable and given to violent whims. He would fall asleep in public or blindly read the wrong speeches in parliament. There was a burlesque moment when media minders tried to get their "fit as two fiddles" master off the hook by explaining that even Jesus would have tripped on the same poorly laid ceremonial red carpet. Most worrying were the deadly fits of hubris—for instance, when the dictator vowed to stay on as president as long as "God wished him to remain there." During a state funeral for one of his ministers, he declared himself to be the new Hitler, who stood for "justice for his own people, sovereignty for his people, recognition of the independence of his people, and their right to their resources."[38]

Compared with the shocking violence, brazen stupidity, and dramatic endings of Mugabe-style dictatorships, the new despotisms tend to operate more flexibly, more subtly, more efficiently, and most probably with greater durability. The new despotisms should certainly not be thought of as rigidly "frozen" forms of power, as despotisms used to be seen by commentators such as Karl Marx, who was struck by the "unchangeableness of Asiatic societies."[39] The new despotisms are in fact marked by a measure of dynamic equilibrium. There are indeed times when they hover between order and disorder, but their powers of survival are formidable. They have staying power. Remarkable is their ability to weather crises and to trigger political and economic reforms, sometimes by springing surprises that leave everybody breathless.

A case in point is Saudi Arabia, where in February 2018 Riyadh's Ritz-Carlton was suddenly transformed by Crown Prince Mohammad bin Salman into a gilded prison for hundreds of kidnapped Saudi corporate tycoons and princes accused of harboring undisclosed assets and unpaid taxes. There was real method to his madness: the lightning strike formed part of a wider move by the young prince to tighten his grip on state power by disbanding the royal assembly and weakening the clerical establishment. While advertising himself as a "modernizer" in favor of lifting bans on women driving, pop culture, and entertainment, he imprisoned rivals and thereby added to his control of a wide range of key political posts: deputy prime minister; minister of defense; chairman of the Council of Economic and Development Affairs; chairman of the Council of Political and Security Affairs; boss of Aramco, the state-owned oil and natural gas corporation; and chairman of the newly created Entertainment Commission.[40]

The dozen-plus Eurasian countries and several unrecognized statelets—Transnistria, Abkhazia, Nagorno-Karabakh, South Ossetia—that emerged from the collapse of the Soviet Union similarly show that while there are roller-coaster moments when the new despotisms are plunged into life-threatening disorder, they typically manage to survive the battering, emerging intact and rather stronger than before.[41] Little wonder that their rulers ooze self-confidence. Convinced that the days of pusillanimous Western democracy are numbered, the new despots, puffed up with pride in their own strength, feel sure of their superior achievements and their resilience. Suckled by strange power alliances, bizarre business deals, and breathtaking political compromises, the new despots mock the weaknesses of their opponents.

They also pay attention to and learn from existing democracies and their current dysfunctions. Despots excel at building into their governing structures mechanisms designed to make them more efficient, effective, and legitimate in the eyes of the people they rule. They set out to prove that resilience, the capacity to survive unexpected shocks, is not the monopoly of neoliberal forms of governance, as scholars sometimes suppose.[42]

A full understanding of the sources of their resilience would require an in-depth grasp of their particular histories, which is beyond the scope and aim of this book. But it is worth noting here a few of the numerous factors that generally feed this resilience. For one thing, the new despotisms are energized by their clever harnessing of inherited local customs and old ways of handling power. Singapore's rulers used the Westminster model of colonial government to build a one-party state, and Alexander Lukashenko's Belarus commandeered the intelligence services of the former communist regime. For another, despots cling to power especially tightly because they see no credible or appealing alternative to current arrangements. And they are aided and abetted by foreign friends bearing military, economic, and "soft power" gifts.

But the resilience of the new despotisms stems as well from their striving hard to be smarter, more efficient, and more effective than so-named democracies. Most striking is the ultramodernity of these regimes, their propensity for self-scrutiny, and their experimentation with locally made democratic practices. The way these despotisms are setting up inspection committees and anticorruption units and integrity bodies and harnessing the internet to control but not stifle online activities—the Iranian and Chinese digital strategies are probably the most advanced—should cause us to be vigilant, wary of Montesquieu's principle that despotisms violently dig their own graves. The new despotisms in fact do the opposite. They strive to become learning despotisms—much more sophisticated heirs of the eighteenth-century regimes historians call enlightened despotisms.

The new despots' efforts to master the arts of nimble ruling often prove puzzling to outsiders, especially Western liberals. These democrats display the bad habit of supposing that despotisms cannot last because they are dogged by bullying, incompetence, and cronyism so toxic that they are incapable of reform and therefore vulnerable to collapse under public revolt. The Western liberal habit runs deep and wide. Mention the word "despotism," and many people nowadays spontaneously think of flimsy governments founded on nothing but reckless predation and unsparing violence.

Influential think tanks such as Freedom House implicitly reason in this way when allocating the new despotisms a "democracy rating." Their presumption is that these regimes are weak and vulnerable transitional types of power whose destiny is, or at least should be, American-style liberal democracy. Statements by outside observers and prominent politicians such as former US senator John McCain, who famously remarked that "Russia is a gas station masquerading as a country," reinforce this impression.[43]

This picture of despotism as wild and unstable honky-tonk government is bolstered by mainstream media fascination with bizarre leaders whose reflexes are thought to be damaged by the lust for power. Power does indeed sometimes go to the heads of those who rule, guide, and manage these regimes. The new despotisms produce villainous demagogues who fight for their right not to be right or reasonable. They like to perform the role of demiurges, substitutes for the sorcerers of yesteryear, masters of "social magic," creators of spells and controllers of the material world, redeemers who are backed by the people.[44] They are also tough-talking, pitiless despots such as Erdoğan in Turkey and Lukashenko in Belarus. Despotism features greedy red oligarchs (*hóngsè guǎtóu*) in China; Russian officials who launder their fortunes in London's property market; factory-owning fat cats in Central Asia; and well-dressed petroleum-industry magnates clustered around Brunei's absolute ruler, Sultan Hassanal Bolkiah, now the world's second-longest-reigning monarch.

It is equally true that there are occasions when the new despotisms pass through a looking glass into a surreal world of shouting sheep and talking flowers, white queens and red kings, hares and hatters, an Alice in Wonderland world with queens roaring at contrarians ("Off with their heads!") and kings ordering subjects more than a mile high to quit the court. Think of the moments when Cambodia's one-eyed, stay-forever prime minister, Hun Sen, calls himself the "illustrious prince, great supreme protector, and famed warrior," or when Erdoğan acts like a sultan and bellows that "Turkey's rise will not be obstructed by anyone but God," or when Vladimir Putin plays the role of a superhero who fancies himself as "second only to God," in the words of Mikhail Gorbachev.[45] All three rulers indulge the fantasy of total state power and messianic greatness.

Then think of the drama triggered by Field Marshal Abdel Fattah al-Sisi's announcement that he was relinquishing his military leadership role to run for the presidency of Egypt and save his country. That moment came during the same week that five hundred members of the Muslim Brotherhood were sentenced to death in one day in a kangaroo-court trial presided over by Judge Saeed Elgazar, whose surname means "the butcher."

Or consider surreal figures like the late Saparmurat Niyazov, the infamous Turkmen despot.[46] Elected to the presidency with 98.3 percent of the vote, he went from strength to strength. He declared himself God's prophet on earth. His face stared out from banknotes, coins, and postage stamps. He ordered the construction of a gold-tinted statue of himself that rotated so that it always faced the sun. He regularly ordered his cabinet ministers to take five-mile-long walks. Niyazov banned ballet, opera, and cinemas; banished dogs from the capital, Ashgabat, because of their "unappealing odor"; and published a four-hundred-page guide to the people of Turkmenistan. Passages from this book, the *Ruhnama*, were plastered on mosque walls. He renamed the months of the year (September, the month when he finished writing his magnum opus, became Ruhnama) and banned listening to car radios, which he claimed were being used to camouflage subversive talk by citizens. When a string of weather forecasts proved unreliable, he personally dismissed the country's head meteorologists. His funeral proved no less dramatic. Prior to being buried in a grand tomb in his home-village mosque, Niyazov's body lay in state in the presidential palace, in an open coffin, to be honored by mourners. Many of them were ordinary citizens who wept uncontrollably as they walked by. Some loyal subjects clung desperately to the coffin. A few even injured themselves after collapsing to the ground or fainting from excitement.

Wealth, Money, Power

Patronage

It is easy to chuckle at the absurdities of unrestrained power. Little wonder that some analysts of these regimes describe them as "autocracies." That term entered the English language (from the French *autocratie* and originally Greek *autokráteia*) in the mid-seventeenth century and came to mean a type of government in which one person has uncontrolled or unlimited power over everybody else, leaving them to wallow in their powerlessness and to draw the grumbling conclusion (as the contemporary Russian joke has it) that autocracy is Putin plus a daily diet of three packets of cheap cigarettes and a liter of vodka. Actually, the old term "autocracy" is misleading, and shouldn't be used when probing the new despotisms. As we're about to see, the sobering fact is that quite a few of them show signs of turning themselves into highly resilient "enlightened" despotisms.

Their rulers are arrogant, no doubt. They boast. They peacock. Impeccably plumed with long tails, some fancy themselves as popular leaders walking in the giant footsteps of Moses and Solon, Lycurgus and Cyrus, Philip and Alexander. The new despots like to sidestep institutional rules by exercising their power through trusted and willing vassals and clients. They enjoy triggering uncertainty and confusion that they alone think they know how to resolve. Yet their extravaganzas are not solo performances. Striking is the way the new despotisms survive because they find clever new ways of ensuring that their subjects let them survive. Their resilience is guaranteed by people's willingness to conform, to do nothing to disrupt the regime and its routines, to nurture blind eyes and cloth ears when faced by dysfunctions and injustices. Durable despotisms are systems of voluntary servitude. As Thomas Paine long ago spotted, despotisms turn their subjects into carriers of despotic ideas, ways of speech, and other symbolic practices that serve to lubricate the machinery of arbitrary power.[1]

But how in practice do they manage to do this? What are the magical secrets of success of these smart new despotisms? Many outside observers understandably find the questions difficult to answer. It is safe to say that among the new despotisms' prime sources of success is the way people's daily lives within these political orders are shaped by connections, webs of patronage protected and managed by government, business, religious bodies, and other gatekeeper organizations. Our muse Montesquieu was on to something important by noting, for instance, that all despotisms foster subjects' entanglement in intricate spiders' webs of power. The sway of despots, he pointed out, always requires dependence upon others. Despots thrive by dishing out favors to their dependents. They feed upon the "busy laziness" of diligent sycophants. Despots suppose that their "sovereign grandeur" entitles them to disburse favors to anyone who displays loyalty, regardless of merit, so obsequiousness is rewarded according to the rule that dependents are "made excellent simply by the decision to honor them."[2]

The point is bigger than Montesquieu imagined, bigger than the influential English liberal democrat John Stuart Mill, writing a

THE NEW DESPOTISM

century later, could comprehend when insisting, in a moment of biting sarcasm, that a "good despotism" cultivates to perfection the art of "relaxing and enervating . . . the thoughts, feelings, and energies of the people."[3] From a distance, and even up close, the webs of patronage that hold together these new despotisms are more-or-less invisible to the naked eye of outside observers. They are certainly difficult to measure. Despotic states are marked by the trimmings and trappings of well-governed polities. They appear to be bound by well-defined laws, institutional rules, and agreed-upon procedures; they have presidents and prime ministers, cabinets and parliaments, chief executives, boards of directors and shareholders. There are courts and laws, police, prisons and probation systems. Daily life is saturated with flows of information emitted by television, newspapers, radio, and digital platforms. These kinds of institutions appear to lay down the rules for the power games people play; they enable and set limits upon what individuals and groups can do. Or so it seems.

The lived reality is different: despotisms are in fact political systems energized by connections. The patronage radiates down and out from the top, all the way to the bottom. Those who govern the new despotisms avoid what has been called the tyrant trap. These are not systems of government by one person whose concerns are merely self-interested, concentrated on their own material desires or those of their family and friends. Quite unlike (say) the Central African Republic under Jean-Bédel Bokassa, or Rafael Trujillo's Dominican Republic, or Haiti in the grip of the Duvaliers, the new despotisms are not examples of what has been called "sultanism," discretionary governments run by interfering and whimsical megalomaniacs.

The new despotisms also cannot be defined as tyrannies, at least not in the exact sense that the ancient Greek historian Thucydides described the generations of tyrants that arose in Greece and its Italian tributaries in the seventh and sixth centuries BCE. These tyrants of the Hellenic cities, he wrote, were obsessed with "the security of their persons, and the aggrandizement of themselves and their families."[4] The definition offers one clue as to why the despotisms of our age are different: today, those who rule do not rule alone. It is a mistake to see these regimes as tyrannies gripped by tyrants inebriated by absolute power. Journalists commonly say that Vladimir Putin, Xi Jinping, and Recip Tayyip Erdoğan are autocrats and dictators, but the truth is that the despots of our age are not old-fashioned pharaohs. The belief that they alone are in charge of state affairs is a delusion, for they are always surrounded and pushed and pulled by clusters of well-organized associates and potential rivals who exert influence and control over their masters. Little wonder that leaders often lament privately how they yearn to lead normal lives of their own choosing; or that if the despot-in-chief is deposed, a basic continuity of sorts prevails. Things carry on, sometimes in their name, despite talk of "handovers" and "transitions" and "new eras."[5] Despots know the dangers of self-aggrandizement. That's why they give some part of themselves away, as it were, by becoming dedicated practitioners of patronage: huge favors, sums of money, and other resources such as jobs and access to contracts are disbursed through the political order with the help of semiofficial fixers and project managers (Russians call them *kuratory*, or curators).

The tight links between Hungary's Viktor Orbán (known locally as the "Viktator") and the mayor of his hometown, Lőrinc Mészáros, are platinum-plated symbols of this top-down favoritism. Over little more than a decade, Mészáros, a friend of Orbán's from primary school, went from being a pipefitter on welfare to the fifth-richest oligarch in the country. His business portfolio

　　　　　　　　　　　　THE NEW DESPOTISM

extends from construction, agriculture, and mineral water production to hotels and golf clubs. His vocal opponent in the 2014 municipal elections died in circumstances that remain mysterious. Mészáros attributed his rise to wealth and fame to "the good Lord, good luck, and the person of Viktor Orbán."[6]

Close connections at the top count, but they don't stop there. If we had a computed tomography (CT) scanner large enough to examine the way things work in the new despotisms, we would see that connections run through the whole body politic. At all levels, in everyday life as much as in the fields of formal law, governmental administration, and business enterprises, cultivated connections to well-placed others really do matter. Unlike twentieth-century totalitarian systems, which cultivated "the atomisation and isolation of the individual," rendering people "more easily manipulable" by destroying civil society associations and replacing them with "huge and undifferentiated mass organizations," the new despotisms thrive on privatized connections.[7] Contacts, bargaining, deals, kickbacks, favors, and gifts both of money and in kind are a common currency of power.

Many institutions, including government bureaucracies, parliaments, and the courts, are captured by these networks of patronage. Universities are no exception; in Oman, reports an observer, "intellectuals are employed by the university, they read books and at 14:30 they go back home and sleep. The government forbids them to carry out interviews and investigations. And in exchange they earn their salaries without any problem."[8] Patronage decides appointments to office and access to privileges. It enables people to get their hands on goods and services that are needed or in short supply. Under conditions of despotism, formal rules and informal practices are mixed together. And those who govern from the pinnacles of state power dispense government resources to win the loyalty of their client subjects. They treat their official positions as personal prebends, wellsprings of material benefits for themselves, their current supporters, and future potential allies.

Much the same disbursement of patronage happens in the middle and at the bottom of the political hierarchy, where individuals, households, and groups depend upon the informal connections that pervade everyday life. With the help of these connections, people solve problems that formal rules and institutions manifestly fail to address. The upshot is that under conditions of despotism, the functional importance of patron-client connections, as they are technically called, casts doubt on the old social science idea that webs of patronage (clientelism) are a vestige of political underdevelopment, a traditional form of getting things done that modernization and modernity will sweep away. The new despotisms show otherwise: these ultramodern regimes prove that patron-client bonds and ties are neither things that belong to the past nor symptoms of economic and political backwardness. Patron-client connections have a deep functional importance in people's lives. They transform everybody into beggars of others' gifts. Goods, services, and money are exchanged among subjects operating within nested power arrangements that are developed and ultimately protected by the political rulers of the system.

Despotisms are systems of patron-client connections. Such a sentence may feel unfriendly, but these are the words needed to make sense of a basic fact of life under conditions of despotism. Matters such as securing a government contract, finding a job, winning promotion, enrolling a child in a prominent school, arranging a quick passport renewal, or dodging an overdue tax payment are typically taken care of by intermediaries, go-betweens, small men, big men, and other assorted fixers and power brokers. They help bail out people in sticky situations. In Uzbekistan there is reportedly widespread reliance on friends, acquaintances, and other networked contacts (called *tanish-bilish*) when drivers are pulled over by a traffic police officer. The drivers' first move, typically, is to make a phone call to someone they claim to be prominent. If merely being seen to place the call doesn't work, they hand the phone to the police officer. If that fails to yield results, more phone calls are made, or a bribe is offered directly to the officer.[9]

The dynamic of *tanish-bilish* illustrates the way that favors are typically arranged and dispensed within the mesh of connections that run from top to bottom and from side to side throughout the structures of power framed by despotic states. The point is that who gets how much, when, and how in life is heavily determined, though not by officials following strict bureaucratic rules (pedantocracy, as John Stuart Mill called it). Nor is the distribution of life's goods primarily decided through open market competition, or by educational merit and achievement, or by shows of hands and secret ballots in public meetings. Things happen because of whom you know, by means of informal personal connections—what Russians call *blat* and in China are called *guanxi*. In Turkey, these connections are known as *torpil* or *destek* or *arka*, in Vietnam *móc ngoặc*, and in Cambodia *khsae* ("strings"), while in Arabic the preferred word for them is *wasta* (jokingly known as the sexually transmitted disease of the Arab world).

It's important to understand that patron-client connections are not to be confused with friendship, charity, or bonding by open and unforced consent. While favors are often arranged by friends and are sometimes infused with charitable qualities, such as helping friends build their house, their basic logic is different. Patron-client bonds are exercises in mutual back-scratching: someone requests, another person offers, and a deal is struck such that something is given or gets done in return for compensation; in the end (runs the logic), all parties benefit. Patron-client connections are power games whose logic seems eminently democratic: everybody in the system, from top to bottom, is involved in daily navigations through the reefs and islands and archipelagos of connections, favors, setbacks, failures, and successes. These navigations are always complicated by official rules and regulations, but the fact is that people inside these despotisms spend a great deal of time bending and breaking those rules, figuring out clever ways of getting stuff and making sure things happen.

Under these conditions, nothing can be taken for granted; outcomes are often uncertain. Despotism might even be defined as a peculiar type of power that intensifies people's uncertainty about how they lead their lives and how they can best get what they want. Like the fabled labyrinth built by Daedalus for King Minos of Crete, connections fling everybody and everything into a state of suspension. Just one thing is certain: everybody knows that everybody knows that this is how things happen and why, so it seems, things have to be this way and can't be otherwise.

The point is that connections make the world of despotism go around. In a strange way, their pervasiveness lends them a measure of acceptance and legitimacy. They have a perversely egalitarian feel, in that all actors are equally entangled in behind-the-scenes ways of doing things on a daily basis. What could be more fair-minded than the working formula "I offer you something; when you accept, both of us benefit"? The formula implies that "we're all in this together," that there is equal opportunity to extract favors and to make things happen. Its sense of equivalence is reinforced by the fact that everybody's entanglement within these sticky webs of influence functions as an antidote to corrosive feelings of isolation, loneliness, and uprootedness. In matters ranging from buying food, finding a job, and renting an apartment through purchasing theater tickets, avoiding army conscription, and arranging a funeral, patron-client connections really count. They are talking points; and there are moments, in quiet corners or over a meal, when connections are the butt of rollicking jokes—for instance, about individuals who sleep or drink or lie their way to the top, or second-rate characters who become famous for being famous. But connections are normally serious business. They draw everybody together, into a cat's cradle of power. In the game of life, all the players are gripped by the sense that they are entangled in a much bigger world of links, tie-ins, and attachments.

This shared sense of interdependence doesn't automatically make things easy for the subjects of despotism. Attachments dirty lives and reputations; nobody is innocent. Each soul is implicated in nested circles of soiled solidarity. However, strange as it may seem, connections also offer a sort of comfort: they provide the reassuring daily reminder that everyone is in the same boat. Yet inside the belly of the new despotisms, reality is less forgiving. Life can be stressful. It can be dangerous. And there are times when the world of connections resembles pure unreality. Everybody is forced to drink from the waters of incertitude: it feels as if the political order is riddled with ambiguity. People easily lose their bearings. Daily existence is a maze of locked doors, tall hurdles, and high barriers. Much time and energy has to be expended squeezing through loopholes, scraping under fences, scaling walls. Under these trying conditions, staying positive is imperative: when the boat hits the bridge, Chinese people say, there's still a river (*chuán dào qiáo tóu zì rán zhí*). There are ways through and around, but avoiding the game altogether is impossible. In this sense, everybody must be on guard. Connections are synonyms for complications, annoying traps, and worrying troubles. That's why everyone is forced to practice the art of what Arabs call *shaatir* and Russians call *pochuya*: sussing out situations.

A complicating factor is that connections among patrons and clients breed corruption. If by corruption is meant illegal or extralegal transfers of money and other resources in exchange for favors, then not only does despotism promote corruption, but corruption feeds despotism. To put things this way may seem tautological, but within the new despotisms getting things done usually involves rewarding people who really matter in any given situation: friends, neighbors, acquaintances, journalists, bureaucrats, legislators, judges, opinion pollsters, celebrities, gangsters, and businesspeople.

Iran's Mohammad Rasoulof captures the point in his bitingly revealing film *A Man of Integrity* (2017). Everybody behaves at every point as if they are courtesans of power. From top to bottom, everybody in the system is corrupt. There are willing sellers and willing buyers everywhere. Ethical numbness flourishes.[10] It's normal to be unconcerned about the plight of others who are not family and close friends. Nobody gives a shit. In order to live and to thrive, everybody is drawn into gluey webs of lived lies from an early age. In Iran, a country full of kind and courteous people, young children learn to swear that their fathers do not have a basement booze cellar; teenagers fib about their spent virginity; during fasting months, shopkeepers allow friends and customers to drink, smoke, and eat as usual in their back rooms. The lines between loyalty and betrayal, religiosity and profanity, honor and disgrace are gossamer fine. Under conditions of the new despotism, it is as if everybody lives the proverb in Sa'adi Shirazi's landmark of Persian literature, *The Rose Garden* (1258): "Better the lie that keeps the peace than the truth that disrupts."[11] Evils fueled by little fibs consequently spring up everywhere. What seems like an innocent rule—

everybody should give each other this, both of us take that, and each of us benefits from giving this and receiving that—has the perverse effect of promoting double-dealing and duplicity, lying and cheating, callousness and outright sadism. Hence the shrewd moral conclusion of Rasoulof's protagonist: "You are the suppressed," he says, "or you have to join the suppressor to survive."

Decadent dynamics of this kind are most pronounced within the connections that flourish in the shadowy criminal worlds of despotism. Naked to the invisible eye and unrecorded by official government statistics, these hidden zones of connections are proof that unchecked power can be dangerous. Payments for the sale of government offices and to seal large business transactions, commissions for arranging procurement deals with government agencies, and transfers of funds from state budgets are examples of kickbacks that operate as a system of negotiated bribery. The payments are rarely isolated, one-off deals. They happen within an organized meshwork of bribery and extortion run by money- and power-hungry entrepreneurs and government poligarchs. Such operators are typically backed by subcontractors and suppliers, stooges, sidekicks, and other corruption brokers who do the routine but sometimes unpleasant work of bridging gaps, fixing or unfixing deals, recovering debts, and providing protection against other criminals.[12] Sometimes these underground networks attract the attention of government regulators, prosecutors, judges, and police. But rather than dismantle the networks, or even merely turn a blind eye to such organized bribery, they provide it with protective "roofs" (what Russians call krysha). They benefit like parasites from what is in effect a shadowy mafia state within a state. An example of how things work is the soccer stadium and academy complex built and operated using government funds, tax breaks, and protection money on the private family estate of Hungarian prime minister Viktor Orbán (an ardent football fan) in his home village, Felcsút.[13]

Life within this murky world of wheeling and dealing is oiled by more than personalized kickbacks. Organized extortion, prostitution, drug running, and protection rackets are usually part of the game. A strange but striking feature of this dark universe of criminal power is that it comes wrapped in local versions of *omertà*, the mafia code of silence. Things are decided behind closed doors and kept camouflaged. Connections require what Russians call "understanding" *(poniatiia):* everybody is expected to follow the informal rules of the game. Just as early modern mafia networks refused to tolerate the "private thief," the new despotisms are not describable in terms of a life-and-death struggle of each against all.[14] Rather, the shadowy connections have a kinship-like quality about them. Those who question or transgress the rules of political kinship become vulnerable to verbal threats, blackmail, even acts of physical violence. Well aware that they are taking risks and supping with the devil, they prepare for the worst—they look for escape routes, ways of exfiltration, ratlines. In a world of parasites and thieves, winners can take all, and servility has its limits. Things can end badly. Gang wars are possible. So is bloodless liquidation. And murder happens.

Plutocrats

Within this rough reality of organized bribery, some players are evidently much more equal than others. Opportunities and outcomes are unevenly distributed, and structured by chains of command. Mighty are those who manage to position themselves as patrons lording over their clients. Under conditions of despotism, everybody knows that the cards are stacked in favor of the powerful, the organized upper world of big shots. Government leaders, business oligarchs, high-level bureaucrats and their advisors, and senior army and police officers enjoy great privileges. Oligarch capture by state actors is reinforced by state capture by oligarchs. The upshot is that patron-client relations are not just mutually beneficial relationships of exchange but asymmetries of predatory power.

In Hungary, the Orbán government cultivates a nouveau riche, a privileged "bureaucratic new middle class" who offer political fidelity in exchange for beneficial tax exemptions, business opportunities, and good jobs.[15] In the nearby Republic of North Macedonia, where facilitation payments and gifts are strictly prohibited under the country's Law on Prevention of Corruption, businesses regularly pay bribes to get things done: to cut through red tape, win favorable legal rulings, obtain construction permits and government procurement contracts, pay for police protection, and shake off customs restrictions and state-imposed operational delays.[16] The slick moves by the Erdoğan government to destroy opponents and transfer assets to political allies, using various state agencies, are equally exemplary of a much broader trend in which the new despotisms cultivate selective access to key resources, such as money, schooling opportunities, reputations, jobs, business deals, thugs, and guns. The point is those who enjoy access within the tangle of patrons, subpatrons, and brokers both desire and functionally require the subordination of clients. It follows that more than a few people find themselves marginalized, their life chances reduced to a low level or even zero.

The despotisms of our age are vertically arranged pyramids of privilege and systems of injustice. Russians call it the *sistema,* and it has its own rules: get even with your enemies, get rich, and then make it legal. The saying serves as a reminder that just a few people determine the fates of the rest. Despotisms are twenty-first-century iterations of what the ancients called chrysocracy, government by and for the rich. In the language of our time, we could say that the new despotisms are plutocracies, governing arrangements mixed with concentrations of private capital, wealth, and income. These top-down regimes follow to the letter Chinese leader Deng Xiaoping's famous first principle: "Let some people get rich first." Actually, they amend and extend the rule, so as to justify a permanent wealth-based rule greased by the desire for material gain. "Let those who have grown rich keep their wealth" runs the mantra of those skilled at using the machinery of the state to nurture their private business interests. "Let we the rich rule. The first must be first, for we are the source of our country's wealth, power, greatness, and pride." Cambodia's despot-in-chief Hun Sen, who fancies himself as a man of merit *(neak mean bon),* pushes things further, urging his subjects to "make the bosses rich" because if "a country has no millionaires where can the poor get their money from?"[17]

This mentality of plutocracy feeds a wide range of practices that work to the systematic advantage of the wealthy. It keeps them at the top of life's pile. Secret deals based on access to insider information, the bending and exploitation of ambiguous laws and legal loopholes, and the bribing and manipulating of rump legislatures and judiciaries and state bureaucracies are among their favorite tactics. Tax evasion and money-laundering schemes, embezzlement of state funds, and graft and kickback arrangements on government contracts are equally attractive. The net effect of all these arrangements, as former Putin advisor Andrei Illarionov famously pointed out, is a political system that privatizes profits and nationalizes costs. Wits build on the point by saying that all this collective fiddling at the top means that, in effect, the rich enjoy a form of socialism while at the bottom the people are forced to practice the ways of dog-eat-dog capitalism.

The tomfoolery makes one thing clear: when it comes to matters of wealth and power under conditions of despotism, there's no level playing field, only the rapacious accumulation of wealth and profits in the hands of plutocrats, rich oligarchs known as bosses, mafia, or clans who are always intimately linked to those who govern. Extreme cases of the resulting collaborative predation are often found on the fringes of the world of despotism, as in Cambodia, where a pact among the local ruling elites is guided by "Hunsenomics": a strange potion of shameless patronage mixed with enforced evictions, foreign capital investment, elite philanthropy, impunity-fueled violence, and large-scale forms of rapacious privatization. In the name of peace, order, sovereignty, free markets, and economic growth, some 45 percent of the country's landmass was sold off in quick time by the Cambodian People's Party government led by strongman Hun Sen, who enjoyed the backing of fat cats like Keat Kolney—a politically connected businesswoman renowned for hoodwinking villagers into parting with their land to make way for rubber plantations and honored officially as an *oknha* (tycoon) for her "contributions to society"—and Teng Bunma, the billionaire entrepreneur and suspected drug trader who, in a fit of rage, shot out the tire of a grounded airliner in a dispute over lost luggage and at gunpoint forced an airline crew to delay takeoff until his late-arriving plutocrat friends were onboard.[18]

Despotisms elsewhere feature more measured figures like Sultan Qaboos in Oman. In this gas-and-oil regime, he was flanked by a circle of leading Muscat families and large companies, like the Khimji Ramdas group, who are routine beneficiaries of state infrastructure projects and the licensing of overseas companies such as Fujitsu, Pizza Hut, and Philip Morris.[19] Despotisms like Singapore have more than their fair share of "three-comma club" members (those whose net worth is figured at $1 billion or more)—figures such as Philip Ng Chee Tat, CEO of the Far East Organization and a real estate baron. There are local moneybags characters known as Chuppies (Chinese yuppies) and HNWIs (high-net-worth individuals), figures that featured in the film *Crazy Rich Asians* (2018), based on Kevin Kwan's best-selling novel of the same title. Despotisms provide room for characters such as Turkey's Alp Gurkan, CEO of the Soma Holding Company, a coal tycoon linked directly to the ruling party's election tactic of handing out free coal to voters. Gurkan symbolizes Turkey's grimy underbelly of corrupt links between business tycoons and officials in the Erdoğan government, relationships punctuated by lavish champagne dinners, carefully vetted marriages, luxury holidays in secluded locations, and access to the right people in power.

Iran has its plutocrats too. There is pious Sayyed Mojtaba Hosseini Khamenei, the rich second son of Ali Khamenei, the supreme leader, who himself presides over Setad, a business juggernaut worth tens of billions of dollars, with stakes in telecommunications, oil, finance, birth control products, and even ostrich farming. And there is Asadollah Asgaroladi, a tycoon whose massive fortune was made through investments in real estate, Chinese retail banks, health care, and exports of agricultural produce such as pistachios, spices, and dried fruit. He was helped by a 1990s trade license deal (supported by the Iranian Ministry of Commerce, at the time run by his brother Habibollah Asgaroladi) that enabled him to buy large quantities of US dollars at a heavily discounted rate and then sell them on at an estimated 300 percent profit.

Last but not least there's Hassanal Bolkiah, the sultan of Brunei, whose lifestyle of splendor seems materially insatiable. His residential palace, the largest in the world, reportedly contains more than 250 bathrooms, five swimming pools, a mosque, and an air-conditioned stable for 200 ponies. He is the proud owner of fancy hotels, private jets (among them an Airbus A340 fitted with a conference room), and a collection of five thousand luxury cars, including a custom-built, gold-plated Rolls-Royce.

These minted characters are part of a much wider picture. Under conditions of despotism, vast private fortunes are made, unmade, and remade. It's true things sometimes go wrong for entirely local reasons, as when inner-circle oligarchs fall afoul of the ruling structures and end up in serious legal trouble or behind bars. That was the fate of Chu Hao, Vietnam's former technology vice minister turned publisher, who was found guilty of publishing books out of step with the party line. And Russian oil oligarch Mikhail Borisovich Khodorkovsky, once the wealthiest man in Russia, was charged with fraud, sent to prison, pardoned after an international outcry, and forced to live in exile in Switzerland. These oligarchs may even find themselves on death row, the fate in 2014 of Iran's richest man, Mahafarid Amir Khosravi, for alleged "corruption on earth," embezzlement of state funds, money laundering, and bribery.

There are also moments when word gets out that the ruling oligarchs are badly divided, and the titans bicker and quarrel openly. Life at the top then becomes a zero-sum struggle. Their bitter spats and wranglings are made public. Jokes, rumors, and harsh words against the regime soon irrupt and go viral on social media. As the drama unfolds, great surprises often happen. A prominent political oligarch steps forward to call for more "freedom" and "democracy." This is music to the ears of the street crowds. Foreign journalists flock to the country like hungry birds to a harvest. Their briefings, often superficial, speak of "openings," "political breakdown," "revolution," and a possible "transition to democracy." Confusion, panic, and excitement spread. The mice begin openly to rebel against the cat. Regime change seems just around the corner. But then—as happened during the so-called Snow Revolution protests against electoral corruption in Moscow in 2011 and the bread riots that erupted in Iran in late 2017—the pandemonium fades. The crumbling castle is repaired. Order is restored. Police dressed in riot gear take care of business: swooping down onto their prey, they clear the streets, breaking limbs and cracking heads. Intense behind-the-scenes political jockeying yields a new compromise among the big power players. The rich oligarchs get real and come to their senses, resembling the sick drunkards from the parable by the eighteenth-century Polish writer Ignacy Krasicki, who were forced temporarily to give up drink so they could carry on drinking.[20] The oligarchs' political noses tell them that preservation of the ruling order is their number-one priority. This necessitates high-level losers: political barons who suffer demotion, in extremis a prime minister or president forced to resign. The amputations help the body politic recover, in reshaped form. The governing arrangements are rescued by a realignment of forces. The political rulers, business oligarchs, and their faceless allies within the various state ministries are bound together anew. The local despotism survives, but on a different and more durable footing. What looked like the end of the despotism turns out to be its dynamic renewal.

State Capitalism

The capacity of rich plutocrats to retain their grip in these exceptional situations is remarkable, and it shows just how misleading is the commonplace saying that money makes the world of the new despotisms go round. In fact, these despotisms are labyrinthine systems of government in which *politics* is always the deciding factor. Within these systems—which in reality are a strange new

THE NEW DESPOTISM

species of capitalism, a type of economy that morphs humans into buyable and sellable commodities—markets are hardly free or competitive. To speak in the language of economists, competition is typically impure. True, there are pockets of purer unregulated capitalism in the form of market competition, such as among local traders. Despotisms are dual economies. That means that at the peripheries of economic life there is space for small- and medium-sized enterprises, for instance open markets in taxis, restaurants, street food (Vietnam's famous *buôn bán* and *chợ cóc* spring to mind), agriculture, and tourism; bazaar, souk, and (in Kazakhstan) *baraholka* merchants selling brightly colored clothing, gold and silver jewelry, electrical equipment, and antiques inside settings shaped by arches and winding alleyways, fast-food cafes and places of worship. Under conditions of despotism, this kind of petty capitalism is supported and often encouraged, yet small businesses are generally marginal and parasitic upon the wider political economy that is best described as a new kind of state capitalism.[21]

What does this phrase mean? Simply put, the new despotisms are big-business states. They are a novel brand of capitalism that in practice blurs the boundaries between market and state, between economy and politics. Under conditions of state capitalism, the means of investment, production, and exchange are heavily controlled by state officials, who are themselves closely connected with big-business circles. Despotisms are heavily regulated regimes of accumulation. High-ranking officials sit on the boards of large state-run and private companies. Business oligarchs bribe state officials in order to do business, making these officials de facto participants in the management process, almost always to the detriment of uncorrupted corporate governance. Government officials help run state-owned companies for private gain, amassing enormous wealth, although they do what they can to conceal their riches from the public in order to maintain the illusion that they are on some level public servants. Government officials and private business tycoons dine at the same tables and enjoy strategic power positions together in sovereign wealth fund management schemes (state-controlled investment portfolios), state-owned enterprises, and privately owned corporations operating in such fields as the production of carbon- and solar-based energy, military weapons and equipment, and telecommunications.

The state is meanwhile the champion of economic growth and the principal distributor of both its fruits and its environmental consequences. It is the reliable buddy of big business. While bitter tensions sometimes erupt when state officials are tempted to squeeze private companies, so violating the principle of what the Chinese call "co-management by state-owned enterprises and private firms" *(gōng sī hé yíng)*, government generally refrains from issuing decrees covering who should produce what, when, and how. There are moments, as in the live-streamed retrial of the oligarch Gu Chujun by the Shenzhen Supreme People's Court, when the state even strives hard to be seen as the legal defender of property rights.[22] The point is that the state provides the broad functional framework of the big-business environment—for instance, through the provision of cheap loans, as in Russia, where giant state banks such as Sberbank, VTB, VEB, and Gazprombank control more than half of the country's banking assets.[23] State banking loans are in effect subsidies for companies and whole industries, granting them a competitive edge. Government also places heavy restrictions on outside investment and pressures foreign companies to share locally their technologies and production methods. The state is heavily involved in local and global stock markets and generally promotes global investment and trade. It extracts taxes from the population, decides where to allocate or reinvest profits, and negotiates international loans, remittances, and various forms of foreign aid.

Note that, within the new despotisms, government-controlled companies are strategically important players, and leading businesses must be on good terms with powerful politicians and officials. Despotisms are not states that have been kidnapped by business but the converse: such states, armed with "a stick" (Vladimir Putin), specialize in what Russian analysts call business capture. Despotisms make property rights thoroughly conditional upon political favors. That means there is no independent business community, no bourgeoisie in the sense described and analyzed by Karl Marx and other European political economists. Business and government are mingled and mashed together. Note as well that the new despotisms are not closed economies, as in the former Soviet Union, where within an imperial setting the state owned and controlled the means of investment, production, and exchange and defended the whole political economy against outside capitalist forces. The new despotisms do not practice autarky in this sense. Their heavily regulated systems of state capitalism do discriminate against foreign investment in certain locally sensitive fields, such as telecommunications and the handling of big data, but they are comparatively open to the world. They actively participate in regional and global markets, and many of their "national champions"— companies like Russia's Gazprom, the chief provider of natural gas to the European Union, or Vietnam's military-run, state-owned telecommunications giant Viettel, which does business on three continents under the slogan "Say it your way"—are competitive on a global scale.

The entanglement of business and government under conditions of despotism drives home the point that capitalism in despotic form is a power system that cares less for public good and much more for private gain. Despotism is wealth-powered rule lubricated by the desire for material gain. Little wonder that wealth and income patterns are so skewed in favor of the rich. Defined by lopsided patterns of property ownership, wealth, and income, the new despotisms are in effect wealth creation and protection rackets for the privileged. Inequality, as measured by the Gini coefficient, runs high (although official figures are typically unreliable because of incomplete and doctored data). The rich care first and foremost about manipulating the machinery of the state and doing deals that serve the growth of their business interests and their wealth holdings. The wheeling and dealing are for the most part hidden from the public eye. They go on behind closed doors, with investigative journalists nowhere to be seen.

The rich hide behind tall walls and gated communities. They mix within narrow social circles. They have the mentality of slave owners: their self-esteem rests upon the degradation of others. Sure that the elite must remain few in number, they wrap themselves in upbeat talk of the national interest and national solidarity. They speak of the need to respect the law and of protection from foreign enemies. The plutocrats talk hypocritically of divine inspiration and make allusions to climbing Jacob's ladder to heaven; they yammer on about the need for anti-imperialism or ethnic mobilization, and there's lots of post-truth talk of the need for benevolence and "serving the people." In China, officials peddle words and phrases such as "socialism," "harmonious society," "ancient Chinese civilization," and the "China dream." There's abundant talk of the "people" and "democracy." But none of this stylized language bears much relationship to the harsher reality in which institutions, connections, and everyday life are marked by great gaps between the rich and the rest.

Cutthroat struggles for political and economic advantage are commonplace. Rent-seeking, dark money corruption, and cronyism are normal, especially at the summits of governmental power.[24] In countries such as Tajikistan and Kazakhstan, despots live parasitically off the earnings and profits of state capitalist enterprises. They stash huge sums of cash in offshore accounts; Kazakh tax dodgers have deposited outside the country an estimated $138 billion in individual assets, more than four times the country's estimated state revenues.[25] Price, profit, and tax considerations are of little concern to them; all they care about is feathering their nests with riches extracted and stolen using all possible means.

The details reveal a more general pattern whereby despots' first priority is to manipulate the machinery of the state to serve their own financial interests. Private business interests do the same: their aim is to sidle up to the governing institutions in order better to extract resources and profits from their state patrons. Consider the case of China, where each week, on average, two new billionaires are minted, thanks to a combination of rapid urbanization, productivity growth, leveraged new technologies, and the growth of financial services, retail, and health care industries. In 2017 the number of Chinese billionaires reached 373, one-fifth of the world's total.[26] China has now overtaken the United States as the country where wealth is created at the fastest rate. Given these trends, it is not surprising that many of the three thousand Party-appointed members of China's National People's Congress are filthy rich by both Chinese and global standards. Despite the talk of socialism, the fifty richest delegates are collectively sixty times wealthier than the fifty richest members of the US Congress. The combined net worth of these Chinese delegates is estimated at $463.8 billion, more than the annual economic output of Austria.[27]

Wealthy oligarchs like Aleksey Mordashov (co-owner of the world's largest tourism company, TUI Group) and Leonid Mikhelson (a natural gas and petrochemical tycoon) similarly enjoy political prominence in Russia, where the executive arm of the state, the dominant force in the whole political order, jealously protects the interests of big business and guards itself against challenges from independent-minded judges, voters, and journalists.[28] While the regime selectively displays some market economy features, it allows these to operate only to the extent that they benefit, or do not harm, a ruling group that is corrupt to the bone. In power-sharing constitutional democracies that enjoy a robustly independent judiciary, the ruling group would be subject to criminal prosecution, with hefty fines or imprisonment. Yet in Russia, as well as in countries such as Saudi Arabia and Iran, wealthy oligarchs escape these elements of monitory democracy. The plutocrats are serial tax dodgers. They steal taxation revenues, practice large-scale graft and kickbacks on major contracts, use insider information, engage in influence peddling, and manipulate ambiguous laws and pliant courts.

These particular countries are no exception to the general rule that the new despotisms are larcenous states, more or less. Their founding often involved brazen theft and brutality, as for instance during the collapse of the Soviet Union, when the breakdown of law and order, the freeing of prices, and wealth-grabbing through privatization suddenly produced a new class of hyperrich oligarchs. In the space of just a few years, the size of the Russian economy shrank by half. A decade into the transition away from totalitarian rule, amid top-level talk of "rule by the people" *(narodovlastie)*, organized criminality controlled an estimated 25 percent of Russia's gross national income.[29] Thuggery, kidnappings, protection rackets, and hit-squad murders (the cheapest way to deal with business opponents) flourished. More than half of the oligarchs who acquired their status during the postcommunist years under Boris Yeltsin lost their wealth or their lives. Yet the number of billionaires tripled. Half of the country's wealth was expropriated by 10 percent of the population. The lives of millions of citizens were badly damaged. Some lost their entire life savings, and their shirts and skirts, in just a matter of weeks. On the streets of Moscow, not surprisingly, the disgruntled reportedly denounced privatization as "grab-it-ization" *(prikhvatizatsiya)* and understandably cursed democracy as "shitocracy" *(dermokratizatsiya)*.[30]

Vassals

Concentrated wealth in the hands of poligarchs is a defining feature of the despotisms, which is why, to put things bluntly, these systems of power specialize in dishing out harms, if by harmful acts we mean the transference to the ruled of the corruption that the rulers bear in themselves. Their machineries of government are stacked heavily in favor of private splendor and the protection of plutocrats, who in effect take the rest of the population for a ride. There are despotisms, Qatar and Saudi Arabia for instance, where a big majority of subjects are migrant workers who are typically treated as indentured wage slaves in what are in effect systems of brown apartheid. Yet it is a mistake to think of the new despotisms as large-scale brazen stealing machines. They are not tin-pot kleptocracies or "gangster states" that enable a few rich people and their families to operate an "organized crime ring masquerading as a state" that robs the rest of the population blind.[31]

They have a kleptocratic quality, certainly, but despotisms learn to operate in more subtle ways, in effect by concealing their larcenous features through crafty statecraft. An important way they do this is by adopting measures designed to imbue the bulk of the population with the vague feeling that over time their standards of living are improving. State sovereign wealth schemes backed by substantial reserves of hard currency and gold are among the favored strategies. So are state infrastructure projects of the kind promoted in Putin's Russia, which in recent years built stadiums for the 2018 World Cup, constructed a new ring road around Moscow, and modernized the Trans-Siberian and Baikal-Amur railways. These projects are not just investment and wealth-generation schemes. They have propaganda value for the regime. Guided by the principle that the subjects of power need to be calmed, reassured, persuaded, and politically seduced through managed communication, these schemes suppose that reality is not given, but made. That means in practice that public consent must be engineered by presenting the wealth funds and their linked infrastructure projects in the most favorable light. Old Machiavelli warned that a ruthless prince must do everything to avoid stirring up popular resistance by "interfering with the property of his citizens and subjects or with their women." Clever princes surprise their subjects with gifts. "Nothing causes a prince to be so much esteemed as great enterprises and giving proof of prowess," he noted.[32] Impressing their subjects with breathtaking gifts is exactly what the new despotisms do.

Despotic power wants to be seen as munificent. It purports to give, not take; to reward, rather than to rob. The Kazakh government's construction from scratch of a brand-new capital city, Nur-Sultan, exemplifies this gifting. The city features flashy grand signature buildings that are monuments to riches and repression: a glass pyramid, towering apartments, a Disney version of the US White House, a finance ministry shaped like a US dollar bill, and a vaselike tower with a ball on top that the president apparently designed on the back of a napkin during a state dinner. There's also the Norman Foster–designed Khan Shatyr shopping center; housed inside the world's largest marquee, it features a temperature-controlled artificial beach with sand imported from the Maldives. Exemplary as well is the Saudi government's effort to stem the decline of petroleum revenues by adopting a much-publicized reform blueprint known as Vision 2030, backed by a showpiece $2 trillion Public Investment Fund. Planned to be twice the size of Norway's sovereign wealth fund, currently the world's largest, the Saudi fund includes the assets of the giant state-owned oil firm Aramco and private equity funds generated through global partnerships with robotics and artificial intelligence companies such as Japan's Softbank and giant US health care and real estate equity firms such as Blackstone. The Public Investment Fund has something for everyone. In the desert sands of the country's northwest, the state is erecting a $500 billion city called Neom that is designed to be a carbon-neutral innovation hub for engineering, science, and technology firms. The fund has launched an entertainment investment company to oversee the development of a massive theme park outside the capital, Riyadh, and to incubate companies that cater to the needs and wants of Saudi youth. The Public Investment Fund is backing small and medium-sized businesses, setting up real estate companies to build new hotels at the holy pilgrimage sites in Mecca and Medina, and carving out new beachfront resorts and artificial island retreats in the Red Sea, where women can dress, move, and mingle among fellow subjects more freely than elsewhere in the kingdom.

Government-provided handouts and welfare programs are also among the favored strategies of despots. These are not to be understood as welfare state measures cross-linked to guaranteed democratic entitlements and rights of citizens, as applied during the brief Keynesian welfare state capitalism of the mid-twentieth century in countries such as Britain, Germany, and Canada.[33] Rather, these handouts and programs have a vassalage quality, resembling the medieval European practice of lords handing out benefice in exchange for their subjects' loyalty. Once upon a time, perquisites functioned to strengthen the bonds of servitude between rulers and ruled. Those who governed paid special attention to the ruled in order to turn them into followers. Allegiance of subjects to the system was everything. Satisfying them was imperative. In the much-changed circumstances of the twenty-first century, despots are well aware that their subjects are capable of restlessness and disloyalty. The allegiance of the powerless must be bought using a range of welfare measures designed to guarantee that the vassal subjects serve their lords in return for *honores* and *beneficia,* as they were called during the early medieval period.

In those times, there were ceremonies known as *commendatio* in which bareheaded and unarmed vassals knelt respectfully before their lords, clasped their hands to signal their unconditional submission, then extended their hands toward the lord. The master reciprocated by grasping the hands of their vassals, thus affirming through an act of homage (in Latin it was called the *immixtio manuum* and in German the *Handgang*) that lord and vassal had entered into a sacred relationship of mutual dependency at once protective and possessive.

The despotisms of our age dispense with such ornate rituals, but their preoccupation with vassalage and the loyalty of their vassal subjects is strikingly similar. Surplus government revenues generated by agriculture, mining, and energy exports certainly come in handy in dampening opposition and transforming people into subjects, subordinates, and servants. Loyalty is purchased. An example is the way the Arab uprisings during 2011 prompted the despotisms of the region to bump up welfare payments in an effort to calm nerves and head off social resistance.[34] The Saudi monarchy nearly doubled state spending by investing a whopping $130 billion in salary increases for state officials, job-creation schemes, a minimum wage for Saudi workers, and infrastructure development projects. Public employees and military personnel in Qatar received generous pay and benefit increases. The government of Jordan kept food and fuel prices low while boosting public salaries and job creation. Kuwait's regime, under Sheikh al-Sabah, granted each citizen a lump-sum payment of $3,500 along with free foodstuffs for a year. With the help of the United States, the despotisms rallied to the side of their endangered neighbors. In Bahrain, where a major social uprising in fact took place, grievances linked to joblessness and inequality were countered by the Saudi-led Gulf Cooperation Council with military intervention followed by a $20 billion aid package to Bahrain and Oman that looked rather like a regional Marshall Plan in support of despotism, not democracy.

The vassalage is practiced by other despotisms on a more permanent basis. The government of Singapore regularly issues cash payments such as GST Vouchers, lump-sum bonuses to civil servants, and baby-bonus payouts. In Russia, the lives of an estimated 50 percent of the population are primarily dependent on direct or indirect payments provided by the regime. State expenditure in Oman is around 30 percent of GDP, among the highest rates in the world. Vast oil rents have been splurged on schools, health centers, asphalted roads, and special one-time payments, such as increased social security family allowances and raises in basic salaries for state employees.

The People's Republic of China is perhaps the most developed case of popular dependency on government. State provision of public goods and services is a defining feature of daily life under one-party rule. There are huge social and regional inequalities in what the state provides (average pension payments for a retired state employee are around fifty times greater than for an elderly rural dweller), and education spending favors urban elites. Large-scale measures such as health care and protection for the unemployed fail to alter the fact that the country is a species of state capitalism that feeds local billionaires. And yet the rulers of China plausibly lay claim to important social achievements, such as the massive expansion of higher education and the lifting since the 1980s of perhaps 200–300 million people above the poverty line (given China's share of our planet's population, that achievement accounts for three-quarters of the global reduction of extreme poverty during the past four decades). Less well known are the efforts by the central government to consolidate social policy provisions that first appeared in piecemeal fashion during early reforms under Deng Xiaoping. Major recent innovations include the adoption of a single national pension plan for urban areas, improving rural health care coverage, standardizing unemployment insurance, the introduction of trilingual education policies in some ethnic-minority regions, equalizing social welfare spending across provinces, and HIV / AIDS awareness programs. Official statistics show that state spending on health care, education, and pensions increased from 6.3 percent of GDP in 2007 to 11.6 percent in 2016—faster than spending on policing and military programs.[35]

The social reforms have reinforced the Party state's deep involvement in economic life, to the point where the state / economy distinction makes little or no sense. Statistics are notoriously unreliable—official data in China is often "man-made" and "for reference only," Premier Li Keqiang confessed with a smile over dinner with the United States ambassador—but available figures suggest that the Chinese government extracts through taxation a minimum of 25 to 30 percent of GDP.[36] The high-tax regime is succored by revenue extracted from the profits of state-owned enterprises, land transactions, social insurance payments, and party and union membership dues. Social spending is also covered by revenues generated from household savings, which run at the highest rate in the world and are heavily taxed (at a rate of around 20 percent) when deposited in banks. Local governments, meanwhile, borrow heavily to pay for local social services; they also extract levies and fees from land sales, development projects, and other schemes. The combined effect is that in the name of "socialism," "development," and "democracy," nearly two-thirds of GDP is consumed by the Chinese state, "second to none in its extraction and taxation."[37]

Middle Classes

The lavish megaprojects and welfare schemes hosted by the new despotisms help us understand why they are not to be thought of as tin-pot plutocracies that rob their dependents blind. These are state capitalist systems well aware that capitalism cannot survive unless its losers feel included. Fashionable talk of kleptocracy is doubtful for another reason: the most stable despotisms nurture a sizable middle class that usually lends its loyal support to the political order. We could say that despotism specializes in promoting *embourgeoisement,* and it often does so with important local and cross-border effects. These middle classes live in interconnected cities such as Guangzhou, Shanghai, Bandar Seri Begawan, Moscow, Budapest, Ho Chi Minh City, Singapore, and Dubai, where they can be seen rubbing shoulders in airport lounges, fancy hotels, and shops. They are usually educated to at least the secondary level and enjoy the use of credit cards (on Huawei phones, if they are Chinese). They own or rent a house or comfortable apartment, and they have some spare cash to spend on themselves and their family.

When measured by Marxist standards, they are a motley crew. They are hardly a class at all. They comprise salaried and self-employed people, including medical doctors, small business entrepreneurs, journalists, academics, executives of nongovernmental organizations (NGOs), administrators, and functionaries in state and private bureaucracies. The middle classes of the new despotisms usually constitute only a minority of the population (around 15 percent in Vietnam, 20 percent in Russia, 40 percent in Turkey), but they have a definite public visibility and they are certainly a political force to be reckoned with. Who exactly belongs in the category of the middle class is of course a matter of wrangling among scholars and statisticians. Putting a firm figure on the definition (such as a $5,000 annual income) makes little sense, if only because of great variations in the standard of middle-class living among despotisms. The Hungarian middle classes live more comfortably than, say, their counterparts in Vietnam and Uzbekistan. Other experts therefore say it is better to define middle classes as people who in matters of consumption find themselves between the 20th and 80th percentiles of the population, or whose per capita income stands between 0.75 and 1.25 times that of other people. This makes more sense, since what must be remembered is that being middle-class is a felt disposition. Middle classes sense that they live somewhere in the middle of the hierarchy of power, wealth, and status. They hold certain attitudes and values in common, intermingle and intermarry, and feel that ultimately their lives are wedged between the rich and the poor of their society.

Classic discussions of the middle class typically underscore its good sense and moderation. Aristotle thought those who owned "a moderate and adequate property" would be "most ready to listen to reason." The middle class would be the "steadiest element" and "least eager for change" within any given city-based polity. Self-government "is attainable in those states where there is a large middle class," he added.[38] His observation underpinned confident claims by later observers that the middle classes usually opt for self-government of the people. "No bourgeoisie, no democracy" runs a famous formulation. The same idea has featured in historians' descriptions of classic (European) middle-class bourgeois virtues, which were said to be centered on such norms as work, private property, thrift, religious commitment, patriarchal family life, public respectability, and disciplined order. Bourgeois culture also emphasized the importance of education, music and literature, table manners, titles and dress, and representative government.[39]

The Atlantic-region middle classes were bulwarks of power-sharing democracy, and they remain so, according to some current-day observers. They acknowledge that these middle classes are sometimes tempted to "align themselves with authoritarian rulers who promise stability and property rights protection." Yet more usual and striking is their support for legal rules and institutions that guard their property, civil rights and daily lives from predatory government. Finding themselves in the social middle inclines them to moderation and balance. That is why they like the rotation of representatives and governments by the pendulum swings offered by free and fair elections. Especially when their numbers are large, and they command substantial public influence and respect, "a broad middle-class" is "extremely helpful" in sustaining "liberal democracy." The conclusion: "Middle-class societies, as opposed to societies with a middle class, are the bedrock of democracy."[40] Or so runs the argument.

It turns out the middle classes of the new despotisms defy modern social science predictions. Their education, occupations, and assets incline them to be loyal to the system; they show few signs of wanting to walk in the footsteps of the independent-minded, property-owning citizens of the early modern period. Why? How do these middle classes think? What is their philosophy of life?

Generalizations are hazardous. Minimally, one thing is clear: these middling classes don't have a common life philosophy. Fickle pragmatists, they are skilled at navigating mazes of connections. They value elasticity when handling the unexpected. They're good at mental acrobatics and at practical writhing and wriggling. They scale walls, unlock doors, and open windows of opportunity. The middle classes have few scruples. Their ranks contain more than a few pedants, hairsplitters, and hard-boiled skeptics. They can also be hardheaded; they are prone to feel their reality is the only reality that counts. They can be "simple-minded avoiders of complexity," but this disposition is both a product and a support of despotism, not a "*natural* variation in human 'political character'" that is "largely heritable and relatively immutable."[41] And the middle classes are opportunists. When they speak about being middle-class, they say it is less about actual wealth and more a mindset that believes in education, hard work, personal resolve, and (of course) whom you know. Sometimes their willful ignorance about things begets a sense of innocence. They scoff at the privileges of the rich and kick down at the poor, who fail, they say, because they lack guts and gumption sufficient to change their lives.

These middle classes are self-employed, run small businesses, and hold down professional jobs. They dream of a lifestyle where things are comfortable—where, as the Turks say, their salt is dry *(tuzu kuru)*. In reality they earn enough to live comfortably, not extravagantly, and they expect their children to do well in life. In families with children, both parents usually work and their hours are typically long, which means they rely on relatives or hire domestic help such as a housecleaner and cook. Pressed for time, they still manage to squeeze annual vacations into their busy schedules. They have access to reasonable medical care, and they own a car or two or a scooter. They enjoy good dinners with friends and family. They are not especially religious, though they find Buddhism, Christianity, Islam, and other forms of spirituality congenial. Their consumption of alcohol and drugs isn't unknown. It would be unfair to dub them "philistines" (as Hannah Arendt said of the broken-down bourgeoisie of totalitarian regimes) marked by nothing more than "single-minded devotion to matters of family and career."[42]

These middle classes yearn for a good and better life. They want it to be fulfilling and fun. Yet they often complain, though with a wry sense of humor. They are the first to laugh at the old joke that when optimists say a bottle is half full and pessimists think it is half empty, the middle classes conclude the bottle is fully empty. Their humor and cynicism are not to be underestimated, nor is their melancholia. In conversation, their pulses often seem unexcited by pros and cons. They sometimes feel jaded, especially when gripped by the feeling that they're on their own; and there are times when they express their irritability about the world because it feels as though the whole system is so rigged that the best thing to do is get on with their own lives.

When it comes to democracy, the fickleness of these middle classes is remarkable. Indulging private life, skilled at creating sanctuaries for themselves and their families and friends, happy in the hives of their homes, they watch what they say and to whom. Life under conditions of despotism is a constant masquerade. Keeping silent about personal convictions is part of the chess game of existence. There are moments when they applaud their leaders, as if they really believe in the whole system. They sometimes complain about excessive state meddling in their lives, yet they admit that their daily lives are heavily dependent on state policies, regulations, and edicts. They are often the first to defend state-enforced law and order. They say they like democracy but in the next breath they curse the "corruption" of politicians and the disorder born of "politics."

Their reticence about power-sharing democracy and their taste for tough leadership and top-down rule should come as no surprise. Writing in the first half of the nineteenth century, the astute early analyst of democracy Alexis de Tocqueville feared the advent of a peculiarly modern form of "democratic despotism" backed by a bourgeoisie and its selfish individualism and live-for-today materialism. The coming despotism would encourage "citizens to enjoy themselves provided that they think only of enjoying themselves." Its foundation would be a middle class feeding upon their "bourgeois pot of stew" and "constantly circling for petty pleasures," a stratum of so-called citizens willing to embrace an "immense tutelary power" that treats its subjects as "perpetual children," as a "flock of timid and industrious animals" in need of a shepherd.[43]

Tocqueville's warning that the sheepish middle classes would plump for despotism proved prescient. One lesson of the new despotism is that the middle classes have no instinctual love of open power-sharing. Guided by a mixture of motives, including greed, professional and family honor, respectability, and anxiety about the future, they seem happy to be kidnapped by state rulers, willing (as per the Stockholm syndrome) to be bought off with lavish services, cash payments, and invisible benefits such as being left alone to live their lives. That's true for state-revenue-rich countries such as Saudi Arabia, Brunei, Kuwait, the UAE, and Iran. It is equally true of countries such as Russia, Vietnam, and China, whose expanding middle classes, all things considered, definitely have a taste for regime stability plus private comforts. Protected by the "immense tutelary power" of the state, they strive after "petty pleasures" centered on the trimmings and trappings of conspicuous consumption. In bold contrast to the "uniformly gray and uniformly indigent" Soviet-type regimes of the twentieth century, plagued as they were by the "chronic lack of consumer goods" and cursed by products of "a single second-rate quality," the despotisms of the twenty-first century are consumer paradises, at least for some.[44] Priority is given by governments to paving the road to paradise, as in Turkey, where the number of shopping malls jumped nearly eightfold during the first two decades of rule by Erdoğan. Little wonder that shopping is a source of middle-class spiritual comfort. Shopping malls and online retail portals are places of pilgrimage, glitzy labyrinths of color and sound designed to dazzle pilgrims into lingering in expectation, to spend to the hilt so as to earn absolution through consumption. From within these temples they chant the litanies of Singles Day (China), Harajome (Iran), and Russian Black Friday, with their refrains of "hurry, buy now, everything must go." Kitchen gadgets, paintings for the walls of the living room, designer clothes, smartphones, same-day delivery services, thirty-day return policies, free size exchanges, and 24/7 customer service support are their salvation.

A Phantom People

Ruling Anxieties

The cynical conformity of the middle classes helps explain their role as shock-absorbing barriers against hotheaded and rough-minded disturbances erupting from the lower social ranks. Yet it is important not to overstate their anchoring and stabilizing role within despotic states. "It is an error," wrote our muse Montesquieu, "to believe that any human authority exists in the world which is despotic in all respects. There never has been one, and never will be, for the most immense power is always confined in some way."[1]

Nearly three centuries later, the sobering point about the confinement of despotic rule remains pertinent. Frailty is a curse of despotism. Stalked by rivalrous poligarchs and haunted by wide gaps between rich and poor, despotic power is vulnerable to fragmentation and disorder, popular resistance and breakdown. The general rule is that despotic regimes appear legitimate and stable until they collapse or are overthrown, which is why we now take a turn toward strangeness, in order to make sense of one of their oddest qualities: the anxiety attacks suffered by their rulers.

The popular impression that despotisms are top-down "authoritarian" dictatorships, autocracies, or tyrannies, run by a small group of leaders who impose their will by force, is misleading. It has little basis in reality, for a striking feature of life within these regimes, at all levels, is the way officials worry about losing power over people. Despotisms indeed have a pyramidal shape, with power and influence peddling ordered vertically. Rulers know the old dictum that power is the ability to get one's way in the world, to overcome opponents, to enjoy the capacity not to have to learn from previous mistakes—and to ignore their costs or heap them onto others, or postpone dealing with their consequences until a later date.[2] Yet those who occupy the tip of the pyramid are mindful of their vulnerability to those they push and pull. They sense both the powerlessness of their power and the power of the powerless. That is certainly why they spend vast sums of money on domestic policing and surveillance, usually much more than on their military forces, who they fear can become too big for their boots. Yet in a big paradox, this is also why those who govern are acutely aware that rule by violence, fear, and directives is not a workable recipe for durable government. Violence is the fist in the pocket of despots, but they know it cannot be overused, especially because by breeding resistance its effects can be counterproductive. Despots understand the maxim that what can be won by deception and seduction is preferable to what is won by force.

The cleverest despots strive to be what the Chinese scholar Yu Keping calls "learning" rulers.[3] Their advisors, if they are competent, alert them to the disorder, dysfunction, and signs of disunity and contestation within their realms, and they remind them, if reminding they need, that leaders' power to act involves the ability to get people to do things without constantly bossing and bullying them. Smart despots and their inner circles are interested in smart power. They are familiar with the advice of old Machiavelli: "A wise prince will think of ways to keep his citizens of every sort and under every circumstance dependent on the state and on him; and then they will be trustworthy."[4] Much the same counsel was proffered by the seventeenth-century Croatian scholar, adventurer, priest, and diplomat Juraj Križanić. "Kingdoms were not created for kings, but kings for kingdoms," he dared say in his *Politika* (composed during the years 1663–1666). "Rule over the people so that they will never seek a change."[5] Smart despots think the same. Their aim is to rule by manufacturing voluntary servitude among the ruled. They buy rather than bully, deflect instead of deny, co-opt rather than confront. They are keenly aware of the dangers of hubris and the need for durable government based on performance and popular legitimacy. That is why they tread carefully, why they look ahead, and why they are fascinated by the techniques of "adaptive governance" and experimentation with the arts of ruling others.[6]

The propensity of the powerful to learn how better to rule is remarkable. So is their skittishness. The pangs of impotence felt by the powerful are palpable. They know that governing is less like hammering nails into wood and more like balancing on slippery eggs, as the Chinese saying goes. They worry about the demoralization and decay of the state. From heads of state downward, government officials understand well that powerful people are condemned to worry about loss of power. It is said that Xi Jinping fancies the joke about Brezhnev bringing his mother to Moscow for the first time. He proudly shows her the Kremlin state apartments, his swanky Zil limousine, and other fripperies of the life of luxury he now lives. "Well, what do you think, Mama?" says Brezhnev. "You'll never have to worry about a thing, ever again. I'm so proud of you, Leonid Ilyich," says Mama, "but what happens if the Communists find out?"[7] The old Chinese proverb that when trees fall monkeys scatter *(shù dǎo húsūn sàn)* not only captures despots' fear that they could lose everything but also explains their tough-mindedness. "I've learned," Viktor Orbán told a group of ambassadors, "that when you have the chance to kill your rival you don't think about it—you just go ahead and do it."[8] Within the ranks of despots, that attitude is typical, and it helps throw light on why power-sharing is not their thing. These rulers have no taste for monitory democracy—a robust style of politics and way of life committed not just to open, free, and fair elections but also to greater social and political equality and, hence, active citizen and media support for the public monitoring and restraint of hierarchies of power, wherever power is exercised.

Yet here's the strange thing. Trepidation about loss of control explains why the despots of our era, with their immense monopoly of power, are still skittish. They typically act as if they are blessed with superhuman qualities and therefore stand well above ordinary mortals, yet their all-too-human insecurity runs deep. How come? First clues are provided by the ancient Athenian historian, philosopher, and soldier Xenophon, whose fragment *Hiero* (written around 474 BCE) questions the presumption that power over others always breeds pleasure, almost an erotic satisfaction in knowing that ruling can inflict distress and ruination on subjects' lives. Written as a dialogue between the Syracuse tyrant Hiero and a wise lyric poet named Simonides, Xenophon shows that arbitrary power tends to make tyrant rulers miserable. "Day and night," he reports, tyrants "live as if they are condemned by the general verdict of humanity to die for their iniquity." The "glamor of a tyranny" is more symbol than substance. In practice, omnipotent rulers have few or no true friends. They are plagued by flatterers. Tyrants have to keep their known enemies "at arm's length, and yet be compelled to lean upon them." They have to be wary of their own armed guards. They must harbor suspicions about honest, honorable, and wise public figures, all of whom are prone to turn their talents into

THE NEW DESPOTISM

disloyalty. Even family, lovers, and visitors bearing gifts cannot be trusted.[9]

Xenophon had a point. Today's despots suffer bouts of insecurity. They know well the double curse of isolation and paranoia, and they can cite local versions of the Chinese proverb that powerful people should fear fame just as pigs fear getting fat. And so it should come as no surprise to learn that when dining, just to be sure, Vladimir Putin is protected by a food taster (the Romans called this role the *praegustātor*) and that when he is out and about he surrounds himself with *siloviki,* "force-men" with a security or military service background; or to discover that, when on state visits, Kim Jong-un regularly orders his aides to bag his feces and urine and bring the whole malodorous lot back to North Korea, to prevent details of his health from reaching the hands of present and future enemies. Despots are surrounded day and night by secret agents, and by secret agents watching the secret agents, plus highly trained and well-armed guards. An obvious example is Xi Jinping, rumored to be the world leader who has survived the highest number of attempts on his life. He travels surrounded by an enormous posse of hand-picked men dressed in black suits, elite bodyguards directed by the several-thousand-strong, highly secretive body known as the Central Security Bureau. In Vietnam, the Communist Party leadership is protected by the body it directly controls, the intelligence and police forces of the People's Public Security of Vietnam. In equally tight and no-nonsense style, Orbán guards his bodily flanks through a range of agencies: security services that protect his family estates, a well-organized and politically reliable mob of Ferencváros soccer fans who specialize in disrupting public demonstrations against the government, and the Counter Terrorism Center, a sword-sharp body with unlimited powers of search, surveillance, and arrest established after the 2010

Fidesz election victory and led, unsurprisingly, by the ruler's former personal bodyguard, János Hajdú.

For obvious reasons, details of the mechanics of these secretive security arrangements are in short supply. What's far clearer is that the precautions reveal the way despots at the top are neurotic, or perhaps proto-democratic, in their constant self-examination, self-justification, and relentless attention-seeking. They must handle a difficult policing dilemma: should their priority be a security force designed to protect them against popular unrest, or a security force whose job is to protect them against spies, informers, high-level plots, and coup attempts?[10] Behind the scenes, no doubt, they also fear that they and their prime officials are fated to become victims of the Peter Principle, the axiom that powerful ladder climbers win promotion until they reach the level where they are no longer competent. The old adage that mediocrity knows nothing higher than itself applies to their own security forces.

There are times when rulers reveal their anxieties and behave as if their time in power is running out fast, such as when they purchase overseas property.[11] Their skittishness is compounded by the symptoms of something we can call office dependency. Despots hardly need reminding that leaving or being pushed from office equals the collapse of a personal world. "You know how hard it is. I've given my whole life to politics," says the key character in Václav Havel's *Leaving,* a tragicomedy scattered with references both to Chekhov's *The Cherry Orchard* and to Shakespeare's *King Lear,* two plays that deal with the theme of the painful personal costs when power slips through fingers.[12] What triggers office dependency under despotic conditions? It is not just the perks of office: mountains of personal wealth, chauffeured time management, good dinners, free access to bed partners, bountiful bribes. The deep personal satisfaction of winning public recognition also plays a role. Despotic power functions as an aphrodisiac. Despots are hooked on the snuff and stuff of office. Sooner or later, they usually become easy meat for the vultures of hubris. Arrogance, the flipside of insecurity, gets the best of them. These soldiers of high politics see no need to shoulder their arms. They detest talk of time limits on their power. Unblessed by the wisdom that political genius consists in knowing when to stop—"In der Beschränkung zeigt sich erst der Meister" was Goethe's way of saying that the master triumphs by holding back—they live the illusion of their own indispensability.[13] Hence their hostility to the democratic art of conceding power gracefully to others and other democratic mechanisms for preventing office dependency and the abuse of power, such as the periodic rotation of officeholders, accredited leaders of the opposition, public exposure through investigative or muckraking journalism, laws against the acceptance of bribes and payments, recall and initiative mechanisms, impeachment procedures, benefits after leaving office (such as a retirement pension, travel privileges, medical benefits, and security protection), and restrictions on membership of supervisory boards or management of companies in receipt of state contracts.

All these mechanisms are seen by despots as rubbish from a bygone democratic era. Their fear of losing power understandably oozes arrogance. Forced departure from office risks much more than irrelevance or mourning the loss of accumulated wealth, long days where once minutes were sliced thinly, empty calendars and silent phones, regret at the inability to make up lost time with families and loved ones, or the emotional stress and outright depression caused by exiting a macho world where thick skin is a job requirement and confessions of vulnerability are reckoned a liability. The great fear of despots is not just actual death, either from natural causes or from assassination by their opponents, but political death, once described by Yugoslav strongman Josip Broz Tito as "the most horrible death of all."[14]

The fear of political death helps clarify why the new despots tint their hair (Chinese leaders' thirst for black hair dye surely is unmatched), sport gleaming white false teeth, and regularly use sun lamps to top up their tans, as if to prove their grandiose selves know no ending. That's also why these men (they are mostly men) like younger women on their arms, and why they indulge deep massages and stimulants and endure face lifts, gym sessions, polo sessions and workouts. Political death is bound with bodily death, which is no laughing matter. It stalks the lives of despots. Perhaps some of them privately are consoled by versions of the old Epicurean adage that the living should not worry about death when they are alive, and that in any case after death they won't be able to. And they may know the old joke that death is no more frightening than the moment just before birth. But still they fear the demise of their own bodies. Despite the prophylactics, despots suffer moments of mild or intense panic when they realize their mortality will at some point pose a succession problem, or perhaps a regime crisis. Mortal impotence is the absolute limit of absolute power. It pinches and claws at the body of every despot. It is the moment when rust gets the better of iron, the point when time is no longer eternity, the moment of transition from "Absolute Power to Absolute Impotence."[15] Even the most powerful despots know death's clutches are ineluctable. Creatures who catch cold in winter and snore at night, they are well aware that they cannot escape the truth of the Arab proverb that death is a black camel that sooner or later comes unbidden to kneel at every door. All of them are acutely aware that assassination is in the cards.

So here we encounter one of the most fundamental weaknesses of despotic regimes: their difficulty in getting rid of rotten rulers and (under emergency conditions) finding a solution to the succession problem if the despot dies in office. Montesquieu long ago spotted that even the most powerful despots are powerless when it comes to determining their successors. Propped up on their deathbeds, they can stipulate who should replace them, as Oman's childless Sultan Qaboos did in the form of a sealed letter containing a last will and testament, opened at the moment he passed to paradise. Yet Montesquieu noted how even the most ruthless sultans (he had in mind Ismail II), who had consolidated their rule by blinding or strangling their brothers and other male relatives, were, at the point of death, unable to prevent power vacuums and violent usurpations. Pouncing on this frailty, pranksters nowadays understandably arm themselves with cruel deathbed jokes, as when a dying despot asks, "What will my people do without me?" An advisor, keen to comfort the ruler, says he should not worry about the people, as they are so resilient they "could eat stones." After a brief silence, the despot orders his advisor to issue a presidential decree giving his eldest son a monopoly over the stone trade. Another deathbed joke features a despot reportedly saying that he will rule the country "till his last breath." The doomed despot is quietly informed by an aide that the people want to see him one last time, and to say goodbye. Surprised, the despot asks, "Why? Where are they going?"

Sovereign People

Note how both jokes feature the great phantasm that despots are both masters and servants of the people. Despots indeed fear violent unrest, and they're acutely aware that among their own subjects there is only a fine line separating cowardice from civic courage. They know, as the Russians say, that a spoonful of tar ruins a whole barrel of honey. By instinct, despots also know that food on the table, skyscrapers, shopping malls, and vacations abroad aren't enough to consolidate their power. Hence the rulers' constant public declarations that they believe in the people, and that their sole purpose as rulers is to serve the people, whose support they enjoy.

Perplexing is the way officials from top to bottom of the new despotisms regularly deploy the rhetoric of "the people" and refer constantly to them as the presumed source of sovereign authority. They do so not simply because they are mousers who like to play with mice. The cleverest rulers know it's not enough to have the army, secret police, journalists, and censors on their side; they know they must pay lip service as well to the fundamental principle that it is the support of people that ultimately enables the governing institutions of a country to function with a measure of effectiveness.

Talleyrand, the eighteenth-century Frenchman who worked at the highest levels of successive governments, most commonly as diplomat and foreign minister, explained that no government can survive for any length of time without enjoying the agreement of its subjects. He called this the principle of legitimacy. By this he meant that the "strength and duration" of government depends always on winning the support of its population, whereas government based on what he called usurpation produces "no end of troubles, revolutions, and internal calamities."[16] The new despots are well aware of this principle of legitimacy. Privately, far from the microphones and cameras of meddling journalists, they may think or say that the people are nomads, idiots, prostitutes, vagrants, conspirators, migrants, faint hearts, and idlers who crawl on all fours toward destinations unknown. Publicly, they speak differently. They do everything they can to nurture their own legitimacy using means that give them a strongly democratic feel. They say that the people are in need of protection from outside corrupting influences. They swear the people are the country's inner strength. There is a point to all this specious talk of the people. The new despots work hard to secure, in the name of the people, the unquestioning recognition that obedience to the leaders' dictates is right and proper, and that all institutions of the polity are the materialization of the people's collective power.

Reflecting on how "the people" is used in the People's Republic of China, Yu Hua's *China in Ten Words* notes that there isn't another term in the modern Chinese language that is such an anomaly, in that "the people" are "ubiquitous yet somehow invisible."[17] That's an important point: despotisms thrive on representations of the people as a living phantom. In the imaginary of despotism, the people are both being and nonbeing, of supreme political importance and of little or no importance at all. In Belarus, supporters of Lukashenko's regime regularly call him *bats'ka* (daddy) and say he is "a man of the people." In tiny Brunei, an oil-and-gas-rich kingdom where there are no taxes and no elections, only free education and health care and heavily subsidized housing, Sultan Hassanal Bolkiah often invokes the mantra of "the people." "The responsibility of the king is to his people and the people have a responsibility to the king," he says to audiences at his palace. "Together, the king and the people hold the trust of the nation."[18]

In China, as Yu notes, officials from top to bottom of the political system regularly refer to "the people" *(rén mín)* as the source of sovereign authority of the state. The terms "the people" and "democracy" *(mín zhǔ)* are part of the prevailing language of the Party state, which is said to be the living embodiment of "the people." In briefings, seminars, and workshops, officials wield such formulations as "serving the people wholeheartedly . . . is the leading purpose of the Party," and the Party represents the interests of the people "rather than special interests of certain vested groups." The Party leadership says that its fight against corruption *(fŭ bài)*, its organized pursuit of "tigers and flies" at both upper and lower levels, is a direct consequence of "what the people demand and what they support." The "mass line" purge launched by Xi after he was elected general secretary of the Party Central Committee in mid-2013—a top-down campaign against corruption within Party ranks—came couched in these terms. So did his widely covered February 2016 appearance in the studios of China Central Television (CCTV), during which he emphasized that state media is "a reflection of the voice of the people" and therefore must "protect Party power and protect Party unity."[19] There are even moments when the people are appointed the fortune-tellers of the future. Shortly after the eighteenth National Congress of the Chinese Communist Party, Xi announced the China Dream project. "I believe that realizing the rejuvenation of the Chinese nation has been the greatest dream of the Chinese people since the beginning of the modern era," he reportedly said. "This dream concentrates a long-cherished expectation of many generations of the Chinese people, and encapsulates the overall interests of the Chinese nation and its people."[20]

The mellifluous words nicely illustrate the point that within the new despotisms virtually everything done by those who govern is done in the name of the people. The people are the great ventriloquists of history, past, present, and future, or so it seems. They are even projected back into the distant past, as in Uzbekistan, where Zahīr ud-Dīn Muhammad (1483–1530)—the founder of an empire that lasted more than three centuries, rivaled those of the Ottoman Turks and the Persian Safavids, and included the Mughal dynasty that ruled most of the Indian subcontinent until the mid-nineteenth century—is today known as "Babur" (the lion) and officially worshipped at lavish public ceremonies as a "great ruler of his people" and "true son of the Uzbek people." Living people are certainly not safe from the clutches of the fictional people, either. The well-noted troubles that befell a Chinese citizen nicknamed "Brother Banner," who dared in 2010 to hold a banner that read "Not Serving the People" outside the gate of his local Wuxi New District labor relations office to protest its failure to resolve his pay dispute with his former employer, show how talk of the people can have a sinister phantasmagorical quality.[21] Chinese writers report strange and contradictory censorship restrictions, including official instructions to alter the phrase "Chinese people" to "some people" in their writings (presumably to preserve the unsullied purity of the key phrase), or to scrub references such as "Gansu people" or "Xinjiang people," presumably because they carry the air of regional differences or discrimination, a violation of the sacred abstract principle of "the people."

There's something else that's intriguing about the organized worship of the phantom people under conditions of despotism. Close observers often note the moments when outsiders could be forgiven for thinking that the rulers who say they love and respect the people secretly fear and despise them. One example: During early July 2013, with the approach of the fourth anniversary of public disturbances in the far western province of Xinjiang, a harsh new form of martial law began to be imposed in the name of the people. Chinese officials called the crackdown a "people's war." Here, as in many other cases, the ode to the people seems to harbor deep ambivalence, even secret contempt, for flesh-and-blood people. Real people are viewed as selfish, slavish, mendacious, timid, and prone to ill temper, but ultimately deferential to reigning power. Hence the warnings that the opinions of the people can get out of hand and slide toward "soft violence" that feeds disorder. Hence, too, the insistence that the people need unambiguous guidance, if necessary by the ears.[22]

Showboating

So the practical question arises: how can actual people be guided in the name of the people? The challenge is formidable, especially because despotic systems of power are plutocracies that distribute people's life chances in markedly uneven ways. Leading the people by their ears isn't easy. Things can go wrong. The people are combustible material; they can suddenly explode in flames, as the bushy-eyebrowed, balding despot and self-declared democrat and friend of the Kyrgyz people Askar Akayev discovered in early 2005 when Tulip Revolution protesters stormed his presidential compound in the central square of Bishkek and forced him and his family into exile in Moscow. Fearing similar fates, clever despots strive to be both agile and attractive to those they seek to master. Their task is to magnetize flesh-and-blood people, to encourage them to pay attention to their leaders and to be charmed by their tunes. Real people must be persuaded of their rulers' rightness, convinced that their leaders' authority and the system are good for them and their country, and that they have no serious alternative. Despots operating at all levels of the system know that to govern well requires nurturing a kind of governmentality among their subjects.[23] That means prescribing for them right ways of doing things, inscribing the rules of the game within their lives, seducing them, persuading them to accept the governing power, even getting them to crave their domination by embracing it as their own. The ruled must be productive of the power of the rulers.

Until quite recently, most textbooks and manuals of politics were straightforwardly clear about how this could happen. Popular deference to rulers was presumed to be "natural." Aristotle's *Politics* (written around 350 BCE) helped dictate the tone. Its typology of "pure" types of power (monarchy; aristocracy; and polity, or citizens' self-government) supposed that the great danger threatening every polity is the insolent stupidity of the masses: their mindless attraction to demagogic leaders, wizard tyrants like Pisistratus skilled at flattering and seducing the masses with promises of redistribution of wealth and power in their favor. Tales of Roman emperors ruling through bread and circuses (*panem et circenses*), followed by medieval Christian (St. Augustine) and early modern secular European doctrines of the original sin of fallen humankind (Hobbes), kept this ancient prejudice alive. So did fears of "violence of the majority faction" and mob rule, something that worried James Madison and other architects of the new American republic.

Until the early decades of the twentieth century, modern social science kept alive this same belief in the innate deference of the masses. Crowd theorists such as Gustave Le Bon, upon whom the much more famous Sigmund Freud drew in his *Group Psychology and the Analysis of the Ego* (1921), peddled the belief that when people assemble they submit to the "group mind" logic of mob behavior. Individuals come to resemble grains of sand swept asunder by the winds of strong leaders who play to the crowd's fickle feelings of nervous invincibility and contagious loss of self. Magnetized by Great Leaders, the excited crowd succumbs to the madness of a people who "do not possess clear and reasoned ideas on any subject whatever outside their own specialty." The leader-follower relationship is based on the masses' deep yearnings for an idealized protective and loving parent figure who can do no wrong. The leader is a spiritual guide who multiplies their strength many times over. Le Bon concluded, "The type of hero dear to crowds will always have the semblance of a Caesar. His insignia attracts them, his authority overawes them, and his sword instils them with fear."[24]

This hypnotism model of popular servitude, sometimes called brainwashing, makes little sense when trying to understand how despotisms work. Their dependence upon "the people" is more complicated, more tenuous, and more sophisticated. Yes, there are indeed people gripped by masochistic desires to fling themselves into the arms of a reassuringly strong leader. Millions of Russians will surely shed tears when strongman Putin bites the dust. More than a few Chinese citizens will mourn Xi's passing, as many Turkmenistan subjects did when their chief despot Saparmurat Niyazov moved on to a higher (or lower) place. But it is a category mistake to suppose that the new despotisms are grounded in popular hypnotism. Despotisms sup on the souls of many different character types who have one trait in common: their willingness to conform to top-down power. The skeptic, the scoffer, the pessimist, the brown-noser, and the sycophant who sucks up to the powerful and despises the weak (who "kisses up and kicks down," as Carlos Fuentes put it) are high on the list.[25] So are cynics who trade in overstatements and paranoiacs sure that there are hidden realities and concocted conspiracies. Fatalists, those sure that the world has its own ways, that everything falls after it rises, and that little or nothing can be done to fix things, are equally useful allies in the cause of despotism. So are apathetic people, propagators of ennui, listless noncitizens who stay quietly locked down in circles of work, family life, sport, and other private forms of self-celebration.

There's plenty of room for people who are actively complacent, mildly pretentious, and boorishly banal—middle-class figures who resemble Nikolai Gogol's Chichikov, a character in *Dead Souls* (1842) who is the incarnation of such qualities, which Russians still today call *poshlost*. Despotism needs dreary rectangular minds, conformists born and bred to harness, crawlers who do what they are told and accept things as they come. It likes people who comply by minding their own business and letting others get on with theirs. Despotic power most definitely needs authoritarian personalities: men (typically) who aggressively embrace hierarchy, say they like order, shun introspection and critical thinking, desire strong leaders and admire powerful states, and have a rigid outlook on life that "has no room for anything but a desperate clinging to what appears to be strong and a disdainful rejection of whatever is relegated to the bottom."[26] Just as useful are those characters who practice the rather tricky art of performing *ketman*, moral acrobatics that combine self-contradictory opinions with the pleasure derived from hairsplitting and the willful deception of others.[27]

Perhaps the personality type most welcomed by and most central to the whole experience of despotic regimes is the grumbler. Preoccupied with their private lives, struggling to get by and to get on, grumblers leave things undisturbed. They are noisy barrels emptied of content. Their talk, talk, talk is hollow. They bellyache, wave their arms about and clench their teeth. They curse, whisper, and complain, but in reality they are gullible agents of blind conformity. They seem strangely unaware that their grumbling enables virtually everything done by the rulers to be done in their name, on behalf of them as "the people." In effect, by doing nothing to change things, bellyachers grant the rulers a daily vote, offer them encouragement, and teach them that the powerful can rely on the powerless to grant their power freely. Grumblers license the power of the powerful.

But here's the special challenge faced by the new despotisms. Since power is no rabbit's foot, a lucky charm that grants its holder the magical ability to perform wonders without resistance by others, despots are forced to find clever ways of winning the support of grumblers, hairsplitters, authoritarians, the apathetic, scoffers, and fatalists. We have seen already that despotisms feed upon middle-class resignation and patron-client relations, the personalized exchange of benefits and punishments among acquaintances, but this is not support enough. Rulers find as well that the early childhood socialization of their subjects within families doesn't supply the popular support rulers functionally require. Freud was surely wrong to insist that most adults in every culture are "horde animal[s]" gripped by unconscious wishes "to be ruled by one person." Yet he was right to say that bossy political rule typically rests on deep foundations and that people shaped by certain early childhood experiences are attracted to a figure of arbitrary power "they can admire, to which they can submit, and which dominates and sometimes even ill-treats them."[28] The new despotisms undoubtedly munch on deep-rooted (not inborn or innate) emotions. The subservience of subjects to despotic power isn't superficial. It runs deep inside them. Despotism dwells within people. It shapes both the external and internal lives of its subjects. More research is certainly needed to understand better how this happens.

To understand the new despotisms, we cannot rely on simple formulations such as the contrast between "democratic" and "authoritarian" personality types, or facile presumptions that authoritarianism nurtures a "cluster of values" that include beliefs in "collective security for the tribe," "the value of group conformity to preserve conventional traditions," and "loyal obedience toward strong leaders."[29] Such simplified formulations are misleading, for life inside the new despotisms is different and much more complicated than is supposed. That is why those who think of themselves as shepherds of the flock find themselves continually searching for different ways of keeping their livestock obedient and contentedly grazing. Using a now-obsolete term last in fashion in the eighteenth century, as Dr. Johnson's 1755 *Dictionary* records, we could say that the measure of the "despoticalness" of a despotic regime is its propensity to manufacture willing compliance in multiple ways: to combine the threats and promises of "external power" with the "internal power" of a great variety of subjects who carry despotism inside themselves and are therefore willing to comply and obey.[30]

A common way despots construct their subjects is to win their hearts and minds through democratic style. Supposing there's something like a tacit or unwritten contract with the people they govern, leaders strut their stuff on the public catwalks. They display their power for all to see and hear; they show off. In the past, power brokers often hid from the gaze of those they ruled. It is recorded that certain African kings were once considered by their communities as rainmakers, harbingers of excellent harvests, and deliverers of general plenitude, so the reverence they expected, and to which they felt entitled, required them to govern at a distance from their subjects; they had to refrain from displaying themselves to others and were never to be seen eating or drinking.[31] Today's despots, by contrast, seek to close the gap between the ruler and the ruled. They act as if the state is what it appears to be. They mount the public stage and pay meticulous attention to body language, diction, decor, manners, and charm. In the name of serving the people, as if they were up for election, they embrace the aesthetics of the permanent campaign. Yes, there are moments when, resembling dictators from the past, they dress in uniform, mount the political stage, salute their troops, and send televised signals to the population about the need for popular discipline. But these moments are exceptional. The new despots prefer to do peacock dances before fawning audiences. They step out from behind closed doors and go walking among the people. As if unscripted, they make appearances in unusual locales. There they pause to breathe the local atmosphere, to establish themselves as the guardians of the political order, to measure the loyalty of their supporters, to charm cynics, to shut the traps of people who ask too many questions, to win over those who fear they are being devoured by the jaws of power. In the name of the people, by means of smiles, handshakes, and words of greeting, the rulers showboat.

Why do they do this? The simplest answer is that they know that hiding themselves away is risky. The people chat, whisper, and gossip. They jump to conclusions. Hence they need guidance through flattery. Roman emperors practiced the art of charming crowds by bowing before them, touching their heads, blowing kisses, and "in everything aping the slave in order to become the master."[32] The new despots similarly specialize in theatrics. Their trade is artifice, pose, and performance. Every move they make is in quotation marks. They understand that ruling arbitrarily requires the common touch, as when Belarus's Lukashenko plays the role of an outsider man of the people who loves to be filmed making small talk with miners or sitting atop a combine harvester. Or when Xi springs a well-crafted "surprise" appearance and presses the flesh in a Beijing bun shop, rides on a bicycle with his daughter, embarks on a "poverty tour" in western China, and kicks a Gaelic football during an official tour in Ireland; or when his partner, former singer and opera star Peng Liyuan, triggers a media sensation during her first state visit (to Trinidad and Tobago) and brings high heels and proto-democratic style for the first time into the field of high-level Chinese diplomacy and foreign policy.[33]

The most switched-on despots are master copyists of democratic style. There is the oft-told story of how Orbán, at the time just chairman of his Fidesz party, stayed overnight at a lawyer friend's house. Next morning, to his surprise, the lawyer's wife began cleaning his shoes. "What are you doing, Mrs. Irénke?" he asked, to which she answered, "I'm cleaning your shoes so that I can one day say: I cleaned the shoes of Hungary's prime minister!" The true man of the people responded by fetching Mrs. Irénke's shoes and set about cleaning them. "What are you doing?" she asked in surprise. "I'm cleaning your shoes," Orbán replied, "so that you can say one day: Hungary's prime minister cleaned my shoes.'" Another example: Soon after snatching the reins of his country's leadership, Saudi Arabia's Crown Prince Mohammed bin Salman made carefully choreographed visits to his strategic partners. In London, where he dined with Queen Elizabeth, black cabs, posters, and giant billboards welcomed him through slogans such as "He is opening Saudi Arabia to the world" and "He is empowering Saudi Arabian women." Local lobbyists and public relations firms were equally hard at work during his three-week tour of the United States in early 2018. Flanked by armed guards, he met television star Oprah Winfrey, talked in a California desert about space travel with business magnate Richard Branson, and visited MIT and Harvard. Aiming to rebrand his country's image and attract investment capital, acting as if he was a true democrat, the young crown prince dined with Hollywood stars and Rupert Murdoch at his Bel Air vineyard, mingled with Wall Street financiers, talked in Seattle with Amazon CEO Jeff Bezos, and agreed on the biggest arms deal in the history of the United States with President Donald Trump. The Saudi national flag, green with a white sword, fluttered outside New York's Plaza Hotel, all of whose rooms were rented for the young leader and his entourage. The performing democrat's meet-and-greet was repeated at the Four Seasons in Palo Alto, where the young prince toured the nearby campuses of Facebook and Google.[34]

Quiet Loyalty

Celebrity can quickly melt under the hot sun of public exposure, as the young prince was soon to discover when accused of direct complicity in the grisly murder of a prominent journalist, Jamal Khashoggi. Despots' taste for democratic style has its limits. They are certainly less cocksure than might be supposed. This explains why they experiment with a wide range of locally crafted "democratic" tools designed to win public support.

To deal productively with what they variously call "public disturbances," "mass incidents" (an estimated one hundred thousand happen in China annually), and "seditious activity," the rulers tap expertise from trusted think tanks, as the Orbán government does with the Századvég Foundation. Their experimentation with public forums, consultation exercises, and dialogue projects is equally striking. The Tajikistan Young Leaders Program is an example: implemented by Counterpart International under funding provided by the United States Agency for International Development, the four-year initiative had the stated aim of building "a pro-active, civically-engaged and socially-conscious generation of young people able to take ownership of their future and contribute to the development of their country."[35] The rulers of the UAE have launched a national "happiness and positivity" program backed by "councils for happiness" and public-involvement initiatives designed to collect information about and boost citizens' happiness levels.[36] For three days at the end of Ramadan, the sultan of

Brunei opens his palace to the public, offering free meals and a chance to shake his hand and exchange a few pleasantries (except if you are a woman; then you are offered the chance of meeting his wife, Queen Saleh, in a separate location). In pursuit of "national consultation," the Orbán government has used questionnaires sent to all adult citizens to divine their opinions on such matters as terrorism, refugees, and unemployment.

When it comes to public consultation in the world of despotism, the rulers of Singapore are surely the headmasters of the wizarding school. The People's Action Party (PAP) began in the mid-1980s to experiment with new methods of citizen engagement through the state Feedback Unit, later renamed Reaching Everyone for Active Citizenry @ Home (REACH). Its brief has been to spread information about government policies, to "build bridges" with citizens by taking their suggestions and collecting feedback, and to place government departments on high alert to deal with their anticipated complaints and actual protests. Many clever innovations have since resulted. Their overall aim, reports PAP member of parliament and REACH boss Amy Khor, is to go beyond "gathering feedback to helping Singaporeans feel engaged and that they can make a difference." Government documents speak of such goals as increased "opportunity" and "purpose" for the people, the "assurance" of their basic needs, the building of a more "compassionate" society, and encouraging "citizen trust" in their government. Examples of these people-centered innovations include e-consultation exercises, online public forums, and small-scale informal consultations conducted by government ministers and known as Tea Sessions, Dialogue Sessions, Policy Feedback Groups, and Policy Study Workshops. The rulers operate Facebook, Instagram, and Twitter accounts. Other digital tools include Facebook question-and-answer sessions and online town halls, both of them subject to preregistration rules and input filtering to prevent "abuse and hate mongering." The Youth Ambassador program encourages young Singaporeans to organize their own feedback groups. Consultations targeted at professionals, managers, executives, and technicians deal with such matters as global technology innovations, unemployment among older workers, and developing labor-market shortages. Nearly fifty thousand Singaporeans participated in a year-long Our Singapore Conversation exercise. So-called Listening Point pop-up booths have been established at convenient city locations to raise awareness of government policies and to gather subjects' views in multiple languages on such policy matters as medical insurance, national budget details, and "pioneer generation packages" for the elderly.[37]

These experiments in public engagement show that the new despotisms are structured by a silent contract between the ruling authorities and their subject populations: the rulers will deliver what their subjects need in exchange for their quiet loyalty. Quiet subservience is an organizing principle of despotic power. Note here a key difference with twentieth-century totalitarian regimes. Mussolini's Italy, Hitler's Germany, and Mao's China condemned their subjects to lives of perpetual enthusiasm. The self-appointed philosopher of Italian fascism, Giovanni Gentile, captured well its spirit: "Among the major merits of fascism is to have obliged little by little all those who once stood at the window to come down into the streets, to practice fascism even against fascism."[38] Those times are over. Gone are the days when millions of people were captivated by skillfully orchestrated newspaper, radio, and film performances led by showbiz demagogues dressed in formal attire, military uniforms, or macho riding gear, or stripped to the waist and helping sweating laborers gather harvests (Mussolini's specialty). Public rallies still happen, but they are a second-rate pastiche, not the real thing. Millions no longer celebrate in unity, marching in step across a stage built from the glorification of heroes, cults of the fallen, national holidays, anniversaries, triumphs of the revolution, and electrifying speeches by a Leader who leaves "no place to hide from the Voice."[39] And leaders no longer chillingly suppose, as Hitler did, that mass rallies can "burn into the little man's soul the proud conviction that though a little worm he is nevertheless part of a great dragon."[40]

The new despotisms pay great lip service to "the people," but political cults and public worship of rulers are discouraged. Private adoration is acceptable, but the general rule is that those who govern do all they can to prevent public gatherings of people. There are bizarre happenings, as in Kazakhstan, where a young citizen determined to test the limits of freedom of public assembly was carted away by police after standing silently in a city square holding a blank sign. In Tajikistan, which bans lavish private gatherings on the grounds that extravagant parties strain family budgets, a Dushanbe resident was fined for hosting friends at a local restaurant to celebrate his twenty-fifth birthday. Also in Tajikistan, in May 2016 celebrations marking the Hindu festival of Holi were broken up by police, with some young revelers (according to material uploaded by Platforma, a Tajik- and Russian-language Facebook group) interrogated by police and allegedly beaten.

These examples highlight the general principle: flesh-and-blood citizens are expected to stay quiet, locked down in private forms of self-celebration. Individuals gripped by stubborn desires for justice, Michael Kohlhaas figures who fight until the end against corruption, are blacklisted. Those who feel weighed down by the world, or simply bored with things, can reach for the bottle; some analysts reckon that certain despotic regimes, Russia for instance, could not survive for long if the production and consumption of alcohol were banned. Drink is their democracy. Consumption of goods and services is their next-morning hangover cure. Consumption as a way of life is positively encouraged. Grand shopping malls are the temples where subjects with money worship themselves in the name of their loved ones. "All I want is to live and work in dignity," they say, "to earn enough for me and my family, to raise my children, sometimes to go on vacation, and to be sure my job is safe." The point is that the much-praised people are expected to be dutiful, and to see to it that politics is not their business.

Early twentieth-century totalitarianism expected public displays of duty. In fascist Italy, handshakes were replaced by Roman salutes, right arms outstretched. "Hail the Duce" opened public meetings. Buildings and walls were decorated with the black-lettered words "Believe, Obey, Fight." The Nazis boasted that the "only person who is still a private individual in Germany is somebody who is asleep."[41] The new despotism tolerates private life among those who are awake. It goes without saying that just as oxen bellow under the weight of their yokes, so the subjects of despotism do a lot of bellyaching. But what's vital from the rulers' point of view is that they keep their complaints to themselves, or at most share them with friends and family. A quote of the week presented by the UAE newspaper *The Gulf Today* says it well: "The more you complain about your problems, the more problems you have to complain about."[42]

Elections

The new despots know that the art of governing people into quiet conformity is demanding and learned with difficulty. Hence they do their best to be seen as governors who stand well above the people but like to engage with them and feel comfortable and energized in their presence. The tactic is in effect a species of managed populism: a way of publicly binding together the polity, a method of making the subjects of the realm feel included in the affairs of state, despite the fact that most people are excluded from the hallways and backrooms of governmental power. But as a technique of power it has limits. Even the most skilled practitioners of publicity know that public relations is not enough, and that other means are needed to ensure that the whole system works. Enter the practice of tolerating, staging, and winning elections.

In countries such as Iran, China, Russia, and Vietnam, in the Gulf region, central Asia, and elsewhere, it is a strange but true fact that ruling oligarchs have a definite fondness for elections. It is a commonplace among political scientists and "democracy barometer" assessments by such bodies as Freedom House that these are "authoritarian" systems because they either know no elections or lack free and fair elections. These assessments are superficial and potentially misleading. The scandalous verity is that elections and despotism are conjoined twins, and that the new despotisms stage national elections and tolerate their spread into various subspheres of daily life. Incoming American president John Quincy Adams famously insisted that "the best security for the beneficence, and the best guarantee against the abuse of power, consists in the freedom, the purity, and the frequency of popular elections."[43] Despotism shows that this formula isn't necessarily so, and that subjects can be taught to understand elections as a device for rewarding those who rule their subjects well.

Consider China, where during the past four decades there have been over 1 million elections across more than six hundred thousand villages, with some 3 million Party officials chosen by voters.[44] State officials in metropolitan areas are willing to experiment with secret-ballot elections to smooth ruffled feathers and stifle public disputes, as in the well-known case of Beijing's Chaoyang District, where in 2007 district Party officials working hand in hand with developers tried to resolve a land dispute through the ballot box for the very first time. Local residents were sent an information sheet that explained why people should vote and how they could do so. The flyer stated that voting would "determine the outcome of the rebuilding program." It added: "Please value your right to vote, and vote according to your true wishes!"[45] The words show how Party officials in China typically treat elections as a device for resolving social conflicts, a tool for conducting what they sometimes call "consultative democracy" *(xié shāng mín zhǔ).*[46] Thinking of themselves as the elected elect, they interpret voting in terms of a twenty-first-century rendition of the old Maoist refrain, "From the masses to the masses" *(cóng qúnzhòng zhōng lái, dào qúnzhòng zhōng qù),* according to which the Party mobilizes the people and collects their opinions for the purpose of formulating coherent policies and strategies in line with the Party's own priorities.

For all concerned, the promise and problem with elections is their fickleness—things don't always go according to plan. That is why rulers train a firm eye on the practice of voting, even when it spreads into other areas of life, such as the entertainment and culture industries. Consider the field of television programming, which under conditions of despotism is often far from dreary. Stuffed with talk shows, soap operas, and programs showcasing the intimate details of celebrity lifestyles, television sometimes arouses great audience interest and controversy, as happened between 2004 and 2011 with China's sensational singing-contest series, *Super Girl.*[47] Produced by provincial-government-owned Hunan Satellite Television, the blockbuster series attracted a huge audience (nearly 400 million for a concluding episode) as well as widespread media coverage. Rather in the fashion of song shows such as *American Idol,* with connotations of primary caucusing and balloting during an American presidential campaign, the extravaganza featured sharp-tongued "audience judges" and audience voting by telephone and text message. After the 2011 season, the show was canceled by the State Administration of Radio, Film, and Television. Those who wanted to see the series continue made their views known. Posting, reposting, and commenting on China's microblogging websites, many netizens *(wǎngmín)* insisted that state promotion of "role models" from above was a dying practice and that many of the show's young women contestants were "the voices of our times" and "idols of the people." Others suggested that although the frenzied competition could be cruel and frivolous, the show ultimately celebrated the triumph of the individual over the state. With good reason, still others speculated that the cancelation was a consequence of the show's democratic appeal: millions of people had gotten used to voting by text message before regulators banned the practice in 2007, forcing the show to limit audience participation to those inside a cavernous television studio.

The official nervousness about voting illustrates the point that when despots lose elections, they move to correct the flawed results. They prefer phantom elections—simulations whose results favor the rulers. Despots like safe in-house voting in areas of life that they do not directly control, such as the state-protected world of business. An example is the telecommunications giant Huawei Technologies, whose governing board, called the Representatives Commission, comprises 115 employee representatives elected in a secret ballot by the company's nearly one hundred thousand shareholder employees, who are scattered across more than 170 countries.

The giant company known as Alibaba goes further. The company has become famous not just because it is the leading digital powerhouse within the Chinese domestic economy, the champion of innovations in the field of artificial intelligence, and the world's largest retailer, but because it practices elections. Its managers stress the importance of nurturing trust, openness, and commitment among their employees via a range of schemes, such as providing free medical services for their families, celebrating Alibaba Day (May 8, the same as World Smile Day), and hosting group wedding days and open site visits for thousands of family members. The company trumpets its commitment to commercial integrity through its global intellectual property rights protection body known as the Alibaba Anti-Counterfeiting Alliance (which includes global luxury brand companies such as Louis Vuitton, Burberry, Li-Ning, and Dyson). It strives as well to foster a sense of consultative democracy. Cofounder and executive chairman Jack Ma is of course a public opinion leader with a huge following throughout the country. The company mirrors his cultivated reputation for independence by hosting a Public Interest Committee, whose ten members are democratically elected from a pool of over twenty thousand employees. Any employee can stand for election; the electoral system is one employee, one vote, by secret ballot. Candidates are encouraged to campaign wearing "Vote for Me" badges, and they have to go through a last stage "player kill" rally prior to election day. The mandate of the lucky winners lasts three years, and their job is to decide how to spend the sizable sum (0.03 percent of the company's annual revenue) the company allocates annually for public services.[48] Alibaba extends the principle of voting into other areas of company life, including the allocation of much sought-after parking spaces. Nearly five thousand employees drive to work each day, but the

THE NEW DESPOTISM

spaces available fall far short of that figure. So the management applies an equal-opportunity lottery scheme to allocate annual parking permits to employees (with the exception of the board of directors, whose nine members are granted special permits). No employee has a privileged status: position in the management hierarchy and years of company service simply don't count. In the land of Alibaba's phantom democracy, all employees are treated equally. Each commuter has an equal chance of winning the right to use a parking lot for a whole year. The unlucky ones are provided with alternatives: as valued employees of the company, either they can commute to work on company buses or they can carpool with those who have won their permits democratically, by lottery.

The general point of these particular cases is that despotisms are top-down regimes of power that host enclaves of voting. But this is not the end of the story of how despotic power feeds upon elections. In contrast to old-fashioned dictatorships, which often canceled or postponed elections, despots use periodic country-level elections as a prime instrument for consolidating and legitimating their rule. Why do they do this? The really strange thing is that country-level voting is not understandable in terms of old and familiar theories of democratic representation that see elections as exercises in the popular rejection and rotation of leaders.[49] During elections, say such theories, citizens let off steam. They put their leaders on trial. Dissenting minorities are granted space to defend their interests. People are offered a chance to control the governors by means of open competition for power that lets elected representatives test their political competence and leadership skills in the presence of voters armed with the power to trip them up and throw them out of office. Elections function as weapons for periodically cheering up disappointed citizens. According to this line of reasoning, if elected representatives were always virtuous, competent, and fully responsive to the wishes of the represented, elections would have no purpose. The represented would be identical with their representatives; representation would lose its meaning. Yet since representatives are quite often idiots who get things badly wrong, continue these theories, elections function as a vital means of disciplining representatives for having let down their electors. Through elections, electors get their chance to hurl harsh words and paper and digital rocks at their representatives: to toss them out of office and replace them with more competent leaders.

The new despotisms are not legible in these terms. The only kind of elections they tolerate are phantom elections. Voting is not an exercise in deliberative democracy based on direct participation by citizens, who choose representatives to govern for a fixed term on the condition they maintain the trust and consent of their citizens. Rather, voters are encouraged to think of themselves as loyal subjects of a government that performs well. Elections are designed to protect the government from the people. The whole idea of representation and the principle of the representative serving the represented is absent. The new despotisms practice *elections without democracy*.

There have been previous antidemocratic regimes, such as South Africa's, that utilized elections, but the despotisms of our time do so differently, and in much more sophisticated ways. From Belarus to Azerbaijan and Singapore, despotisms embrace the institutional facades of electoral democracy by universalizing the franchise (except in Brunei and the UAE, where women are banned from voting, and Saudi Arabia, where women can now cast their ballots and campaign for office at the municipal level, but without the right to speak to male voters or mix with men during the campaign).

These regimes offer approved candidates the chance of higher office. The head of government is blessed through electoral confirmation. And they allow a measure of multiparty competition.

Despotisms also bring to perfection the dark arts of manipulation. Living proof that elections can be functional instruments of top-down rule, these regimes harass and exclude candidates considered undesirable, as happened in the 2016 parliamentary elections in Vietnam, when Mai Khoi, a popular young musician trying to run for parliament, was subjected to a range of dirty tricks, including threatened eviction from her apartment, police harassment of her parents, and extended questioning by the immigration authorities when she returned home from a European tour. Despotisms buy votes and intimidate voters. They concoct sensational media events, gerrymander constituency boundaries, alter voter rolls, miscount votes, and make ballots magically disappear.

So why then do despotisms bother with staging phantom elections? It is a mistake to suppose that despotic rulers are disconnected from reality, or that they live in a permanent state of denial, or that the elections they convene are merely bad jokes, propaganda-massaged plebiscites. Elections are in fact useful tools of rule. They have a make-believe quality that materially serves to improve the quality and precision of the government of subjects. Context matters, of course. There are always local reasons at work. In China, the Party's support for local elections was initially driven by the need to rebuild its damaged legitimacy in the countryside following the large-scale violence and social disruption of the Cultural Revolution. In Iran, where revolutionary forces overthrew a cruel, American-backed dictator, the end of war with Iraq and the waning of theocratic rule forced the acceptance of the principle of competitive elections for city council seats, parliament, and the presidency. And in Vietnam, the ruling

Communist Party chose to oil and perfume its reputation by means of multilevel People's Council elections and parliamentary elections designed to appoint candidates on a two-round basis (candidates must receive at least 50 percent of votes cast in the first round, or otherwise face a second round decided by a plurality) to the National Assembly, which chooses the next prime minister of the country.

These local dynamics are important, but there are general reasons why despotism embraces periodic voting. Once they happen, the strategic reliance on periodic elections comes to be shaped by what economists and political scientists call path dependency: although the decision to stage elections is born of specific circumstances, the decision later becomes irreversible, if only because elections lend a democratic feel to the political system, and scrapping them would prove deeply unpopular, judged by many citizens as a sign that the rulers were attempting to sever their dependence upon the people. Elections may result in the felt improvement of the lives of people. In China, for instance, villages with elected officials seem more willing to tax themselves and to spend substantially more (on average around 27 percent, though data quality varies) on such things as tree plantings, irrigation schemes, roads, and primary schools.[50] In Iran, where the supreme leader despot acts as if he is the real thing, elections do yield results: they serve as small but significant triggers of government policy, even though nominated candidates are vetted behind closed doors by the Guardian Council, a twelve-member group appointed by the chief justice and his Excellency the Supreme Leader.

Elections have other politically useful functions. They enable dissenters in the governing hierarchy some room for maneuver. Electoral contests can help settle old scores, resolve disputes, and offer low-cost exit options for discontented regime politicians.

Elections can create opportunities for spotting new talent (that is, budding accomplices of the ruling power). They distribute patronage to supporters and potential supporters, and serve as early warning detectors of disaffection and opposition. Elections also provide much-needed information to those who govern. In one-party despotisms such as Laos and Vietnam, information shortages continually dog rulers, who cannot be sure whether their subject populations genuinely worship them or only appear to worship them because they demand obedience. Elections help solve this problem by enabling rulers to keep an eye on current and potential dissidents and to learn about the performance and popularity ratings of their subordinates, especially subnational cadres and officials who daily operate far from the direct oversight of the rulers. The information so gleaned not only helps guarantee electoral victory but also enables rulers to formulate longer-term plans, readjust their policies, and even ask more from their subjects in such matters as taxation, urban planning, and military service.[51]

In multiparty systems, by contrast, elections can be powerful means of placing opponents in a quandary: their almost-certain loss means they suffer demoralization and a high risk of disintegration. Tajikistan, where roses are lavished on voters as they enter polling stations, is a case in point: there, on a typical turnout of around 90 percent of adult voters, the People's Democratic Party consistently wins a sizable majority of votes and seats in the Assembly of Representatives at the expense of small parties such as the Agrarian Party of Tajikistan, Party of Economic Reforms of Tajikistan, and Socialist Party of Tajikistan. Fringe parties such as the Communist Party of Tajikistan and the Islamic Renaissance Party of Tajikistan are swept aside.[52]

In all despotisms, periodic elections also have the effect of reinforcing the legitimacy of the sultans who rule from the saddles of high power. In much the way a cunning cat about to pounce and kill its prey may choose to bide its time, granting the mouse space in which to run around and to grow hopeful that things will end well (though they do not), rulers use elections to toy with their subjects. Elections offer breathing space for subjects, respite from felt repression. In some quarters, elections may breed hopes for change. Yet in truth they are exercises in voluntary servitude. When citizens vote, they do more than cast votes. They give themselves away. They license the rulers. They lend them authority. The razzamatazz of elections is an awesome celebration of the mighty power of the regime. It may even offer its subjects a chance to behave as if they believe in the regime, through something like an "election contract."

Once victorious, the elected act as if they are the elect. They do not think of themselves as recallable, or as servants of the governed. To govern is to keep the people calm and quiet. Voters must turn out on the great choosing day, but ideally they should show little or no interest in the procedures and timings of elections. They must not complain about government, big business interests and political maneuverings, or vote-buying and vote-rigging. Elections are public rituals, carnivals of domination. The job of those seeking election is to convince people that they are well served, and that nothing else matters. If voters complain about discrimination, government selfishness, and embezzlement of funds, then their bellyaching must not be confused with yearning for the replacement of the present system. They must think of themselves as appendages of a state that is fundamentally on the right track. They must believe that what they want is good, strong leadership from above. This is all in accordance with the despotic principle that the elected know best and that their task is to keep in touch with the people in order to correct their wrongheaded opinions and guarantee their true interests.

Staging elections can be risky business, of course. When despotic rulers hold elections, they expect to win. But things can go wrong. When they do, because voters do not behave as expected, the controlling powers risk a double embarrassment. Not only does their electoral defeat show that the powerful are weaker than was thought, but people learn that elections can involve real choice, rather than merely operating as ritual selection exercises. When things go wrong in that way, the rulers typically resort to election stealing (as happened in 2009 in Iran, in the 2011 Russian Duma elections, and in Wukan, in the Chinese province of Guangdong, in September 2011).[53] They quickly announce victory. In the name of "restoration of peaceful order" and "stability maintenance," officials use every trick in the book to win back control. Leaders of the electoral rebellion are tracked down and encouraged publicly to repent. The dead come to life; the disgraced are rehabilitated. The matter is then settled amid a hail of truncheons, pepper spray, and gunfire. The ballot counters prove by their actions that the really important thing in elections is not who votes but who counts and calls the votes. The police and army are left to show that bullets can trump ballots, proving that in the end elections are raw exercises in bludgeoning the people by the rulers of the people, for the claimed good of the people.

Media Power

Abu Dhabi

General elections can be the crowning moments of the call by despots to rule indefinitely by popular demand. Yet precisely because things sometimes go wrong at the polls, rulers do not depend exclusively on elections. Sly despots know the dangers of relying on fickle voters. They are well aware that history is much bigger than rigged elections and phantom by-elections. That is why they harness supplementary methods of winning popular support. In between the stage dramas of periodic elections, rulers use nonstop media manipulation to win approval from those whom they rule.

To understand how they manage to do this, in distinctive style, we need first to go back, to take stock of things, in order to prepare for some surprises. We have seen that the new despotisms defy the standard textbook categories and classifications of political science. A new species of top-down rule marked by recombinant qualities, these despotisms are systems of state-regulated capitalism in which wide gaps between rich and poor are bridged by top-to-bottom patron-client connections, middle-class loyalty, staged elections, and a great deal of officially sanctioned talk of the people as the veritable source of political order. Yet there is another secret, something else of fundamental importance, vital for understanding how the new despotisms operate: these are systems of rule that manage to weaponize the unfinished digital communications revolution of our time.

Everybody knows that this incomplete media revolution has ended spectrum scarcity, mass broadcasting, and predictable prime-time national audiences. Our age of communicative abundance is structured by a new global system of overlapping and interlinked digital media structures and devices such as mobile phones and artificially intelligent robots.[1] For the first time in history, thanks to smart algorithms and built-in cheap microprocessors, this system integrates texts, sounds, and images in digitally compact and easily storable, reproducible, and portable form. Communicative abundance enables messages to be sent and received through multiple user points, at chosen times (either in real time or delayed), within modularized and ultimately global networks that are affordable and accessible to several billion people scattered everywhere. Viewed historically, the transformative potential of this new mode of digital communication is astonishing. Yet the whole world is slowly learning that its disruptive force and positive effects should not blindly be exaggerated. Communicative abundance does not bring paradise to earth. In the same way that in the 1920s the advent of mass broadcasting (radio and cinema, then television) gave a helping hand to the birth of totalitarian power, so the age of digital platforms and networks and communicative abundance makes possible the spread of despotic rule.

The new despotisms confirm the formula that, historically speaking, different modes of power always take advantage of new modes of communication. How do they do this? Most obviously, the rulers of the new despotisms don't hide themselves away behind

THE NEW DESPOTISM

walls of secrecy, as old-fashioned dictators liked to do, and as early modern commentators typically supposed when denouncing despotism as a system of government shrouded in "the silence which reigns in the seraglio."[2] The new despotisms are just the opposite. They are visual, noisy, and garrulous affairs. They make full use of communicative abundance. Despots like publicity, and liking money as well, they surround themselves with media conglomerates. More than a few despotisms display Disney-like qualities, melding their governments with corporate media, journalism, advertising, and entertainment. The state-capitalist dalliance serves multiple functions. Large media firms depend upon the protective regulatory frameworks established by despotic governments. The media conglomerates like tax breaks, safe havens, business parks, and handouts in the form of government contracts. The effectiveness of governments and their methods of tightening surveillance require secure access to communication infrastructures. Big media conglomerates are serial tax dodgers, but they do generate employment and play a large role as drivers and gatekeepers of the middle-class consumer economy. Not to be underestimated is their role as fairy godmothers blessed with the power of sprinkling incumbent governments with the magic dust of positive media coverage—or of dishing out crusades and bullying, shit lists, character assassinations, black public relations, and other types of rough media treatment.

Remarkably, more than a few despots, with the help of media giants, try to turn their political regimes into works of art. The new despotisms have a fancy for status-driven architectural wonders and construction megaprojects. Prize-winning architects and lucre-loving developers launch projects featuring land reclamation, posh apartment towers, floating seahorse-shaped villas with underwater bedrooms, artificial beaches, beach club spas, infinity pools, even climate-controlled public squares in the desert cooled by artificial snow. The landmarks include Dubai's tree-shaped Palm Jumeirah island; China's Nanhui, a German-designed new city built on land reclaimed from the sea, marked by a beach, forested park, and huge artificial lake inspired by the design metaphor of concentric ripples formed in water by a single drop; and Qatar's Lusail complex, a smart city built for the 2022 World Cup, featuring the Qetaifan Islands, a place advertised as offering "a fresh perspective on life." The islands are a man-made paradise, where the dwellings are "a true indication of style and status, where luxurious waterfront living meets exclusive property and a warm community feel."

The new despotisms have soft spots for the pomp and circumstance of grand sporting events and other entertainment spectacles that radiate the impression that life is good and progress is happening on all fronts. We are going to see that the new despotisms are jumpy about bad news, nervous about the past, and censorial, but that is why, through media spectacles, they strive to add new content and style to the old art of bread and circuses.

Consider the cosmopolitan metropolis of Abu Dhabi.[3] Capital city of the United Arab Emirates, the largest of its seven semi-autonomous city-states, and currently ranked among the richest cities in the world, Abu Dhabi is ruled by royals who have pulled out all stops to move it beyond its reputation as one of the world's largest oil producers and toward being a new skyscraper Hollywood of the age of communicative abundance. Home to Etihad Airways, state-controlled mosques, and nearly a million people, including a wealthy middle class and a large majority of nonunionized and often badly treated migrant workers, Abu Dhabi has become a haven for global media conglomerates. It is home to the world's first graduate-level, research-based artificial intelligence university (MBZUAI). The city aspires to be the kingpin in a media production and supply chain that "unites the world." Huge oil and gas revenues and sovereign wealth funds (among the world's largest) have been pumped into Abu Dhabi Media, the state-owned group that owns and directs much of the domestic media, including the world's first fiber-to-the-home network, mobile phone services, newspapers, and television and radio stations, including one that is devoted to readings from the Quran. Abu Dhabi Media has working partnerships with Fox International Channels, a unit of News International, and enjoys Arabic-language programming deals with such giants as National Geographic and Comedy Central. Abu Dhabi Media also hosts Image Nation, a body that underwrites the production of feature films. A free-zone office park project called twofour54 (named after the city's geographical coordinates) houses foreign news agencies, including CNN, which produces a daily news show for its global channel. Twofour54 boasts state-of-the-art production facilities as well as a venture capital arm to invest in promising Arabic-language media start-ups, and it hosts a world-class media training academy that offers short skills-based courses targeted at talented young media workers.

For culture consumers, there is the government-controlled Abu Dhabi Exhibition Center; the Abu Dhabi Grand Prix; the Abu Dhabi Classical Music Society, which boasts a strong and visible following; the Louvre Abu Dhabi; and the Abu Dhabi Cultural Foundation, which works to preserve and publicize "the art and culture of the city." Of vital strategic importance to the ruling authorities is the government marketing and entertainment body called Flash Entertainment, whose motto is "Put simply, we make people happy." It has presented big-name musical acts like Beyoncé, Christina Aguilera, and Aerosmith, and sporting events such as the AFC Asian Cup 2019 (with its slogan "Bringing Asia Together"). Vexed questions about whether, or to what extent, the citizens and noncitizens of the UAE are happy, what happiness means, or whether they or their journalist representatives might freely be able to remedy their unhappiness remain unanswered. More than a few Western expatriates living there simply don't care about answers.[4]

Abu Dhabi fancies itself as the new Hollywood without the old California. Governed by leading members of the ruling family, open public monitoring of power is *haram* (forbidden). Its citizens are rentiers and vassals, beneficiaries of state-guaranteed jobs, transfer payments, and other forms of untaxed income and wealth. Free and fair elections are regarded as a thing from yesteryear. Democracy makes no political sense, say members of the royal family privately, as it causes unwanted social divisions. Hence the priority they give to blocking hundreds of websites considered publicly offensive and to routinely cleansing local media infrastructures of pornography and blasphemous commentaries on the God-given noble blood of the rulers.

Vaudeville

Operating within media-saturated environments serviced by large media conglomerates, rulers do all they can to be seen and heard constantly on multiple media platforms. Communicative abundance feeds despotism in ways unimaginable to thinkers of the past. The ancient Athenian tyrant Pisistratus (608–527 BCE) won political fame using dirty tricks, such as slashing himself and the mules hauling his chariot with a sword just prior to staging a bloody entrance into the agora (public marketplace) to show why he deserved the support of the assembly of male citizens; they voted him use of a public bodyguard of club-wielding citizens, who then helped him seize the Acropolis and control over Athens in 560 / 559 BCE. Machiavelli recommended that rulers should strive to become skilled practitioners of *simulatore e dissimulatore,* the art of appearing to others what in fact they are not. He cited the case of the early fourteenth-century Roman senator Castruccio Castracani, who assumed office dressed in a brocaded toga bearing on its front the words "God wills it" and on its back "What God wills shall be."[5] Writing in the age of the quill, ink, and parchment, when rulers divined their subjects into believing that monarchs were the earthly head of their realms just as Jesus Christ was their Savior, Machiavelli could not have anticipated how life under conditions of despotism is a permanent public relations bombardment campaign. Cunning old Pisistratus and Machiavelli would be astonished at the new rulers' taste for omnivorous self-publicity. The new despotisms are theater states: everybody and everything is entangled in printed texts, sounds, and images designed to function as props of ruling power, without respite.

Why the intensive publicity? The most obvious reason is that under conditions of despotism the powerful know they must never be spotted naked. Power denuded is power taunted. Despots learn from hard experience that no polity can survive over time unless it has public support. Here there is a more general point, with a particular twist. Following Talleyrand, historians and political thinkers refer to the political problem of legitimacy faced by all rulers.[6] They remind us that insofar as power exercised over others easily induces fears of corruption, disorder, and violence, fears that engulf rulers and the ruled alike, stable and secure government requires the tempering of fear by cultivating shared feelings ("spirit," Montesquieu called it) among the governed that existing power arrangements are backed by principles of good government, and are therefore right and proper, and should be honored and respected. According to this way of thinking, principles of legitimacy are justifications of power. They are magical formulae that have alchemical effects. Arbitrarily chosen rules come to seem wholly reasonable. Contingent principles pass for timeless truths that are self-evident and unalterable. Monarchy, aristocracy, democracy: these and other sets of incommensurable principles of legitimacy, the historians and political thinkers tell us, imply a contract between rulers and ruled, who are duty-bound to obey rules reinforced by the prevailing set of governing institutions.

Note the presumption in this way of thinking about legitimacy that each set of arbitrarily defined rules directly corresponds to a particular set of governing institutions. Things are not like that in the new despotisms. Their poetics of power are different. Remarkable is the way they manage to break with the one-regime, one-mode-of-legitimacy principle. Despotisms take a leaf out of the book of Charles V, the legendary sixteenth-century Holy Roman Emperor who chose to learn so many languages in order to rule over his vast empire that he was said (according to contemporary anecdotes) to speak Spanish to God, Italian to friends, German to enemies, and French to lovers. The new despotisms similarly practice the art of ruling through multiple sources of legitimacy; their ships of state are powered by winds blowing from many directions. Twentieth-century totalitarian regimes ruled through a combination of all-purpose terror and a dominant "glorious myth" ideology that claimed "to know the mysteries of the whole historical process" and its supposed "natural" laws, such as the coming triumph of the classless society and the inevitability of a war between "chosen" and "degenerate" races. The new despotisms ditch ideologies.[7] Their rulers come draped in colorful magic coats made of different languages and styles. The colors are those of a scrambled sunset. To switch images, the new despotisms resemble an impressive political show, a souped-up version of early twentieth-century vaudeville, performances that featured strongmen and singers, dancers and drummers, minstrels and magicians, acrobats and athletes, comedians and circus animals.

The big despotism tent show is a new type of vaudeville government, let's call it. The rulers parade their magicians, drummers, and dancers. They preach the national interest, national solidarity, and the recapturing of "national dignity" and "national pride." "Sovereignty" is a favorite word in their arsenal. So are weaponized phrases such as "law and order," "peace," "anti-imperialism," and protection from "foreign enemies." Acting like open-door cages in search of unsuspecting birds, despotisms encourage their subjects to say things like "We don't have any problem with this government and our leader. We respect him. He's strong. The government has brought stability. It has done a lot for our country." The worship of country means that past national catastrophes and failures must be forgotten; as in Chinese author Ma Jian's fantastical story of the search for "China Dream Soup," government-enforced denial and forgetfulness are compulsory.[8] There is instead pragmatic, businesslike patter about "stability" and "growth." Forced redevelopment, earning money, growing rich, and general prosperity are articles of faith. Loyal subjects say: "Our lives have improved. Millions have been lifted out of poverty. Even if hard times come, we'll support the government."

There is much talk of revealing "truth," and it often comes mixed with divine inspirations, allusions to climbing Jacob's ladder to heaven, and stern calls to "obey Allah and obey the Messenger and those in authority among you" (Quran 4:59). In an age marked by the death of God, the powerful can be viewed with greater suspicion, hence their efforts to cling to religious scriptures, proverbs, and sayings. In Saudi Arabia, where seventy thousand mosques and the *mutawa,* or religious police, back the rulers' stated adherence to the ascetic principles of Wahhabism, more than a few subjects count themselves lucky that they are not getting the government they are promised. There is widespread awareness that since official religion has become a clunky ritual, there is room for parallel worlds in which Christianity, Sufism, and Shiite Islam are de facto tolerated; where middle-class Saudis shop, drink whiskey, and sleep with sex workers when on vacation in Bahrain and Lebanon; and where there are even spaces for young people (around 60 percent of the population is twenty years of age or younger) to do a spot of online "fatwa shopping."

In Erdoğan's Turkey, officials encourage musicians, radio and television programmers, teachers, and chefs to join the campaign to cast aside old feelings of inferiority and to make the Ottoman fatherland *(vatan)* great again by renewing Islam as a central pillar of public life. Oman's Ministry of Tourism sells its country as a place of authentic "heritage" *(turath)* expressed through "traditions" *(taqalid)* like those displayed at fine hotels, where staff in ceremonial dress warmly greet tourists with invitations to lounge on locally made carpets and sip coffee flavored with cardamom, rosewater, and dates, the air perfumed with the sweet, woody scent of burning frankincense. In Iran, a country often misdescribed as a theocracy, vaudeville is everywhere. Candidates in fiercely fought elections take religion for granted, as a common language, yet secular, this-wordly language is also spoken in abundance. Elections are of course strictly vetted by the Guardians Council, and references abound to sacred Shiite principles and practices: pilgrimages to shrines, intercession, mourning for Hussein (the grandson of Muhammad), and the reappearance of the Mahdi (the "hidden" imam). But there is simultaneously much profane talk of peace, welfare, economic growth, national stability, serving the people *(mardum),* advancing the status of women, the dangers of corruption, and the need to honor election outcomes.[9]

Under conditions of despotism, there are public displays of benevolence, national holidays, and ritual celebrations. The rainbow performances are designed as light entertainment that has the serious effect of putting blinkers on the eyes of public doubt. Turkmenistan's elected leader, Gurbanguly Berdymukhamedov, races fast cars, rides horses, publishes books, performs hospital operations and rap videos, writes serenades for women, strums his guitar at workers' rallies, and hands out televisions and other gifts to local citizens.[10] In China, leaders at all levels spout the mantras of "socialism," "harmonious society," "rule of law," "ancient Chinese civilization," and the "China dream." There's also lots of mellifluous chatter about "people's democracy." Elsewhere there are vocal expressions of nostalgia for pasts treated as paradise lost combined with calls for fresh beginnings and breakthroughs defined by greater respect from the wider world, territorial expansion, greater power, and more glory. And there are plenty of references to enemies, as in Orbán's Hungary, where the government-controlled media machine denounces "liberalism" and "liberal democracy" as the accomplice of a wide range of ills, from foreign disparagement of the Magyars as a great "global nation" to fractious party-political rivalries, dependence on the West, greedy multinational corporations, the criminality of Gypsies and the unemployed, and the public order threats posed by big banks, demonic Jewish financiers, homosexuals, and pedophiles.

The rulers mobilize communicative abundance to mix and stir different political languages at all levels of the polity. Despots know well that their power is suckled by the milk of symbols. Pomp and performance are not mere means to life but life itself, living proof that power is the servant of pomp, not the other way around. Despots understand that power is the ability to do through others symbolically what they are themselves unable to do alone. They know that language, broadly understood, is the medium of their power. That is why, like Dr. Francia, the figure at the center of the classic Paraguyuan novel *I, the Supreme* by Roa Bastos, despots grow nervous when confronted by public satire and lampoons. They dislike contrarian pasquinades because they understand that poetic language can assume a public life of its own, and that their loss of control over this medium will prove to be the decisive source of their downfall and defeat.

It is possible to imagine that despots dream in their beds of new ways of purifying the official language of politics; in their wildest dreams, some of them may secretly contemplate banning language altogether.[11] They don't in reality act upon such hallucinations. In the age of communicative abundance, making that move would require self-liquidation, and the liquidation of their subjects. Gone are the days of the crazed fantasy of the purification of language through its abolition, or (its flip side) concocting one big Glorious Myth propagated through endless repetition of organized drumbeat euphemisms, neologisms, and prefixes.[12]

Seen through the eyes of the rulers, the switch to vaudeville government wrapped in multiple languages has tactical advantages. For a start, despots don't necessarily suffer the fate of Hamlet, engulfed by the personal tragedy of having a duty to act but crippled by his inability to make up his mind and by his unwillingness to act on his convictions. Actually, vaudeville government is for the new despots liberating. They come steeped in the spirit of Shakespeare's Duke of Gloucester, confident in their ability to exercise power by adding colors to a chameleon and changing shapes with Proteus. Vaudeville government, by ditching ideological self-righteousness, enables despots to be different things to different people at different times.

Fans of despotism in Singapore typically praise its founding father, Lee Kuan Yew, as a tough-minded realist, an archetypal "benevolent dictator" who learned from the British and Japanese colonizers "how to govern, how you dominate the people," and who disliked yes-men because his favorite question was not "Is it right?" but "So what?" His eldest child and third prime minister of Singapore, Lee Hsien Loong, tellingly told *Fortune* magazine that while a "leadership pyramid" is needed to "hold the system together," governing is best conducted through "diversity and different views" rather than from "a single point."

Despots fancy themselves as purveyors of "reality without ideology," as Orbán put it.[13] The truth is that their vaudeville performances blur the boundaries between reality and fantasy. The political language of their performances is neither straightforwardly Orwellian nor describable in terms of what Michael Walzer famously called "failed totalitarianism," tyrannies "dressed up in fascist or communist clothing and acting out haphazardly some aspects of fascist or communist ideology."[14] Vaudeville government is more complicated, more willfully confusing than these thinkers could have imagined. Yes, there is the controlled government language of restricted grammar and vocabulary typical of newspeak. Yes, the dominant broadcast media are free—but only to say what they are told to say. And there is plenty of the euphemism, intentional ambiguity, semantic inversion, and sheer cloudy vagueness that are characteristic of doublespeak. But vaudeville government is far more slippery. It is pinned down with difficulty. It feels indescribable. Its kaleidoscopic language is not easily falsified. That is why it lends the regime a people-friendly quality.

The reality of despotism isn't negotiable, of course, yet opponents of the way things are do not need to be crushed outright. They can be mentioned, acknowledged, and even praised for a time. Surprise moves can be made, as when the Hungarian government led by Viktor Orbán, himself an atheist in his youth and then later an adherent of the Reformed Church, takes part in a Catholic procession and pardons the Muslim murderer of an Armenian Christian in the hope of securing a deal with the nearby despotism of Azerbaijan. The hypocrisy is normal, for the political aim of the rulers is to sail with the political winds, to outflank opponents and to get inside their heads, to exploit them, and, in the end, to make them look like marginal figures or outright fools.

The rulers are equally gripped by a powerful sense that in a world crowded by public stories jostling for attention, whoever tells better stories more aggressively and unscrupulously, whatever their degree of veracity, has a good chance of coming out on top. But closer inspection reveals that their storytelling is motivated by much more than playing factions off against one another in order to defeat them. Rulers know that cant corrupts. Their embrace of contradiction and speaking in tongues has a purpose: to gaslight their subjects into bemused submission.

The term "gaslighting" is indispensable when making sense of vaudeville government. It was coined in the 1950s, a reference to the 1944 film *Gaslight,* directed by George Cukor and starring Ingrid Bergman and Charles Boyer, in which a husband tries to convince his wife she is insane. But what does it mean in this new context? For the new despotisms, vaudeville performance is designed to push opponents into submission. It is a political weapon. Vaudeville is not just about winning votes, siding with friends, simulating openness, or managing political foes. Gaslighting is more insidious than the old Machiavellian "art of contrivance," in which government scripts and stages pseudo-stories and pseudo-events that function as illusions, counterfeit versions of things as they actually are.[15] Gaslighting cuts much more deeply into daily life: it is the organized effort to mess with subjects' identities, to deploy entertainment, conflicting stories, lies, bullshit,

THE NEW DESPOTISM

and silence for the purpose of sowing the seeds of doubt and confusion among subjects in order to control them fully and durably. The point is to drown subjects in shit, to flood their lives with gaseous excrement. Elected leaders under democratic conditions are supposed to behave differently. Take the example of American president Franklin Delano Roosevelt, who was well known for his governing strategy of sowing seeds of uncertainty among colleagues and friends. Until recently, Washington staffers and journalists would similarly speak in pragmatic ways of keeping "options open" and making sure that everybody is kept guessing until the moment a decision is made. The public gaslighting that takes place under conditions of despotism is qualitatively different, more comprehensive and intrusive in people's lives, more sinister in its effects. It is not just a tool of pragmatic public policymaking. It aims to confuse, disorient, and destabilize people. It wants to fuel self-doubt and ruin people's capacity for making judgments in order to drive them toward submission. Gaslighting through vaudeville government sets out to disprove those who think that "reality" will always trump falsehoods.[16] When gaslighting works, its victims report that they don't really know what's happening, or that they don't care. Without firing a shot, citizens are turned into complacent subjects. They buy the tactics of the manipulator. The subjects of despotism fall by default under the spell of their master wizards.

Magicians

The wizards who produce and direct the vaudeville stage show typically operate backstage, with the help of media conglomerates and well-organized media machines. Their job is to disprove linguists who say that language evades command management because it always functions as a protean, dynamic, self-regulating system of symbols that never sits still. Orbán's regime entrusts the job of symbol management to a ruling party stalwart named Antal Rogán, baron of the National Communication Office, which pumps out nonstop government messages and conducts campaigns against its opponents through radio and television advertisements, newspaper editorials, bus stop posters, chain emails, tweets, and Facebook posts. Bespectacled, youthful Võ Văn Thưởng, boss of the Central Propaganda Department of the Communist Party of Vietnam, similarly runs a tight operation that dispenses messages about the need for all organizations and the population to study and follow the "guiding principles" of Ho Chi Minh and to work for greater "innovation and efficiency and winning human hearts"; it spreads bon mots such as "laughter is the manifestation of political decadence." Erdoğan's image was curated by a master magician of signs, Erol Olçak, an advertiser who (before his death in the failed 2016 coup d'état) won public fame for a shrewd propaganda video, *The People Won't Bend Down, Turkey Won't Be Divided*. Among the chief gaslighters in China is the Shandong-born kung fu fan Wang Huning, a former university professor and now a member of the Politburo and frequenter of Zhongnanhai, China's equivalent of the White House, who for some time has peddled advice to the Party leadership about the need for a "China dream" in the form of a strong and resilient and uncorrupted state that promotes economic growth and deals with the dangers of environmental pollution.[17]

Surely the title of Master of the Dark Arts of Gaslighting goes to Vladislav Surkov, a drama graduate of the Moscow Institute of Culture and Vladimir Putin's former chief court magician, a "gray cardinal" political strategist and champion of "sovereign democracy" *(suverennaya demokratiya)*.[18] During Putin's first two terms in office, the novelist, playwright, political technician, and public relations fixer worked hard to turn the Russian state into a work of art better suited to "new realities." The media spectacles resembled a Theatre of the Absurd performance. Surkov helped create new political parties and pro-Kremlin youth organizations (like Nashi) skilled at destroying opposition to Putin and working toward a new type of democratic rule that he considered uniquely suited to "Russian political culture." The word "democracy" left the lips of Surkov riddled with ambivalence: unaccompanied by the adjective "sovereign," it is a synonym for "distrust and criticism," political weakness, low quality, and "leveling" (Russians speak of the "democratic prices" of chicken sandwiches and french fries from McDonald's). That is why Surkov liked to quote the Ukrainian-Russian author and playwright Nikolai Gogol: "If there isn't one head managing everything it becomes a complex muddle. It's difficult even to say why; evidently, it's something about the people. The only meetings that work out are the ones held for revelling or a bit of lunch." He adds that Russian-style democracy is "rule, strength and order, not weakness, confusion and disorder." The contrast with Western democracy, which is based on the "illusion of choice"—the "main trick of the Western way of life in general and of Western democracy in particular"—is stark. The great strength of "the modern Russian model of statehood" is that it "begins with trust and rests on trust. This is its fundamental difference with the Western model, which cultivates mistrust and criticism."

In practice, Surkov's thinking implies full support for Putin, the ruler who issues constant reminders that "the national agenda calls for active work to modernize the country, not a public holiday to sit around talking about how great it is." According to Surkov, the "Russian political algorithm" proves that sovereign democracy requires "an effective, leading class." It strives to be "sophisticated, but not malicious" (the words once used by Einstein when describing God). Hands-on grooming and manipulation of the local mainstream media are especially significant in securing its effectiveness. Pretense is power. Winning the "informational battle . . . for minds" is imperative for defending the "spirit" of Russia: "a desire for political cohesion through the centralization of authority, the idealisation of goals and the personification of politics."[19]

The quintessence of the "personification of politics," the crowning media moment of the struggle to gaslight subjects, is the annual press conference featuring Putin. Meticulously choreographed, watched by millions, the show lasts several hours. Putin is at center stage, relaxed, serious, sometimes grinning, without a teleprompter, indefatigable, and the master of ceremonies. He knows he is the breaking news, the main story, the country's fortune-teller. The courtier journalists come equipped with brightly colored banners and toys, some dressed in smart suits or short skirts in order to catch the president's eye. They fawn; they feel graced by his presence. Nothing fazes him. He is beyond good and evil, pride and humility. General questions are commonplace. "Dear Mr. President," runs a common type of non-question, "are things going as well as you expected in the difficult war against terrorism?" Or, "How is the strength of our economy?" The man spouts homilies: "There have always been issues. There will always be issues, but we will surely win. My guide is the interests of Russia. Our country is big and complex. We value relations with China and hope that they will develop." Smiles greet the unobjectionably local questions: "Could you please tell us your favorite color, Mr. President?" "How do you find time to do gym workouts so regularly?" "Are you traveling abroad soon?" At one point, an unbroken three hours of questions and answers behind him, His Eminence jokes: "Love will turn into hatred if we continue this for too long." He carries on. He tells Russians that it's high time they get up off their knees. There are softer moments when he plays the role of paterfamilias (or perhaps godfather) of the whole nation: "It's best not to slap children," he recommends. He is then asked whether the state will address the declining popularity of reading among children—for instance, through its support for libraries. "Undoubtedly," he answers, "they need to be revived. They are important for children." Cute questions are awarded equally cute answers: when asked what kind of robot the Kremlin needs, Putin answers that robots "are important, but so are people. Robots are needed in manufacturing, but we deal with sensitive issues that have an impact on human lives, so we have to be human, and cannot rely on robots." Nebulous questions get foggy answers mixed with factoids, platitudes, and non sequiturs. The pointed questions are stonewalled. "What's your biggest mistake as a president?" a journalist dares ask. "Every person makes mistakes," he replies. "It is important to draw conclusions. Next question."

The vaudeville performances are as impeccably polished as the Russian media world is topsy-turvy. It is as if the new vaudeville tactics are drawn straight from the old book of rules drawn up by Alexander Shuvalov, the prominent chief of the secret police during the mid-eighteenth-century reign of the Russian empress Elizabeth Petrovna: "Always keep the accused confused." One moment there are announcements about new funding for civic forums and human rights NGOs. At the next moment support is given to young skinheads, to rehabilitating old fascist ideas (of intellectuals such as Ivan Ilyin, from the 1920s), and to defending nationalist movements that attack NGOs as tools of the West. Victories in war are announced in speeches that describe Russia as an "encircled fortress" threatened by a "decadent West" and "fascists" in denial of a "Russia that is great again." Strange but striking is the obsession with sexual purity, evident in official rhetoric about the "homosexual" efforts of the United States and the European Union to "sodomize" Russian virtue.[20] All this rhetoric comes mixed with talk of modernization, human rights, and sponsorship of lavish arts festivals featuring provocative hipster Moscow artists before support is switched to black-clad Orthodox fundamentalists who proceed to attack modern art as decadent. "The Kremlin's idea," observes a prominent journalist, summarizing the logic of Russian-style gaslighting, "is to own all forms of political discourse, to not let any independent movements develop outside of its walls. Its Moscow can feel like an oligarchy in the morning and a democracy in the afternoon, a monarchy for dinner and a totalitarian state by bedtime."[21]

The dynamics seem to be replays of the point long ago made by our French tutor Montesquieu, who remarked that under conditions of modern despotism nobody is safe from insecurity. Writing in the age of the printing press, book, pamphlet, and newspaper, he could not have foreseen, let alone imagined, just how in the age of communicative abundance those who live under despotic conditions suffer intense new forms of media discombobulation. In matters of publicity, nothing is fixed, frozen, or forever. Despotisms may seem inwardly calm and stable, but they are pell-mell worlds, regimes of media confusion. Deep uncertainty is a lived reality for many subjects. Those who pay attention often feel dizzy, as if their sense of balance has been disabled by a brain that isn't able to process and coordinate the constant swirls of information. Nothing is straightforward. Nothing is true. In this looking-glass world, everything is conceivable, imaginable, and sayable, especially if the means of manipulation and silencing can be found to say what is wanted and to prevent others from saying and getting what they want.

Media Blackouts

Under these conditions of vaudeville government, making sense of things isn't straightforward. We could say that if real things were embodied straightforwardly in upside-down images, then subjects intent on decoding the world of power would simply have to stand on their heads. Practice would quickly make perfect. The misfortune suffered by subjects of the new despotism is that things are never straightforwardly up or down or across. That is why, as in Saudi Arabia, they have to wear "multiple faces—two, three, four, five, six faces."[22] Most people know they live under a canopy of media spectacles and media blackouts. In some quarters, there is acute awareness that the principle of WYSIWYG (what you see is what you get) simply doesn't apply. It follows that since official definitions of reality are typically kaleidoscopic and in perpetual motion, interested citizens are forced to spend quite a lot of time decoding what is being said, or not being said, or revealed. They practice the art of suspecting and seeing through appearances; some of them rate dietrology (decoding official explanations in order to grasp *dietro,* or what is behind them) among their favorite hobbies.

Talk of conspiracies and cabals flourishes under these conditions. Open secrets—things most people know, spread by gossip and whisperings—are commonplace. Yet people know there are strict limits, electric fences, lines that mustn't be crossed. They understand that some things are better left unsaid. The electric fences are typically as invisible as they are effective. Not only do they protect the ruling powers, but they encourage the regime's subjects to believe that they are acting independently.[23] Willful self-censorship flourishes. It sits like a raven on people's shoulders. So also do skepticism and disaffection. Yet not all the subjects of despotism are easily fooled all the time, or rendered docile by gaslighting, which is why despots specialize in information crackdowns and careful gatekeeping to regulate when and where who says what to whom.

The means of censorship are formidable. Despotisms harbor well-kept secrets. Secrecy is indispensable for their successful operation as top-down modes of power. Subjects must be kept in the dark by a system of secrets and regulated information flows reinforced by unusually well-coordinated political dos and don'ts. The media blackouts are backed by a smorgasbord of sanctions familiar to all journalists: a cup of tea with the censors, sharp reprimands by editors, sideways promotions, physical attacks by unidentified thugs, disappearances, and imprisonment (sometimes in "black jails" operated by outsourced mafia gangs employed by the rulers). The pattern is evident in the regime of Ilham Aliyev in Azerbaijan, where investigative journalists, human rights activists, and civil society activists are regularly pressured, beaten, or jailed as "traitors."[24] Within all the new despotisms, tight-fisted controls are most obvious in the field of television. In China, for example, more than a billion people access programs through countrywide, provincial, and metropolitan stations. Foreign satellite channels such as CNN are not widely available and are subject to periodic shutdown. The Publicity Department and the State Administration of Radio, Film, and Television regularly intervene in matters of program content throughout the country, for instance by ordering channels to limit the length and frequency of entertainment shows, to carry state-approved news items, and, in tricky situations, to disregard audience ratings when deciding on program schedules.

Controls on the content of radio programming are equally strict. Under despotism, there is no real "live" broadcasting; transmission delays are used to filter out possible damaging news items, especially when the rulers are under pressure. Things are more complicated in the field of newspapers, where a combination of regional and linguistic differences and commercial pressures often results in significant variations, even the evasion of controls by editors. A censorship-avoidance game is played hard in the exceptions. The labyrinthine structures of regime control within the world of newspapers are difficult to grasp, even for insiders, in part because market competition provides space for a variety of mastheads, but also because the likes and dislikes of readers are important. In consequence, despite state controls, funding shortages, and the atmosphere of physical intimidation, in-depth investigative journalism sometimes still happens.[25]

Strict state controls flourish in the field of digital communications media, where thanks to the unfinished digital communications revolution rulers find censorship a trickier affair. Things are changing fast. Consider the most important case of China, a global empire-in-the-making. ChinaNet, the first internet service provider (ISP) in the country, was officially launched only in 1995. Back then, the internet provided a select few users with a limited range of basic services, such as email, web surfing, newsgroups, and chat rooms.[26] Since that period, helped by state intervention and support, the field of digital communications media has expanded at a remarkable pace. There are now more than 800 million users (57.7 percent of China's population), who spend on average more than twenty-six hours per week online, more time than on any other medium. The Party's desire to promote "indigenous innovation," to use only technologies manufactured by homegrown companies rather than being reliant on foreign manufacturers, has helped make Chinese technology companies such as Lenovo, Huawei, and Xiaomi major competitors within global communications markets. The

Party's stated goal is for China to become an "innovation ori-
ented society" and a "world leader in science and technology" by
2050.[27]

The figures are dizzying, but the sobering fact remains that the
governors of despotic regimes remain concerned about the dishar-
monious effects of digital media on the political order. They are
profoundly ambivalent about communicative abundance. With
good reason, as we are about to see, they fear that the more citizens go online, the more the power monopoly of the rulers is open
to challenge. That is why the frightened rulers of Iran for the first
time (in November 2019) shut down internet access to 95 percent
of the population but kept open internet usage to government departments by using their National Information Network, a restricted domestic digital infrastructure sometimes referred to as
the "halal net." The fear of public resistance explains why despots
put political pressure on national and foreign information technology companies to censor, filter, and control the expanding
flows of data exchanged on the web. It is also why officials in practically every despotism insist that a key government priority is to
establish a firm regulatory framework that (in their jargon) im-
proves "management of new network technologies and applications," especially through improved "emergency response" systems
that handle "sudden incidents" and (as Chinese Communist Party
officials say) "maintain stability" *(wéi hù wěn dìng)*.

It's also why citizens who refuse to play the game are subject to
a wide assortment of informal and legal punishments, ranging
from official warnings, daily harassment, and hefty fines to years
spent behind bars. Networking citizens who actively raise and engage issues of public concern can quickly find themselves in trouble.
Exemplary punishment of individuals is a favorite deterrent. Not
even netizens backed by millions of followers are automatically

safe, as Charles Xue, an outspoken, wealthy Chinese American entrepreneur known online as Xue Mansi, found to his great personal cost. In 2014, in a well-known case, he was arrested and imprisoned for eight months on charges of "soliciting prostitutes." Few independent observers believed this; rather, they judged that he was being punished for blogging complaints about the Party's failure to promote political reform. Xue was paraded on television and forced publicly to admit his sins, which included, among other charges, spreading online rumors and losing sight of his place in society. He was told to admit that his huge online following (more than 12 million people) didn't make him superior to the state, and that his online behavior deserved punishment because it risked producing "social chaos" *(shè huì dòng dàng).*[28]

Easily the best-known censorship tools used by the new despotisms are elaborate electronic surveillance systems, known officially in China as the Golden Shield *(jīn dùn gōng chéng)* but commonly referred to elsewhere as firewalls. These countrywide electronic barriers filter and control information flows so that all digital data traffic in and out of the country passes through a limited number of gateways controlled by ISPs, specially programmed network computers, or routers. The architecture is sometimes likened officially to a system of rules and regulations for policing automobile traffic, but the key difference is that under these conditions digital media users are often left in the dark about the routings and rules of the road.[29] Invisibility is the controlling norm; the banned keywords and websites are kept secret. Unless users have access to leaked memoranda, they never know whether the pages they are searching for are unavailable for technical reasons or whether they have encountered government censorship. Their computer screens simply display a common error message (such as "site not found"); or they are greeted by these words: "According to relevant laws, regulations, and policies, the system doesn't show the content you are searching."

The algorithmic filters used by despotisms in Russia, Iran, China, and elsewhere spot homonyms and synonyms used by activists to tunnel through censorship walls. The filters are continuously reviewed and upgraded, with added features such as the ability to detect, discover, and block virtual private networks (VPNs), which are used routinely by citizens to access web services beyond the established firewalls. The tussles confirm the rule that uncertainty is a key ingredient of the spirit of despotism: consistent with their gaslighting methods, censors use "flexible" or "open" censorship to keep everybody guessing. Although some websites (such as the *New York Times,* the *Guardian,* the *Financial Times,* or Wikipedia) may be permanently blocked, especially because they publish material deemed politically too close to the bone, official lists of censored websites and keywords are not fixed. Some sites are normally accessible but then blocked at more sensitive moments, as for instance happened in early 2013 when the Guangzhou-based *Southern Weekend* published an open letter criticizing the Party's rewriting of its New Year's editorial, headed "China's Dream, the Dream of Constitutionalism." The newspaper's website was promptly shut down, officially because its license had expired, and such terms as "Southern" and "Weekend" were suddenly blacklisted.[30]

Under despotic arrangements, such measures are normal; constantly tweaked, "flexible" controls that predetermine which information citizens can download, read, publish, or distribute are commonplace. Censors frown upon anonymous users. Government regulations demand that users wanting to build a website must register with internet regulators in person and present their ID. Real-name registration is often a legal requirement for internet users when uploading videos to online platforms. The same rule applies to all mobile application developers and users of micro-blogs and instant-messaging tools.[31]

The systems of censorship naturally require the cooperation of digital technology companies. Official documents stress the need to be permanently on the lookout for threats to "sovereignty" or "social order." Foreign companies, such as Cisco Systems, the world's leading supplier of networking management and equip-ment, are caught up in this system; so, too, are tech giants such as IBM, Google, Amazon, and Microsoft.[32] They are expected to share their surveillance technologies and user data with the state; they are also required to exercise self-restraint and to act as zealous gate-keepers of the political order. Companies that refuse to cooperate with the state may find their business operating licenses with-drawn. Refusal to comply with official requests can be costly, which is why many foreign companies (or their local legal subsidiaries) cooperatively share information stored in their own databases with the ruling powers. Prominent cases of collaboration have included Cisco's sale of internet surveillance gear to the Chinese govern-ment in the early 1990s; the support of California-based Yahoo! Holdings for Chinese prosecutors who sentenced the journalist Shi Tao to ten years in prison for leaking a government censorship memo on the anniversary of the Tiananmen Square massacre; and Google's prototype Project Dragonfly app, designed to conform to Chinese censorship rules by automatically "blacklisting sensitive queries" and filtering websites blocked in China.

Local media companies tend to be just as compliant. Not only do these merchants of media blackout offer up information when it is officially requested, they also fuel the whole censorship and surveillance system by zealously filtering data and/or storing users' logs for future use by the authorities.[33] In China, Sina Corporation and Tencent are examples. Offering microblogs and instant-messaging services to millions of users, they operate rumor-control and website-cleaning teams that employ thousands of staff (perhaps up to seventy thousand censors, the rule of thumb being two censors per fifty thousand users) whose job is to block forbidden content day and night.[34]

Media Seduction

We return here to a foundational idea of this book: despotisms are not systems of denial and repression. Censorship and internet shutdowns aren't their whole story, or even the most interesting part of the story of how they handle the unfinished digital communications revolution. Despots in fact make every effort to beguile and bewitch their subjects into accepting their regimes of power. The most sophisticated despotisms—Saudi Arabia, Singapore, Russia, and China—strive to be publicly attractive. They want to be cool. Seduction, not repression, is their preferred method. It is an old art in new forms. Historians tell us that the despots of the Byzantine Empire were always decorated in pearls and the colors purple and white. Early modern Russian despots bathed themselves in the splendor of glorious entries, coronations, weddings, name days, funerals, and sumptuous ceremonies such as the Blessing of the Waters. The new despots practice the old art of seduction using new technical means. Television, radio, print, and digital platforms are the media of their political performances and their political calculations.

The most obvious examples of media seduction are those moments when the leaders act as if they are Dolce & Gabbana models who mount the catwalk and stride with their heads high, purposefully looking into the distance, moving their hips to impress. Why do they stage performances in this way? How come Viktor Orbán likes soccer so much that he arranges for television channels to film him watching matches live with political friends (his team, Puskás Akadémia, usually wins)? Why do leaders want to join Vladimir Putin by flaunting their athletic abilities to score goals at the local hockey rink? Why does Prime Minister Lee Hsien Loong daily feed his million-plus Facebook friends with reassurances about building a strong and united and secure Singapore, a vibrant global economy backed by a more caring and inclusive society? It is hard to know to what extent the rulers do so out of fear of the people they rule, but their skittishness is unmistakable. They are well aware that wrong moves, like a shout from a mountain, can unleash an avalanche of revolt.

Hence leaders think and talk in terms of "guiding the people" by experimenting with novel communications methods, shepherding the people by winning their hearts and minds. They do more than try hard to control the flows of information upon which their means of administration and popularity depend. The cleverest despotisms go beyond firewalls, censoring information, and government propaganda, drawing on state-of-the-art tools for "smart filtering" of the internet. In Iran, for instance, the rulers know that their attempts at blocking American-based social media such as Twitter, Facebook, and YouTube are routinely bypassed by tech-savvy Iranians using VPNs. So, rather than institute a blanket ban on these sites, they experiment with strategies of censoring what the official news agency IRNA calls "criminal and unethical" content. This has the added advantage of treating public communications as an early warning device, as the raw material of total surveillance, even as a virtual steam valve for venting grievances.

Operating within a tangled and tortuous media topography, the ruling powers build twenty-first-century equivalents of the petitioners' bench cantilevered from the wall of the Palazzo Medici in Florence, a gesture to public space by the Medici rulers that ensured that their complaining subjects sat and waited in full view, fully exposed, against giant walls that made them look utterly insignificant. Despots of our time use infinitely more sophisticated versions of the same practice of repressive toleration. Yes, they vigorously guide and control digital media, and they keep millions in the dark. Rough hands are reserved for the dissenters, who face wall-to-wall public indifference and hostility; they are a minority that always ends up flamed, jobless, disappeared, or behind bars. But so long as information producers and spreaders stay inside the published rules and regulations, and keep their distance from the invisible electric fences, they are safe, and tolerated.

Here another difference between the new despotism and the old totalitarianism is clear. These are not systems of power whose rulers crudely order firefighters to locate and burn books while most subjects are glued to their two-way spying televisions (worlds dramatized a generation ago in George Orwell's *1984* and Ray Bradbury's *Fahrenheit 451*). Despotism grants subjects the freedom to bellyache and vent their concerns. Blowing off steam on the internet is functionally useful for the rulers. So is carrying on noisily about problems. Steam and noise are more than early warning detectors. They enable rulers to learn how better to rule.

Digital Mutinies

Scholars and human rights activists living beyond the borders of these despotisms often ignore the artful new strategies because they fail to see that all's not calm within the new despotisms, which tend to generate substantial social resistance. Why? Simply because one of the unintended effects of the rulers' taste for tight surveillance and control is that they spark organized public pushback by digital activists who are less than satisfied with the way things are. These are China's *wăngmín*, or web people; in Russia, famously, they were dubbed by a popular TV presenter, Vladimir Solovyev, as "two-percent shits"; in Iran, the world's leading jailer of female journalists and bloggers, online activists are called "webgardan" *(web-bāzān)*. Harnessing a wide range of available tools, including smartphones, tablets, computers, and sophisticated software, and brushing aside the risks of punishment, these digital activists fling themselves into daring campaigns that spread messages to a wider imagined public, sometimes with dramatic effects. Their actions demonstrate that state censorship can be interrupted. This they do by cleverly applying so-called circumvention technology, including mirror sites and VPN software, to sidestep state censorship and gain secure and full access to banned websites and unfiltered search engines such as Google. Media storms are the result.

It is important to grasp that this online resistance isn't simply the refusal of censorship. Lives online are linked; activists never walk alone. Every denunciation of the rulers' incompetence, every picture or video of officials abusing their power, every single whisper of discontent has the potential to go viral, to become a digital mutiny. The complaints are always difficult to control because their content is copied, shared, commented on, and expanded with other information. An example: the netizens of Iran who use Instagram, the filtered but not blocked photo-sharing site owned by Facebook, create @RichkidsofTehran, a page brimming with photos of rich young Iranians flaunting their wealth. The censors take down the site. Then a cat-and-mouse game begins, with the launch of a new dedicated account, @RichkidsofTeh, that publishes much the same material. Workarounds are common, as when the Turkish government ban of Wikipedia prompted activists to spread the counter-news to millions of users that they could still have access simply by typing a "0" or "1" before a Wikipedia link—either 0wikipedia.org or 1wikipedia.org. Users in Turkey and elsewhere take screenshots of deleted posts and then upload them as images. If certain keywords are blocked, users invent new coded terms, such as, in China, "getting rice drunk" (committing a crime) and "grass-mud horse" (f—k the Party).[35] The examples highlight an important and unending dynamic: as government censorship tactics grow more sophisticated, so do activists' strategies of cat-and-mouse resistance, which sometimes have "swarm" effects, which can quickly turn into rowdy media tempests the rulers call "mass incidents."

Like their geomagnetic counterparts, the digital mutinies are brief, politically charged disturbances that suddenly erupt online and quickly spread through daily life in "media events" that rattle officials and may even rock the foundations of the whole political order.[36] The arrest and trial of Chongqing Communist Party boss Bo Xilai in early March 2012 had this effect: online media carried many tens of thousands of anti-government comments and even rumors of a possible coup in Beijing, to the point where the government was forced to resort to social media blackouts.[37] Impressive is the way digital storms of this kind can and do erupt from local posts. During the past two decades, scores of protests known as anti-incineration campaigns began in this way in various parts of China.[38] Storms sometimes quickly take on a life of their own. In January 2015, a sanitation worker in the Chinese city of Zhengzhou was savagely beaten by a fellow citizen who was asked to stop spitting seeds onto the street pavement being swept. The government-run television network CCTV reported the story through its Weibo account. It beckoned its viewers to show sympathy for the hospitalized worker by sharing these posts with friends. This produced a wholly unexpected reaction: many online activists used the invitation to criticize CCTV's style of reporting and the government's ineptitude in improving the living conditions of sanitation workers.[39]

Digital mutinies can suddenly erupt from far graver matters too, especially when citizens demand that government officials do a better job of listening and make good on their own stated goals of improving the lives of the people, rather than just focusing on the wealthy. During the twentieth-anniversary independence celebrations in Kazakhstan, riot police dressed in black fired on striking oil workers in the town of Zhanaozen. The resulting massacre (dozens of workers died and nearly a hundred were seriously injured) triggered a digital media storm, which grew so serious that the government of President Nursultan Nazarbayev invited bloggers to visit the town in the hope that their online reports would help quell the disturbances spreading like wildfire to other cities. The president's son-in-law Timur Kulibayev, head of Kazakhstan's sovereign wealth fund, Samruk-Kazyna, which manages energy companies and state assets, was fired, along with the regional governor and heads of the national oil company Kazmunaigaz and several local officials held responsible for the massacre. Public relations were later handled in accordance with advice proffered by Tony Blair, who was paid for his suggestions.[40]

There are moments when the whole People's Republic of China is similarly rocked by people power in digital form. A striking example was the mid-2018 vaccine scandal centered on Changsheng Biotechnology Company, whose *baibaipo* vaccine was found to be below required standards. The previous year this company had received 48.3 million yuan in new government subsidies designed to boost the market position of vaccine companies throughout China. Its executives had financial interests in other vaccine corporations. That was why Changsheng was initially protected by the State Drug Administration and by the local Changchun drug administration, which ordered only a small fine (3.4 million yuan). "We are deeply ashamed," said the company in a stock exchange announcement, adding that the defective product had been discontinued. There was no mention of a recall.

Such obfuscation triggered mayhem on social media. All hell broke loose. Within hours, a WeMedia article attacking the company was viewed over one hundred thousand times, the limit displayed by WeChat. The public mood was well summarized by a Weibo user: "If the state does not protect its citizens, how can we love our country?" By the next day, Changsheng's website displayed a 404 page, and the WeMedia article had been scrubbed. Lawyers Tang Jingling and Yu Wensheng, who had previously been convicted of "inciting subversion" for exposing previous corruption affecting other vaccine products, remained behind bars. Then Chinese state media and local authorities sprang into action. They urged Weibo users to "not let anger and panic spread." The *People's Daily* called on local regulators to "rapidly take action, do a complete investigation, and announce authoritative information in a timely manner to pacify public anxiety." Premier Li Keqiang chimed in with talk of "illegal and criminal acts that endanger the safety of people's lives." Xi interrupted his state visit to Rwanda to order severe punishments "to safeguard the public interest and social security."[41]

An earlier incident displayed the same media-storm logic. In Zhengzhou, Henan province, Lu Jun, the head of a city planning office, saw his career swept away in 2009 by a digital media storm triggered by a questionable response he gave to a radio journalist. When asked during an interview why his council had redirected funds originally allocated to build houses for the poor toward a new plan to build luxury apartments and villas, the bureaucrat planner refused to give reasons, instead attacking the journalist with an ill-chosen taunt: "Who are you speaking for? The Party or the people?" he asked. There was mayhem, with *wǎngmín* all over China weighing in, many of them reminding Lu that the Party *is* the people.

The public occupations of Hong Kong's streets and squares during the summer–autumn 2014 Umbrella Movement, and the equally dramatic protests of 2019 in support of civil society, social justice, and free and fair elections, were undoubtedly the most serious digital storms the rulers of China have so far faced. The networked (dispersed, flexible, and distributed) qualities of the nonviolent protests relied heavily on creative experimentation with digital media. Drones and the encrypted Telegram app were used for the first time in China to organize and publicize crowd actions; at one point during the protests, citizens even responded to rumors that the local Hong Kong government was about to cut the city's cellular networks by downloading the Firechat app, which uses Bluetooth and Wi-Fi technology to allow smartphone users to connect anonymously by relaying messages from one user to another without a cell signal or internet connection.[42]

These digital mutinies prompt obvious questions: Why are the massive media apparatuses of the new despotisms unable to prevent media storms from happening? How come despots, far from exercising complete control over their subjects, occasionally find themselves cornered, as they did during the huge public debate in early 2015 triggered by *Under the Dome (Qióng dǐng zhī xià)*, an online documentary about pollution from coal-fired power plants that was watched by at least 150 million Chinese viewers, then later blocked by government censors? Why is it that such censorship sparked even greater fury, which resulted eventually in an assurance by Premier Li during a press conference that the Chinese government would do much more to tackle pollution?[43]

The sharp questions require measured answers. We have seen repeatedly how rulers who proudly claim to be the servants of the people do all they can to silence collective expressions of disaffection and complaint. They understandably worry about media storms and their incitement of collective action; they are well aware these digital mutinies can provoke wider civil unrest and public calls for openness and democracy. Hence all online posts, regardless of whether they are for or against the rulers, are subject to censorious measures. Yet digital mutinies still happen. The reasons are often circumstantial; the courage, technical skill, and sheer determination of digital activists are important drivers as well. But something much deeper is at work, and it has to do with the networked quality of the digital media that are at the heart of the new communicative abundance.

To understand why this is so, we need to consult the Canadian scholar Harold Innis, who long ago noted how different historical forms of communication have different structuring effects on the daily lives of people.[44] His insight that when people communicate with others they are as much shaped by their tools of communication as the tools are shaped by people is vital for understanding why under despotic conditions digital mutinies are chronic. Skeptics who say digital media can be used equally for "democratic" or "authoritarian" purposes, or who say that under "authoritarian" conditions online activists are in effect mere "slacktivists," who stand little chance of changing the world using smartphones, links, and clicks, underestimate this point.[45] They fail to see that although the

THE NEW DESPOTISM

rich and expanding media environments of the new despotism are interlaced with sophisticated business and government control strategies, the digital communications networks upon which they depend are, at their core, distributed networks that defy single centers of control.

The key technical point here is that well-developed, distributed communication networks are integrated through multiple nodes that enjoy a measure of mutual independence. That means that when for any reason nodes "malfunction" or are "disabled," for instance by censors, the rest of the network continues to operate. It also means that any information sent through a distributed network (blockchain, for instance) by digital activists can quite easily bypass a node that is controlled or has been rendered unavailable. In distributed networks, it follows that power, the ability of actors to do things with information, is never fully controllable through central regulation. Communication power is promiscuous. The capacity to act is spread laterally throughout the whole network, which tends to be both dynamic and "flat" in the sense that it has little regard for predefined hierarchies of power.[46]

The deep dependence of the new despotisms upon distributed networks they cannot fully control helps explain the bewilderingly large number of media storms bedeviling their rulers. Of course, the ruling officials always have the option of shutting down the operating networks, as has happened several times in the past in China, in the regions populated by Tibetan and Uighur majorities. The trouble is that such fail-safe firewalling proves in the end to be both self-paralyzing and technically impossible: the digital networks cannot be controlled outright by any single user or group of users. Digital dissent is always possible, especially given that the whole system of state-regulated capitalism is thoroughly dependent upon digital networks. Unplugging them would have ruinous economic and political effects, raising troubling questions about the governing competence of the rulers.

In the age of communicative abundance, distributed information networks tie the hands of despots, which helps explain why they can no longer straightforwardly rely on violence as their ultimate resource. True, power is often viewed as the ability of actors to achieve certain self-defined ends despite resistance from others.[47] The exercise of power backed by force is regarded as a zero-sum battle: the strong triumph over the weak. In this view, the power of some requires the weakness of others, so the greater the rulers' power, the weaker the people's resistance. That, say the champions of this orthodox view of power, is the lesson of the crushing violence used in Chechnya, Tiananmen Square, and Taksim Gezi Park. Its effectiveness in crushing resistance proves the timeless truth of Chairman Mao's famous maxim that political power ultimately comes from the barrel of a gun.

The formula is unconvincing. Even when despots are tempted to use violence to keep order, their growing functional dependence on distributed information networks makes them highly vulnerable to opposition from their critics and opponents. Government censors do use sophisticated algorithms to sift through the personal data of millions of people, but a single post can stop them in their tracks, embarrass them, and force them to recalculate their position. A media storm is often just a quick click away. So too is confirmation of the old rule that power is the ability "not just to act but to act in concert."[48]

Digital Innovations

Under despotism, censors must continuously adapt to this resistance. Remarkably, it forces them to use digitally networked media not just as means of propaganda and control but also in cleverly "democratic" ways. Digital media are used as learning mechanisms, as listening posts, as a means through which people are urged to chat and to vent their grievances against the government, to move closer to the rulers, even to fight against their corruption. In each and every case, the overriding purpose of such tactics is to win public support, to draw digital activists into a cat's cradle of praise, denunciation, and control, all in the name of the rulers serving the people.

Some of these phantom democratic tactics function as early warning devices. Under conditions of despotism, as we have seen, leaders denied free flows of information badly need intelligence. It is recorded that the Baghdad caliph Harun al-Rashid (c. CE 763–809 solved this problem by venturing into his city's taverns disguised as a commoner. What he drank or discovered is unrecorded, but what is certain is that today's despots do much the same, though with great sophistication and on a much-expanded scale. They employ, at various levels and in various branches of the state's bureaucratic apparatus, "cyber units," police agents and hireling bloggers who monitor and influence opinions on the web, sometimes from inside the headquarters of major internet companies. Their aim is to map and understand the underlying causes of dissent, rather than attempting to smash it with an iron fist. Such agents might be described as salaried state meteorologists on the lookout for digital storms that threaten to capsize the ship of state.

Chinese government officials working in "emergency response centers" *(yīng jí lǐng dǎo xiǎo zǔ)* perform much the same forecasting function. They watch for signs of brewing unrest or angry public reactions. Their job is to deal with digital activists who use sophisticated proxies and other methods to avoid censorship, spread salacious tales of official malfeasance, and quickly circulate online jokes, songs, satire, mockery, and code words. So-called rumor refutation departments pitch in, scanning posts for forbidden topics and issuing knockdown rebuttals. Their aim is to take the wind out of the sails of those who accuse the rulers of hypocrisy, who call on them to listen to the people and to live up to their promises to provide harmony, material well-being, and a good life for everyone.

Other innovations go beyond the role of forecasters or early warning devices for those who govern. Their function is instead to deal with public complaints by demonstrating that the rulers listen to the people and are ready to remedy their public grievances, above all by collecting and circulating public information. The field of digital communications is seen by despots as a vital resource for gauging people's thoughts, cares, worries, and grievances, as a medium that makes it "much easier for governments to interact with residents and thus improve their governance."[49] Remarkable is the way government officials publish microblogs to release authorized information and to solicit feedback from people. *Study Times*, the newspaper of the Central Party School in China, speaks of the urgent need for officials to get involved in the business of influencing public opinion—for instance, by employing Zhou Xiaoping, Hua Qianfang, and other big-time bloggers as spreaders of positive energy, paying them according to their productivity as representatives of the "silent majority."[50] Governing officials also cultivate digital means of gathering and spreading useful public information. An example is the official microblog of the Beijing Emergency Medical Center, which earned high praise for its role in quickly informing concerned citizens in the aftermath of the 2011 Fukushima nuclear catastrophe in Japan. The government body known as the Institute of Public and Environmental Affairs does something similar. Its Blue Map app, designed to inform citizens in real-time about water quality, local sources of pollution, and emissions from polluting companies, has been downloaded many millions of times. The data collected through the app, which enables users to input updates via their phone, is then shared with hundreds of companies in the power, steel, chemical, and petrochemical fields, to encourage them to cut levels of contaminating emissions.[51]

Still other digital innovations function to stimulate public involvement by luring bloggers and other subjects inside the structures of government. E-consultations, online Q&A sessions, virtual petitions, and online webcast forums run in this direction. Clothed in talk of "listening to people's voices," "answering people's questions," and remedying "public grievances," these mechanisms show that under despotic conditions digital media can be used not just as tools of top-down decision making and control but also as a way of involving people "from below" in the processes of government administration. The southern Chinese province of Guangdong, known for its innovative public involvement schemes, uses public policy "network hearings" *(wǎng luò tīng zhèng)*, broadcast live, with hand-picked presenters expressing their views on proposed reforms, with the public invited to make comments and to vote online for the policies they support. Similar innovations have happened in the Yangzi Delta cities of Hangzhou and Nanjing, which use electronic "mayor's mailboxes" to promote bottom-up feedback, make public administration more accountable *(gong sí)*, and persuade people that local government is actually efficient and effective.

Another trend appears to be gaining ground in the new despotisms: the deployment of digital platforms for encouraging people to scrutinize government officials and procedures. Here the paradoxical aim of rulers is to expose their own malfeasance and to take firm action against misconduct by governing officials. Pioneering examples are the anticorruption web reporting platform (www .12388.gov.cn) hosted on the official website of the Chinese Communist Party's Central Commission for Discipline Inspection and the Ministry of Supervision of the People's Republic of China (www .ccdi.gov.cn). Citizens are encouraged to engage with these sites to report wrongdoing by government officials at all levels. The range of possible matters is defined widely, to include "political discipline," "democratic rights," financial and tax regulations, family planning regulations, and government procurement and bidding procedures. The sites also encourage complaints about bribery, hidden property and other assets, assaults on other people's rights, pornography and prostitution, and "abuse of power, negligence, and power-seeking."

Velvet Fists

Guiding Public Opinion

What are we to make of all these improbable but tangible experiments in the field of digital communications? Do they have a broader significance? They arguably do, if only because they serve as reminders that the new despotisms are not straightforwardly censorious systems of brute power grounded in violence. These systems are undoubtedly dead set against power-sharing monitory democracy, in the richest sense of free and fair general elections combined with ongoing public monitoring of power by independent watchdog mechanisms. Despots treat more than a few topics as ticklish or taboo. Open public criticism and resistance to the ruling institutions and their leading figures are risky. Fair-minded analyses of "sensitive" topics, such as Putin's hidden wealth, Xinjiang detention camps, and the murder of journalists in Turkey, are banned. And all the official don'ts are backed by pre-digital methods: early-morning swoops by plainclothes police known as "interceptors"; lengthy interrogations of suspects; hostage-taking of relatives; rigged court trials and imprisonment; violent beatings by unidentified thugs; trolls, torture, murder, and bodily dismemberment.

But these forms of top-down control and censorship are not the whole story, as the spread of digital feedback and learning mechanisms illustrates. They come as something of a surprise, especially when we consult our eighteenth-century guide Montesquieu, who was sure that despots had a bad habit of lazily hiding from their subjects. Cloistered in palaces and seraglios, surrounded by trusted courtiers who spoon-fed them information calibrated to please their ears, despots could be tripped up by "natural foolishness." By contrast, the cleverest despots of our time are not "naturally lazy, ignorant, and voluptuous"; they know the pitfalls of cloistering themselves, and they don't suppose that they are "everything and that others are nothing."[1]

Well aware of their own vulnerability in tugs-of-war between their will to control, negotiated change, and outbursts of public resistance, our despots know well local versions of the Russian saying that riding slower takes you farther. That is why the new despots have a taste for public forums and other consultation mechanisms and why they pay so much attention to producing and controlling public opinion. "The correct guidance of public opinion benefits the Party, benefits the nation, and benefits the people," former Chinese leader Hu Jintao famously remarked, before adding: "Incorrect guidance of public opinion wrongs the Party, wrongs the nation, and wrongs the people."[2]

Such statements are not mere official hyperbole. They reveal how the new despots strive to be flexible in how they exercise power, pragmatically adapting to changing circumstances so that they remain on top. In this new twenty-first-century vision of "enlightened despotism," the embrace by despots of organized market research and opinion polling is telling. Most of the new despotisms know that fish are best caught with hooks, baskets, and nets, which is why they build a giant information-gathering apparatus that covers every nook and cranny of their domains, and beyond.

The contraption has many parts, comprising many different types of information gathering. In Iran, for instance, public opinion polling is considered a vital tool of resilient government, even though pollsters and polling agencies find themselves forced to tread carefully. So as to improve the quality of its received intelligence, the regime tolerates the operation of a variety of pollsters. Iranpoll is the most active, and enjoys a reputation for the most reliable polling. In cooperation with the American Association for Public Opinion Research, the University of Maryland, and other outside bodies, it claims to conduct more than 150,000 interviews each year, using methods ranging from landline telephone interviews (notoriously unreliable in a country where barely a third of the population has a fixed line) to online and app-based surveys. Other polling agencies include the University of Tehran's Iranian Students Polling Agency, the official Islamic Republic News Agency, Entekhab, Rooz Plus, and Tabnak. The regime allows outside organizations to sample opinions, as the Washington-based International Perspectives for Public Opinion did a dozen times during the buildup to the 2017 presidential election. On the eve of the same election, even the supreme leader, Ali Khamenei, using his Telegram messaging account, invited his followers to reply to his question about the state of the Iranian economy, which many tens of thousands did.

The regime clearly understands the need for information feedback loops, but here the paradoxes begin. Fearing that negative results might arouse public controversy, the rulers keep a close eye on the pollsters. Polls published at universities, in newspapers, and via online platforms are tracked by the Ministry of Culture and

Islamic Guidance; online poll results are permanently under the surveillance of the Iranian cyberpolice, known officially as the Police for the Sphere of Production and Exchange of Information. Their brief is to apply laws that prohibit such acts as "creating disagreements among the social strata of the population," "disseminating false polls," and "disturbing public opinion." Here the contradictory logic of public opinion polling is exposed. In order to rule intelligently, despotisms depend on free flows of information that come from below. But despotisms do not like bad news, because it can arouse public resistance. So they must suppress poll results not to their taste.

Public opinion is despots' curse. They need it on their side. They must nurture it to prop up their rule. Yet despots fear it. And when it delivers ominous news, they must shoot the messenger. Public opinion must then be ignored, or crushed outright. Examples of the uneasy dynamics unleashed by opinion polling are easy to find. During Iran's bread riots in January 2018, the Office of the President commissioned polls by the Iranian Students Polling Agency (ISPA). Their results showed deep disgruntlement with the policies of the government, which worsened matters by arresting ISPA pollsters as they went about their work. More controversial was the drama triggered by the Ayandah Polling Institute during the so-called reform period under President Mohammad Khatami (1997–2005). When their poll data suggested that a majority of Iranians favored rapprochement with the United States, Supreme Leader Khamenei stepped into the fray. Determined to kill off developing oppositional public spheres, he ordered the arrest of the head pollsters on the grounds that they "lacked national pride" and were "ignorant of the ABCs of politics."[3]

In China, the dynamics are just as fraught. During the first two decades of reform, an estimated eight hundred polling firms were registered, half of them located in Beijing.⁴ Though not all of them survived ruling pressures, some of these organizations are classified as "unofficial" (private, for-profit, not directly part of state structures). Others are semiofficial organizations (for-profit, operating at some distance from state ministries); still others are controlled directly by the state, as is the case with the People's Daily Online Public Opinion Monitoring Center, which harnesses data-harvesting algorithms to send summaries of trends in Internet chatter in real time to Party leaders, often with advice about which language to use, or avoid, in handling hot topics. Some of the polling agencies are joint ventures with media firms and foreign companies operating in China. Practically every institution of higher education hosts a public opinion research unit, chartered to analyze trends and hot spots with the help of social scientists who have swapped their former "redness" for the mantle of expert functionaries in a booming public opinion polling and survey research industry.

From the perspective of state power, the data-gathering and opinion-polling machinery operated by the Party is straightforwardly designed as an early warning system, mainly to protect the governing structures from political resistance and social disorder. Public opinion polling is central to the Party's efforts to kick the habit of keeping the lid on everything by becoming a "learning party."⁵ In the Tibet Autonomous Region, for instance, the Chinese rulers have been experimenting for some time with a new political grid system *(wǎng gé)* of neighborhood information-gathering units, led by grid captains. More than six hundred street-side "convenience police posts" *(biàn mín jǐng wù zhàn)* equipped with computers and video technology have been set up in towns, rural areas, and temples throughout Tibet. These police posts are a vital part of a system that operates 24/7 and is designed to gather information about "special groups," such as ex-prisoners, "nuns and monks on the move," and Tibetans who have returned from exile in India. These police posts are linked in turn to voluntary grassroots civilian networks called "red armband patrols," whose job is to anticipate "sudden incidents" (self-immolations, for instance) and to conduct "doorstep interviews" and searches of Tibetan homes for politically forbidden materials, including photographs of the Dalai Lama. As a reminder to the local population that the mountains may be high but the emperor is close by, available online, the Chinese rulers have announced that they intend to expand the state-of-the-art surveillance system. They say it is designed to "improve public access to basic services." They describe the dragnet as an important component in the countrywide drive toward "social stability maintenance" *(wéi wěn)* and "scientifically guiding public opinion" *(kē xué yǐn dǎo yú lùn)*. Party documents speak of a system of "nets in the sky and traps on the ground" that strengthen the information and intelligence work of the Party.[6]

Elsewhere in the Chinese polity, the data-harvesting machine operated by Party rulers affects all tiers of government. Local Party branches, for instance, function as listening posts, as do the Party academies to which up-and-coming cadres are sent periodically for "study." Higher up within the polity, the network of People's Political Consultative Congresses and other consultative organs is designed to win the support and collect the opinions of businesspeople, intellectuals, and various Party and non-Party people. The information-harvesting machine extends far beyond the territorial borders of China. China's surging foreign press corps is an example: stationed everywhere on our planet, including strategically important countries such as the United States, the press corps comprises more than reporters filing stories from abroad.

Journalists double as providers of regular intelligence to government security and diplomatic departments.

Outside-inside information harvesting by state officials also extends to joint ventures with foreign companies such as A. C. Nielsen, Gallup, and Kantar. For nearly a decade, to cite just one example, the Global Attitudes Project of the Pew Research Center, a nonpartisan "fact tank" based in Washington, DC, has organized surveys in China on directly political matters. "Now I'm going to read a list of political leaders," runs the wording of a standard question asked of Chinese citizens. "Tell me how much confidence you have in each leader to do the right thing regarding world affairs—a lot of confidence, some confidence, not too much confidence, or no confidence at all." The results are understandably pleasing to the Chinese rulers. Between 82 percent and 86 percent of citizens said they had "a lot of confidence" or "some confidence" in former Chinese president Hu Jintao (2006–2012); in a 2014 survey, despite early signs of demagoguery, President Xi Jinping managed to leave the leaders of parliamentary democratic states in the dust by scoring a 92 percent positive rating among Chinese citizens.[7]

These information surveys and opinion polls deserve closer inspection, for they tell us much about the whole strange phenomenon of despotism. The data-harvesting strategies they normally use have proto-democratic methods. They range from doorstep interviews, focus groups, and standard questionnaires to participant observation and telephone, postal, and email surveys. In the peculiar circumstances of heavily mediated rule, these methodologies are debatable: questions are often poorly worded, key terms are left undefined, the methodologies used by the polling agencies are rarely explained, and not much is known about whether and to what extent respondents feel pressure to provide the expected, politically correct, or socially acceptable answers—or to what extent subjects tell lies to pollsters, whether just for the hell of it or to get the data monkeys off their backs.

Given the staggering complexity and various levels of censorship of the official information that flows through the body politic, the opinion samplers can never be fully sure they are asking the pertinent questions or drawing the right conclusions. In Beijing and several hundred other cities just months before the 1989 Tiananmen and related uprisings that threatened to implode the whole political system, most observers considered price inflation to be issue number one. Nobody anticipated the rapid swings of opinion and public explosions that were shortly to happen. In other words, the striking thing about public opinion *(yú lùn)* in China, as elsewhere, is its indeterminacy, its immeasurability, its promiscuity, which is why it is unlikely despotic rulers could ever manage to perfect the art of opinion formation.

In China, things are not helped by the censorship and manipulation of findings carried out by the Party's Central Propaganda Department (tellingly, in 1998 its English name was officially changed to the more democratic-sounding Central Publicity Department). Since the Party controls most broadcasting and print media outlets, survey findings that it dislikes simply go unreleased. Some topics, such as the large-scale cruelty and violence of the post-1949 period, are still out of bounds to polling and marketing agencies.[8] Unsurprisingly, willful self-censorship flourishes under these conditions. Every government department at the central and provincial level contains units dedicated to public opinion research. Yet they often produce reports that reproduce the anticipated views of the officials who are in charge.

When the Party turns to private polling and survey organizations, the bias is not automatically corrected, since they too have a contractual or strategic interest in not incurring the wrath of Party officials.

The upshot is that in China, as in other despotisms, what counts as "public opinion" is a guessing game. Nothing is quite what it seems. There is much pretense, along with cultivation of the art of pretense, fueled by second-guessing. That is why so many people are so busily engaged in interpreting what elsewhere is called dog whistling. In a system of media spectacles in which it is hard to know what is real and what is artificial, what is permitted and what is not, and what will or will not be punished, it becomes imperative to decode surface or official explanations, in order to grasp the hidden meaning behind things as they appear.

Despite such complications, the rulers hold fast to their organized hunt for measured "public opinion," which they seek to correct and control, in opposition to the disruptive forces of "rumor" and "wrong thinking" and "social disharmony." The range, depth, and frankness of some opinion polls can be impressive. The Moscow-based Levada Center uses a countrywide interviewer network to track opinions about a wide range of matters, including daring questions about Putin's overall popularity ratings (they range between 90 percent and 65 percent) and his personal responsibility for "high-level government corruption and financial abuse" (67 percent said "fully" or "in large part" in March 2017).[9] There is considerable freedom to pry into such topics as public order and security, migrant workers, the disabled, beggars, social welfare policies, and the efficiency and effectiveness of local government. Polls are also cleverly used by despots to calibrate proposed policy changes considered potentially controversial, such as measures to reform taxes, restrict car use, or increase the costs of public transport. The rulers know that they cannot simply shove measures down the throats of unhappy subjects, and that public opinion polls are useful means of predicting negative reactions and defusing bitter controversies.

The public rumpus triggered by local government plans to reduce traffic congestion by increasing parking fees in Guangzhou in early 2014 is a case in point. Officials were aware that a survey, conducted by the largest independent public opinion research agency in China, the Canton Public Opinion Research Center (C-POR), had already reported that most Guangzhou citizens (54 percent) were unconvinced that parking fee increases in the downtown area would improve traffic conditions, with an overwhelming majority (69 percent) concerned that increased fees would lead to more illegal parking.[10] So in order to dampen public discontent and to review the proposed plans, the local Guangzhou Bureau of Prices convened a public hearing attended by various invited representatives. Local media were quick off the mark in reviewing the proposed plans, with the *Yangzi Evening News* stirring up trouble with calculations that the average cost of parking for ten years would be equal to the price of a BMW (480,000 RMB).[11] C-POR weighed in with a survey reporting that, while only a bare majority (51 percent) of respondents rejected the government's new policy, more than three-quarters of Guangzhou citizens (77 percent) seriously doubted the wisdom of raising parking fees. A clear majority (60 percent) believed that higher parking fees would actually cause more "illegal/random" parking, but that if parking fees had to be increased, then the revenues generated should be spent on tighter traffic regulations and improved public transport.[12] There followed lively, open, and fairly frank public debate. The Bureau of Prices wavered and began to explore alternative, more equitable schemes, even calling upon citizens to make their views known by email, fax, or mail. This triggered still more controversy, with many hundreds of contributions posted on Sina Weibo. The eventual introduction of higher parking fees in August 2014 did not halt the uproar. Using various media, some citizens asked where the increased revenues were being spent; others complained about the worsening city traffic; still others said that, while public consultation was a good thing, the local government was behaving incompetently, with things made worse by postponed announcements and ambiguous information. One brave citizen even suggested that the best solution to the traffic problem was to arrest and jail the boss of the local Transportation Committee.[13]

Do such public disputes fueled by poll findings have broader significance for how we understand the new despotisms? They do, for they reveal the strange and subtle dependence of the ruling powers on public opinion. It is more accurate to say that the new despotisms pay homage to a "phantom public" (Walter Lippmann's classic phrase) that is both tangible and ungraspable, both real and unreal.[14] They prevent the independent formation of public opinion through nonviolent but rough-and-tumble exchanges of views among citizens who think of themselves as equals. Yet while the institutions of despotism stand firmly against public opinion in this genuine sense, the remarkable thing about these despotisms is how they seek to divine and dowse public opinion through a host of agencies bent on measuring phenomena that are prevented from taking on a life of their own. Put bluntly, those who govern the new despotisms simultaneously honor and do everything to crush the formation of publics with independent views about matters of public concern.

Rulers acknowledge the old maxim that every form of government rests upon opinion.[15] But since rulers such as Recep Tayyip Erdoğan, Alexander Lukashenko, and Sooronbay Jeenbekov (president of the Kyrgyz Republic, whose constitution describes him as "the symbol of the unity of the people and state power") are well aware that the survival or extinction of their regime depends on winning or losing public support, they give the old saying a sharp new twist. Their calculation is clear: if opinion is the foundation of stable government, then government itself must create stable opinion. It follows that the imperative is to watch, to keep ears to the ground, so that the goal of harmoniously guiding public opinion becomes a reality. Despotism must work constantly to stay closely in touch with the people, to ensure that the gap between them and government never grows dangerously wide. Not without a dose of anxiety, the rulers thus acknowledge that when all is said and done, very little props up the political order except people's belief in it. *Potestas in populo* is the classic Roman formulation to summarize this rule. The Vietnamese version might be: the higher you climb, the farther you are likely to fall *(trèo cao, té đàu)*. And the Chinese version: the water that floats the boat can overturn it as well *(shuǐ kě zài zhōu, yì kě fù zhōu)*.

If the resilience of a regime is its ability to get its subjects to act as the rulers choose, then persuasion of people rather than violence against them is ultimately the most valuable governing resource. Command and obedience turn out to be tricky components of any political equation, for power over others functionally requires that they feel comfortable with the instructions, directives, and commands issued by those who rule. Despite their native suspicions of power, the ruled have to be persuaded that they will not be devoured by its jaws. Otherwise, they may be tempted to stir up trouble.

THE NEW DESPOTISM

Measured Violence

If persuasion of people rather than violence against them is key to the stability and long life of despotism, then a salient question arises, one that many consider the quintessential political question: How violent are the new despotisms of our age? Since all states strive to monopolize the means of violence, it seems germane to ask whether rulers are prone to use force on their subjects and on others outside their realm. And since several of these states are armed with weapons of total annihilation, they could be a danger to their subjects, and to all peoples on our planet.

The conventional answer from past thinkers who worried their heads about despotism is straightforward. In the seventeenth century, Thomas Hobbes was the first to say openly that government—"paternal, and despotic"—is founded on conquest and "fear of others."[16] The thought that despotism is a synonym for master-servant government established by violent conquest of subjects fearful of death was echoed in Samuel Johnson's often-cited *A Dictionary of the English Language* (1755). Despotism is "absolute power," he wrote. He went on to say, "Despot: An absolute prince; one that governs with unlimited authority," and "Despotical, Desspotick: Absolute in power; unlimited in authority; arbitrary; unaccountable."[17] The ideas buried in these definitions remain familiar. When the word "despotism" is uttered, what springs to mind is the image of power backed by fear and violence. Despotisms are said to rest upon their monopoly of force. Appearances aside, they are repressive police states.

What we are about to encounter is yet another surprise: the new despotisms are police states, but they do not resemble the police states of the past. The term "police state" once meant a form of government that "policed" (regulated and polished) its subjects. In the mid-nineteenth century it came to mean a government that exercises power arbitrarily backed up by extensive powers of surveillance and force. When used today, the term has negative connotations. It highlights the bullying, fear, and uncertainty that accompany heavy-handed policing. A police state in effect takes the ruled population hostage in deadly games of shadowy, arbitrary power. The commonly used phrase emphasizes how the rulers of a police state are entangled in parallel dynamics, such as fear of rivals, secretive plots, and assassinations. Police states are often symbolized by Hitler's Germany, where terror functioned as "noncalculable violence" hovering daily over the heads of every subject.[18] Violence was an instrument used to attract loyal support, to frighten the obedient, and to destroy defenseless innocents in concentration camps. More recently, when we hear talk of police states, we turn to Augusto Pinochet's Chile, with its unsparingly brutal suppression of citizens' rights to public assembly, independent media, and trade union freedoms. Or we think of Erich Honecker's East Germany, a police state that penetrated every nook and cranny of life by means of a vast police and intelligence service staffed by more than one hundred thousand full-time "sword and shield" officers, noncommissioned personnel, and special guard units and supported by Stasi informers (dubbed *Spitzel*) and occasional stool pigeons that may have numbered up to 2 million people (in a total population of 17 million) drawn from all walks of life, including doctors, lawyers, journalists, writers, actors, Protestant and Catholic clergy, university professors, sports stars, and hotel staff.[19]

Regimes ruled by fear laced with violence are part of a much older pattern. Historians teach us that past tyrannies and dictatorships slaughtered members of their cities' leading families. They exiled, imprisoned, or killed their rivals. Past rulers were regularly tempted to follow the recommendation proffered in an old tale recorded by the Greek historian Herodotus and reiterated in the advice of Machiavelli in his well-known study of Castracani: power with glory goes to rulers who are brave enough to kill even their own friends because at some point they may become revengeful enemies.[20]

The despotisms of our time don't match this description. It is true they are not havens of serenity, gardens of paradise where flowers of peace and harmony bloom. The new despotisms generate plenty of public bellyaching, digital mutinies, and street-level outbreaks of public protest. When public disturbances happen, the police and army swing into action, reminding everyone that when all is said and done these regimes feel like police states. Less obvious is the fact that the new despotisms are a type of police state the world has never before seen.

When it comes to the use of violence, despotic rulers are unusually circumspect, both at the top and in the lower echelons of government. They practice the arts of calibrated coercion.[21] The difference with the past can be observed at the pinnacles of state power, where otherwise-skittish rulers tacitly agree among themselves to something of a peace pact. Despots know they are not truly loved. They may be familiar with the stories of the ancient rulers who suffered death at the hands of plotters, including the Roman emperors Domitian, knifed in the groin by a trusted servant named Stephanus in CE 96, and Commodus, who was fed poisoned food by his mistress, vomited, then was strangled in his bath by his wrestling partner in CE 192. The famous *Encyclopédie* entry on despotism written by Chevalier de Jaucourt (1754) insisted that unrestrained violence at the top continued to be a feature of modern despotisms. Yet since then things have turned out differently.[22] The new despots understand that in a war of each against all, nobody is safe even at the top. Living by the sword risks death by the sword.

The alternative is to practice honor among thieves. Everything is done to prevent the kind of great terror backed by wanton violence that in the Soviet Union during the 1930s resulted in large-scale purges of high-level Communist Party and government officials, who were accused of being "counterrevolutionaries" and "saboteurs" and summarily put on trial, dispatched to concentration camps, executed in mobile gas vans, or shot. The upshot is that at the summits of the new despotisms a strange kind of cold peace breaks out. Rulers remain jumpy, grumpy, and prone to paranoia. As in Saudi Arabia and the UAE, where tribal loyalties, regional allegiances, religious factions, and family conflicts run deep, rulers take for granted, and know in their guts, they are ensnared in wrestling matches among potential enemies. Life at the top is reptilian. There are dangerously two-faced showmen, opportunists, crooks, whisperers, plotters, calculators, cockroaches, and spiders. Surrounded by serpents, rulers have an intuitive feel for the plight of Macbeth, in that they know those they command don't usually obey out of love. They are well aware that there's many a slip "'twixt the cup and the lip."[23] Palace intrigues and full-scale assaults are constants; bitter feuds, promotion-demotion scorekeeping, squabbling disagreements, tilting at windmills, and comic melodramas are commonplace. There are moments when rulers suffer the plight of the Sicilian tyrant Phalaris: sleepless nights racked by anxieties about plots, assassinations, and popular rebellion that would reduce them to rulers of nothing.[24]

The paradox is that in spite of these shenanigans and anxious moments, rulers refrain from using violence against their enemies at the top. They understand the dangers of spreading "rhinoceritis" (the playwright Eugène Ionesco's word for the way murderous violence proves strangely attractive to people who in turn become its justifiers and perpetrators).[25] Since the disease of violence easily spreads and boomerangs on its perpetrators, they have to find more sophisticated ways of fending off competitors. That's why rulers conclude that it's better to be a clever political snake charmer with a flute than to enter the serpents' nest armed with a sword. Since plots at the top are risky, cunning becomes a key weapon. So do secrecy and guarding privileged access to the pinnacles of state power. The concentration of power means that access to its summits must be tightly regulated and carefully guarded. The price of entry must be high, and tickets made scarce. Just as mafia bosses rely on consiglieri, so the despots of our time take great care in surrounding themselves with counselors.

This practice of building chambers of power upon antechambers of loyal and trusted viziers is as old as modern state-building. Cardinal Richelieu, known as the Red Eminence, served as the direct advisor of the seventeenth-century French king Louis XIII. In old age, Frederick the Great reportedly narrowed his advisors down to one: his devoted chamber servant Fredersdorff. Grigori Yefimovich Rasputin, claiming to be a mystic healer, won the trust and protection of Czar Nicholas II. In circumstances very different from the past, today's despots do much the same thing: they look for support and summon to their side people just like themselves, power players who are "reliable elements" (as the Chinese say) skilled at shielding them against potential enemies. Hence despots like to appoint loyalists and family members to senior positions. Recep Tayyip Erdoğan promotes his son-in-law Berat Albayrak to the post of finance minister. Alexander Lukashenko publicly parades his young son Nikolai as if he is the heir apparent. Vladimir Putin surrounds himself with old friends and lackey loyalists, as does Sayyid Qaboos bin Said Al Said, the ruler of Oman who replaced his father in a palace coup. Azerbaijan's despot, Ilham Aliyev, went a step further. He appointed his wealthy wife, Mehriban Aliyeva, as the country's first vice president and his heir apparent. Former member of parliament, busy patron, and ribbon-cutting charity fund-raiser, she is known for her obsequiousness, being reported to have said, "Mr. President, I express my deep gratitude to you for this high confidence in me," quite possibly linked to the "substantial plastic surgery" that left her "unable to show a full range of facial expression.[26] In each and every one of these cases, the rule is clear: favoritism and cronyism are the price of cold peace at the top.

When it comes to dealing with the wider populace, the new despotisms are equally circumspect. Compared with previous tyrannies, dictatorships, and totalitarian regimes, the new despotisms are distinguished by their measured use of violence, and by the way they conceal the fist of force in their pockets. Their mantra is *salus populi suprema lex* (the safety of the people is the supreme law). Keeping subjects safe naturally implies the rulers' use of force against their named enemies. "The question of the death penalty should be kept on the agenda in Hungary," says a prominent government minister, "and we must let it be known that we will stop at nothing when it comes to protecting our citizens."[27] While the death penalty is not a universal feature of despotism (it is practiced in Belarus, Saudi Arabia, and China, where in rural regions mobile execution vans administer lethal injections to convicted criminals), the sentiment that state power is entitled to rob subjects of their lives is commonplace. Despots understand that their duty is to win the obedience of their subjects by ensuring their protection. On the basis of that principle, the rulers display great determination and efficiency in stamping out the first signs of public dissent.

Writers, artists, and public intellectuals are often first in the line of fire—understandably, since they are the ones who are disposed not only to question restrictions on artistic freedom but to protest through their work against the terminal nullity of life, the fact that it eventually ends. Political dissidents and rebel journalists also suffer the whip hand of the state. Sometimes the violence is cleverly concealed in the form of Hitchcock-style murders, as in Saudi Arabia, whose agents entered their government's Istanbul consulate one day in October 2018, waited for the arrival of a prominent exiled journalist critic, Jamal Khashoggi, who had come to obtain a document required for him to get married, and murdered him, hacking his body to pieces. The Saudi regime's religious police, the *mutaween,* are equally shameless. Backed by the custom of public beheadings, and torture methods that include pouring antiseptic cleaning liquid down prisoners' throats and force-feeding watermelon to male victims and knotting their penises, they specialize in striking fear into the hearts of individuals and groups they brand dangerous. Their force rains down hard on brave victims like the human rights lawyer Waleed Abu al-Khair, sentenced to fifteen years in prison for "disobeying the ruler," "insulting the judiciary," "setting up an unlicensed organization," "harming the reputation of the state," and "preparing, storing and sending information that harms public order."[28]

When hundreds of thousands of citizens, including women wearing headscarves, Kurds, liberals, nationalists, and football fans, took to the streets throughout Turkey in the early summer of 2013 to protest government construction plans in Gezi Park, a small green zone on the edge of Istanbul's Taksim Square, Erdoğan delivered on his promise of vengeance: "Whatever is necessary will be done!" In Belarus, President Lukashenko rails against "senseless democracy," while his provocateurs in the KGB (as it's still called in the country) are prone to beat their opponents senseless. Putin, who fancies himself the bare-chested remedy for the past era of "confusion and twilight," the "effective manager" who is making Russia great again, is absolutely intolerant of all "enemies of stability." His rise to power was tightly connected to targeted violence, the clever manipulation of actual and contrived terror attacks to wipe out what he called "the shithouse" of Muslim resistance in Chechnya, where more than one hundred thousand people were killed. Once in power, Putin continued to wage violence against his enemies, for instance at the Sochi Winter Olympics in 2014, when protesting citizens were greeted with lethal cocktails of pepper spray, horsewhips, heavily armed riot police, Interior Ministry troops, and operatives of the Federal Security Service.

In Brunei, the Internal Security Department sniffs out subjects accused of circulating propaganda material, possessing drugs, or playing the local game katam-katam, in which gamblers bet on the outcome of the roll of a dice. Under legislation carried over from British colonial rule, those picked up can be convicted for crimes of "treason," "subversive propaganda," "forgery," and "sabotage of economic stability." In Singapore, police act on the Chinese proverb that killing the chicken scares the monkey. They search homes and detain without trial targeted subjects deemed a threat to "national security." Even an appearance at the famous Speakers' Corner risks arrest and a hefty fine for participating in an unauthorized "assembly or procession." In Kyrgyzstan, people familiar with the famous novelist Chingiz Aitmatov's *The Day Lasts More Than a Hundred Years* (1980) know the continuing real-world relevance of its fictional account of *mankurts,* prisoners of war reduced to brain-damaged slaves by confinement under a hot sun with their heads wrapped in camel skin that dries tight, like a steel band. In neighboring Kazakhstan, it is recorded that human rights workers have been set upon, their chests bared, and a large X—the mark of the censor—carved on their skin. Following an alleged failed military coup in July 2016, the Erdoğan government's purge of its former Gülenist allies resulted in the arrest and imprisonment of tens of thousands of citizens for alleged links to terror organizations, the sacking of 130,000 state employees, the jailing of over 7,000 senior military officers and a quarter of the country's lawyers plus the closure of 200 media organizations, including newspapers, periodicals, radio stations, and television channels.

There is ongoing violent repression of Uighurs in Xinjiang in western China and brutal suppression of the Muslim Brotherhood in Egypt. In Tajikistan, racked by civil war in the early 1990s, the state is constantly on the lookout for signs of what the authorities interchangeably call "Islamic radicalism," "foreign extremism," and "terrorism." Men with beards are stopped on the streets, or arrested on trumped-up charges that often treat faith as terrorism. The wearing of the head scarf, popular among many Tajik Muslim women, is forbidden in state institutions and in some public places and shops. Independent mosques are closed, and state-approved imams are pressured to transform their sermons into paeans to former cotton farm boss President Emomali Rahmon. In his formal 2016 address on Mother's Day, which replaced International Women's Day in Tajikistan, the president criticized women who wear "foreign" clothing, especially the black veils associated with conservative Islam. "Strangers," he said, are using Islamic dress "to promote obtrusive ideas and want to create another new extremist trend in our country." Several days later, following orders from on high, tax inspectors, police, and leather-jacketed spooks from the State Committee for National Security raided Dushanbe's Sadbarg market and instructed shopkeepers to discontinue selling Islamic clothing. State television backed the raids by claiming that sex workers were using the hijab to inflate their prices and to spread "extremist" views.[29]

These few examples suffice to suggest that everywhere in the world of despotism the powerful are constantly on the lookout for subjects who show signs of intransigence or wanting to become public-spirited citizens. The potential for full-on deployment of force by the machinery of state repression means that fear of brutal violence among public dissenters is constant. The army, police, and goons are on constant standby. Yet striking is the way despots' use of concentrated violence is cleverly calibrated, often outsourced, and, until the moment it strikes, a shadowy affair.

Despots surely know the famous maxim of Mao Zedong that only with guns can the world be transformed. Perhaps they are mindful of Thomas Paine's warning in his best-selling *Rights of Man* (1791): "The strength and power of despotism consists wholly in the fear of resisting it." But they are also no doubt aware that the unrestricted or reckless deployment of force harbors grave risks. Experience teaches them that when all is said and done, very little props up the political order except people's belief in it. Russians say that the devil dreamed of ruling the whole world but God granted him not even power over a pig, and many Chinese people know the parable (famously told by the Confucian writer Liu Ji) of the good beekeeper whose foolish son managed their hives so poorly that the bees abandoned the hive, leaving the son to languish in poverty. So if the power of a regime is its ability to get its subjects to act as it chooses, then fear and violence are ultimately limited resources. Command and obedience, which do not happen naturally, as if blessed by the deities, turn out to be tricky factors in any political equation. Power over others functionally requires that they feel comfortable with the instructions, directives, and commands issued by those who rule. The ruled have to be quietly or openly persuaded that they will not be devoured by the jaws of power.

This is why the new despotisms do all they can to camouflage the bodily and mental violence they inflict on their specified opponents. It is as if they take their cue from contemporary democracies, which pioneered ways of dodging public scandal by using "clinical" techniques of torture, such as water, ice, electricity, noise, and drugs, that leave the bodies of their victims unscarred.[30] The new despotisms depend upon targeted—not blanket—force. They annoy and persecute and maim and blind their opponents. They kill. Yet the new despotisms hide the executioner's face. They have velvet fists. The new despotisms strive to be police states in the original meaning of the term: strong states that claim to guarantee order not just via retributive justice (the German scholar Franz Neumann called it *Strafjustiz*) targeted at identifiable real opponents but also through media and policy efforts to protect and improve the lives of their subjects.

How do they actually do this? We have already encountered some of their preferred methods. The rulers talk of the people, foster connections, and tolerate top-to-bottom corruption; they hide away concentrated wealth, rely on the middle class, promote economic growth, and master the arts of entertainment, information flows, and media coverage. When it comes to dishing out violence, the rulers tread carefully. The army is usually kept out of the way; the consequent global decline in military interventions in the politics of the new despotisms is remarkable. The police and the secret police fill the gap. They aren't gentle, but they operate in the shadows. Their targeted and camouflaged violence ensures that despotisms feel more "humane" and "civilized." Unlike the totalitarian regimes of the past, there is no reigning "atmosphere of madness and unreality."[31]

We could say that the new despotisms try to practice to perfection an art that has taken root in actually existing democracies, where (for instance) in the European Union alone, in addition to its use of private "contractors" in overseas missions, well over a million people are now employed in the member states in newly privatized policing and security services, so that (according to recent figures) the ratio of private security staff to police officers is now more than double in the United Kingdom and fast approaching parity in countries such as Germany and Spain.[32] Parallel trends are evident in the United States, whose federal government now depends heavily on mercenaries in war zones, contracts private corporations to run its prisons, and tolerates a presidential candidate using his own private security force to assail protesting citizens.

The reality within the new despotisms is similar. Privatized violence flourishes. It is often invisible. The Qatar way of doing things is every despot's dream. Imagine: the wealthiest country in the world, a place in the Arab world without any recorded political prisoners, a kingdom protected by all-seeing eyes and mostly invisible police repression. Cyberpolicing is strict—Qataris who dare post online materials considered beyond the pale are visited by the police and warned to desist, or in more serious cases summoned for interrogation to the headquarters of State Security. Closed-circuit television cameras are omnipresent. Smart cards, introduced in 2011 by the Interior Ministry, enable citizens to access government services but double as gate passes, national identity cards, residency permits, and tools of surveillance. Undercover agents are active, and private security guards, mostly from Nepal, are found in every shopping mall and office complex. The role for uniformed police officers is consequently slim. Few are publicly visible except at the intersections of Doha's main streets.[33]

Elsewhere, the reality of despotism is harsher though no less camouflaged, as in Russia, where the methods used by its rulers are sometimes crude (slipping radioactive poison into tea; using nerve agent to murder defectors; gunning down a prominent opposition leader in full view of surveillance cameras, just before midnight, at the foot of the Kremlin walls). Most of the work of political violence in that country is done not by the central government but by local political bosses, secret service agents, plainclothes thugs, and organized criminals. The gruesome fate of a hapless Moscow banker in mid-2005 illustrates how justice is typically dispensed. Caught up in disputes linked to land and assets, Oleg Novoselsky, chairman of the Kutuzovsky Bank, was kidnapped by a much-feared paramilitary gang run by Aslan Gagiev, a vain and cunning crook known in the underworld as Djako. Novoselsky was immured in a large barrel of concrete and left without food or water to bake to death in the searing summer sun. A week later, on Gagiev's personal order, the barrel containing the banker's body was dumped into the Moscow Canal. A decade after that, following a tip from a former gang member, his remains were discovered at the bottom of the canal. Gagiev was later arrested and extradited from Austria to Russia, but two decades later the contract murderers had not been apprehended or convicted.

Rule through Law

The brazen lawlessness of dastardly acts stands in contrast to the fact that despotisms typically have fine constitutions, and that there is much trumpeting of the coming of peace and justice at home as the fruit of the fair-minded enforcement of order through law. The doublespeak of the Kremlin refers to "dictatorship of the law." Beijing trumpets "legalization" and "governing the nation in accordance with the law"; it boasts a constitution specifying that every citizen is "equal before the law."[34] But the reality is that under conditions of despotism law is never simply law. There is no independent judiciary. From the top downward, politics under despotic conditions resembles a permanent coup d'état, a steady evisceration of constitutional precepts and rulings, and an unending campaign to destroy "juristocracy." Loaded judicial appointments, demotions and firings, favoritism, and bribes ensure that the courts and the legal profession are hemmed in from all sides and rendered subservient to the reigning political powers.

The dependence of courts on the rulers (in Russia this is known as *telefonnoe pravo,* "telephone justice") means that judges tempted to rule against those in power don't last long. On the other hand, judges who predetermine trial outcomes by daydreaming their way through defense submissions while checking their mobile phones do. Despots have no love for legislatures either. Their parliaments are rump parliaments, not independent lawmaking bodies with teeth. In practice, despotisms gut courts and legislatures, and gutted courts and legislatures nourish despotism. The whole dynamic enables despotisms to deal lawlessly with their targeted opponents. Arrests on trumped-up charges and wrongful convictions of innocent subjects are common, sometimes to the point where the malfeasance of police and judicial officials seems indistinguishable from that of the crooks and criminals they're supposedly tracking and convicting. Despotisms and their systems of law impose few or no meaningful restraints on brutes and bullies. Some are well above the law, or escape the hand of published and publicly available laws. The laws may be stated clearly, but they are rarely observed (Russians say their strictness is honored through noncompliance). Though appearances are deceptive, despotisms are in fact systems of organized lawlessness. "Rule of law" has a phantom quality; it means "rule through law."

What is meant by the much-used, much-abused phrase "rule of law," which—far from being a liberal or bourgeois invention—has hybrid origins, including in the medieval European and Islamic traditions?[35] Loosely put, it refers to institutions and codes of written law that have the practical effect of curbing and balancing the ambitions of the powerful and those seeking power over others. The system of laws imposes meaningful restraints on crooks and thugs. Justitia, blindfolded and wielding a balance and sword, favors nobody. No person is above the laws, or escapes the hand of published and publicly available laws. The laws are clearly stated and consistent. They rule supreme; they apply equally to all, without exception, even to heads of government, judges, and business-people; and their retroactive application is not allowed. The laws are capable of being followed and enforced; they are peace formulae designed to inject a meaningful measure of juridical predictability into the whole political order.

Most twenty-first-century despotisms have been influenced to varying degrees by rule-of-law traditions, as for instance in East Asia, where such traditions began to take root during the Meiji period (1868–1912) in Japan and under the late Qing Dynasty (especially from the 1890s) in China, fueled by the conviction in ruling circles that independent courts were necessary for taming the tigers of power.[36] The same reasoning today grips lawyers, scholars, and citizens working to defend rule-of-law principles from inside the new despotisms. Umbrella groups and networks like Human Rights House Voronezh in Russia, the Hungarian Helsinki Committee, and the loose citizens' alliance in China known as Rights

Defense (Wéi Quán) are convinced that rule of law is a valuable weapon against the corrupting effects of arbitrary power. They say that whenever people act arbitrarily, they decide matters without reference to, or respect for, the existing laws.[37] They think they can get away with things unopposed; they suppose, without losing a wink of sleep, their own power to be self-justifying, or granted by the grace of a higher being, as if they have the heavens, history, or human nature on their side. That is why, cunning and camouflage aside, they treat others with disrespect. Putting themselves on a pedestal, they ditch the dignity principle, the precept that all persons should be regarded as beings worthy of respect because they are capable of publicly explaining themselves and their actions to others. So the merchants of arbitrary power typically rig things to their advantage. Though they may say otherwise, they are antidemocratic: they restrict or ban outright opportunities for others to call into question or actively refuse the rulers' power. Sometimes they even resort to eliminating their opponents through torture, imprisonment, disappearance, or death.

Under despotic conditions, the beleaguered supporters of the rule of law emphasize that it enables the weak to speak against the strong by pressing home their concerns freely in public. Rule of law is an antidote to fear caused by uncertainty. When employers, government officials, or armed police act with impunity, they inject anxiety and paralysis into their subjects' lives. Arbitrary power is unpredictable power. When unleashed, it can operate spitefully, changing direction on a whim, exacting revenge on its victims. Rule of law, they insist, sends signals to the peddlers of arbitrary power that fear is a public problem, and that it can ruin people's lives and therefore must not be tolerated.

Rule of law is seen by its friends as not just a weapon for preventing harm to the body politic. It has positive implications, they say: it is a reminder of the importance of fostering the dignity of citizens. Rule of law rejects the view that people are fit only for bowing and scraping in the presence of masters. Rule of law supposes citizens are capable of defining life's projects for themselves. In this sense, rule of law anticipates and requires putting an end to the practice of people being treated as objects of others' wills. This is another way of saying that rule of law is the ally of the liberty of all citizens, their capacity to live their lives as equals in the expectation that they will not be bossed and bullied by arbitrary power. When citizens enjoy the liberty to express themselves, to say their piece and act upon their words, then they can better make sense of the multiple choices and decisions that are the result of their liberty. Rule of law, say its champions, enables the nonviolent coordination and resolution of potentially conflicting claims regarding who should get how much, when, and how. In sum, they urge, rule of law implies the possibility of democratic politics. They imagine a world in which power is no longer subject to the arbitrary rule of the wealthy, the strong, or the capricious—a world where those who exercise power are required to give an account of their actions and to be held publicly responsible for their fraud, mendacity, lawlessness, and violence.

Enter reality. Present-day despotisms measure up poorly to these standards for rule of law, but in surprising ways. Early modern denigrators of despotism supposed that it "rendered useless all kinds of laws."[38] The new despotisms are different. They cling to law, and do much to reassure their subjects that law is not simply a stick used by the strong to beat the weak. In Vietnam and China, official signs plastered on city buildings and countryside walls urge subjects to pay attention to the laws, steadfastly to uphold the laws, and to obey a state in which rule of law prevails. The slogans seem to be confirmed by the rapid expansion of the legal professions in those countries. In China, for instance, on the eve of the Deng Xiaoping reforms, following a sustained Maoist period of lawlessness when all legal work was condemned as counterrevolutionary, there were just 5,500 lawyers working in 1,465 law firms. Less than two decades later, there were an estimated 110,000 lawyers employed in some 8,300 law firms. The numbers have since grown exponentially.[39]

Despotisms generally seem keen to bolster the trend. They open their legal-services field to Baker McKenzie, to Paul, Weiss, Rifkind, Wharton & Garrison, and to other large foreign law firms, which work alongside local partners. The despotisms negotiate and operate cross-border rule-of-law deals, such as the 1998 Legal and Judicial Cooperation Program with the European Union. There are times when the governing bodies host robust conference discussions about the merits of the rule of law. Judicial reform plans are announced to improve professional training of judges, strengthen the hand of local courts in such matters as commerce and the environment, enhance the openness and transparency of the legal system, and generally strengthen the legal rights of individual litigants, for instance through judicial review and by disallowing illegally obtained evidence. Although stiff penalties for "publishing state secrets," "subverting state security," and the like typically remain on the books, death penalty legislation, where it exists, tends to be used sparingly. There is, meanwhile, abundant talk by officials of the need to "strengthen the law," to "observe" and "respect" the law; there are even calls for locking power in "a cage of regulations" (Xi Jinping).[40]

There are undoubted success stories, where approximations of the rule of law operate as a substantial norm shaping legal practice. Consider the growing domestic use by the Chinese Communist Party of various forms of legal mediation *(fǎ lǜ tiáo jiě)*. Nearly a million legal mediation committees assisted by "people's mediators" now handle most conflicts (perhaps 90 percent) inside and outside courts, at no cost to the litigants, in such areas as economic and labor disputes, divorce, minor criminal matters, and civil disputes at the township level. Moving up the pyramid of power, consider China's escalating global contribution to the field of cross-border legal arrangements. There, against the perceived hegemony of the United States, Chinese officials favor multipolarity and a distinct "transactional" style of diplomacy laced with talk of a stable "community of common destiny" and a "new model of international relations" *(xin xing guoji guanxi)* based on the careful calculation of costs and benefits to the "national interest" of China.[41]

Equally striking is the way these same officials have learned the legal rules of the foreign policy game. With the notable exception of the Organisation for Economic Co-operation and Development, the world's most powerful despotism is now thoroughly entangled in the complex institutional webs of what is called global governance. China plays an important role in the three main Bretton Woods institutions (the World Bank, from which it is now the largest recipient of projects and loans; the International Monetary Fund; and the General Agreement on Tariffs and Trade), as well as in the Asian Development Bank. It extracts investment, loans, and aid from a wide variety of multilateral agencies—larger sums than any other state in the world—and plays a vital role in key global security and arms control treaties. It is committed to building and buttressing new cross-border institutions such as the Shanghai Cooperation Organization (the alliance of China, Russia, India, Pakistan, and the Central Asian states) and to the twenty-seven-member Conference on Interaction and Confidence Building Measures in Asia.

Reports suggest that within most of these organizations, Chinese diplomats, negotiators, and other officials impress outsiders with their knowledge of procedural rules and technical details, their preparedness, and their tough negotiating skills. "China is thorough, exceedingly well-prepared and well organized about executing its responsibilities as an institutional member," notes a US congressional report. "It does its 'homework' and raises detailed, substantive questions about matters which not only affect China's interests, but also on issues of purely institutional relevance. This includes questions about operational issues and structures, staffing and office locations, and a range of administrative issues."[42] Chinese negotiators equally demonstrate their respect for rule-of-law principles and practices within such venues as the World Trade Organization Dispute Settlement Body, in which it has become a highly active participant with a surprisingly low volume of complaints and full acceptance of legally binding decisions.[43]

The trend has prompted respected scholars to ponder the possibility that despotisms such as China, Russia, and Turkey might develop local versions of the rule of law. The evidence is discouraging. Despite all the good behavior, when the businesses and governments of the new despotisms are operating abroad, they often care little or nothing for law. Think of Donetsk, heartland of a Russian-driven military occupation that has resulted in the deaths of more than ten thousand Ukrainian citizens; or Sihanoukville, the Cambodian host city of gambling and prostitution catering to Chinese mafia types; or the Anatolian Kurdish city of

THE NEW DESPOTISM

Silopi, where in late 2015 frightened residents fled a curfew imposed by heavily armed Turkish troops. On the domestic front, the fungus of lawlessness flourishes. The new despotisms contain no effective mechanisms for enforcing well-written constitutions. National legislatures such as Saudi Arabia's Majlis Ash Shura appear to resemble parliaments, but in practice they fail to exercise constitutionally prescribed powers of supervising the rulers. Despots are by definition beyond the reach of the law, especially when they are subject to open public challenges. That is the meaning (reiterated during the several uprisings in Hong Kong starting in 2014) of official statements such as "Firmly safeguard rule of law" and "Democracy without the rule of law will only bring havoc."[44]

Abuses of power by lawless rulers, meanwhile, are well documented on a daily basis. From top to bottom in these systems, personal favors, embezzlement of public monies, bribery, and blackmail are chronic. Public dissent is punished. Take a typical incident: people attend a private event to discuss a matter of public concern. They are trailed, spotted, and nabbed by the police, who instruct them to come for a cup of tea. At the police station, they are interrogated by officers from the much-feared secret police force. Punctuated by periods in which their interrogators leave for cigarette breaks or to make telephone calls to their superiors in order to decide what next is to be done, the questioning can last for hours or even days. Some are let off with just a warning on the condition they switch to offering "constructive advice" to the authorities instead of criticism, "adjust" the tone of their social media postings, or simply shut their mouths. If less lucky, subjects are charged with such offenses as "picking quarrels and provoking troubles" or "gathering a crowd to disrupt public order and undermine law enforcement." The unluckiest are beaten, disappeared, or convicted and sent to prison. Some pay the ultimate price for their civic initiative, with their lives.

Defenders and friends of despotism typically say these events are exceptions, or unwarranted exaggerations made by ignorant foreigners meddling in their country's affairs. They point, with some justification, to the gross legal injustices suffered by religious and ethnic minorities within Western democracies, or they praise progress on the local legal front and say there's still much work to be done. They express pride in what they call the process of "legalization," using phrases such as "governing the nation in accordance with law" and (in Laos, Vietnam, and China) "building a socialist rule-of-law state." Note the clever interpretation of rule of law as "rule by law."[45] Law is a weapon of political command and control.

Anticorruption campaigns well illustrate the point. Conducted in the name of rooting out abuse of power at all levels, these campaigns have the effect of drawing public attention to what everybody knows: from top to bottom, the structures of despotism are riddled with corrupt practices. Backed by tough-minded investigators, these campaigns to slay tigers and swat flies have the effect of familiarizing people with the democratic language of the need for greater "scrutiny" and "probing" of officials. Talk of transparency becomes the new normal. But the stated official commitment to clean up government, as in Putin's anticorruption drive and the high-profile corruption trials that swept Vietnam in 2017–2018, carries with it the serious risk of providing people with plentiful evidence of just how rotten the ruling apparatus is at all levels, and how unfit it is to govern. Encouraging citizens and judiciary officials to be fluent in the language of accountability and transparency might give them ideas about the need for different ways of governing, especially when officials are disciplined or prosecuted in court for their corrupt practices. Hence despots quickly learn that their own anticorruption efforts must be balanced by insistence on respect for "discipline" and "governing by means of law." In other words, the point of anticorruption drives is to strengthen the hand of the rulers by surgically removing from the body politic the spreading tumors of corruption. The aim is to silence squabbling oligarchs, to get rid of opponents, and to impose tougher new practices on both officials and subjects, so that both groups' loyalty and respect for the laws laid down by the rulers are rendered publicly unquestionable. The deep contradiction built into anticorruption drives is telling. It reveals that under despotic conditions law is never simply law. The rule of law has phantom qualities. It is at the same time real but elusive; there but not there; present but absent. Law means the observance, abuse, and non-use of law.

There are indeed spaces in which due process of law is practiced. In Russia, for instance, everyday legal disputes in such routine matters as traffic violations, divorce, and unpaid taxes are resolved in the courts by lawyers and judges guided by procedural and substantive written laws.[46] In all despotisms, official sermons about law and the importance of "legalization" are commonplace. There are efforts, especially at the local level, to strengthen the hand of law through increased court funding, the expansion of law schools, improved training of lawyers and judges, and the provision of legal services to businesses. Yet the truth is that lawlessness, fed by a judiciary twisted and deformed by a ruling apparatus operating in the name of the people, is omnipresent, even in organized sports such as golf.

Again consider China, where during the Mao era golf was banned. Dubbed "green opium," it was denounced as a frivolous, bourgeois pastime of expatriates, a "sport for millionaires." During the Deng Xiaoping reforms, the official position flipped. Although inaccessible to most citizens of China except on television screens, grand golf courses gradually became available for the enjoyment of the country's wealthy subjects. But in 2004, following waves of local protest against compulsory land acquisition and water diversion schemes, the central government in Beijing moved to prohibit the construction of golf courses. The prohibition was trumpeted officially as a blow against lawlessness. Yet during the next five years, things ran headlong in the opposite direction: some four hundred courses were constructed, including Shenzhen's Mission Hills, China's highest-rated golf and leisure resort, host of the region's most important tournaments, and (so runs the boast) the world's largest golf club.[47] In more lawful polities, such establishments could only have been built with difficulty, due to public protest and legal action through the courts. But in China, local governments working hand in hand with developers, blind-eyed judges, and the police rode roughshod over local farmers and confiscated their land in exchange for a few bags of rice, all in defiance of lawful rule. Such practices accord with the ancient power principle that since the mountains are high and the emperor far away, legal instructions from above can easily be neutralized from below, for a handsome profit.

How can we make sense of this odd disconnect between well-written laws and practical realities infused with talk of legalization? Observers are divided. For some, the gap confirms that despotisms are resolutely on the low road toward a future where money talks and arbitrary power rules, camouflaged by law; despotism is likened to a giant corruption machine. Others see things more positively. For the optimists, the strange admixture of legality and lawlessness is a sign of unfinished political business. The new despotisms are on a rocky high road toward a land in which rule-of-law principles prevail in practice. Lawlessness is seen to be gradually withering away; it resembles a rickety footbridge leading toward a more mature rule-of-law system with local characteristics.

A third pathway is most probable: an odd mishmash of legalization and lawlessness that proves durable. Arbitrary exercises of power in many fields come wrapped in fine statements. At the same time, practical experiments extol the virtues of reducing "corruption" and restraining the power of the state through judicial and legislative means and through people's participation in various sectors of the legal system itself. Functioning as a clear alternative to a robust power-sharing, monitory form of democracy shaped by the rule of law, this phantom rule of law (let's call it) may be thought to be a fairy tale, or mere fiction. Closer inspection shows that it is something different, and more sophisticated, especially during those moments when power-hungry despots publicly bathe in the waters of legal reasoning and legal quarrels structured by their own legal codes.

The astonishing show trial and conviction of Bo Xilai in October 2013 was a drama-packed example of phantom rule of law in action. The trial scrambled the line between legality and lawlessness and showed why the new despotisms are not "dual states" marked by a wide gap between respect for law and power based on sheer force.[48] The five-day trial in fact resembled a fine performance of shadow puppetry, a grand show whose players, well aware of the reality of the theater, acted out their scripts perfectly. It was intended by the Chinese rulers as irrefutable proof that their version of the rule of law is at work to hunt down the corrupt, so guaranteeing that China moves unhindered, steadily, and resolutely in the direction of a nation governed in accordance with law.

Not since the trial of the Gang of Four in 1980–1981 was the case of a senior official handled so openly.[49] Bo was accused of embezzling government money and accepting multimillion-dollar bribes from Chinese businessmen, including a luxury villa in southern France. As former Party chief of Chongqing, he was said to have abused his power by dismissing his police chief in order to cover up the murder by poisoning of a British businessman by his own wife, Gu Kailai. The details, including allegations by Bo that he had been tortured and rumors that he had fainted twenty-seven times during pretrial interrogations that lasted seventeen months, proved riveting for many millions of Chinese people. Some details were especially bizarre, including news that the live-in mistress of an official who was being held in a state detention center tried to organize his escape. Court officials whet public appetites by allowing (admittedly incomplete) transcripts of the proceedings to be circulated throughout Chinese media. There was some livestreaming of video footage, and photographs circulated widely throughout every level of official media.

Flanked in every courtroom appearance by gangling policemen designed to make him look short and stumpy, Bo rose to the occasion. Hair dyed jet black, dressed in dark trousers and an open-necked white shirt, he found himself at the center of a courtroom drama that lasted for an exceptionally drawn-out five days. In a legal system that lacks juries, relies on written testimonies, and forbids defendants to contradict witnesses, Bo rejected every charge against him and took every opportunity to challenge the state prosecution point by point. Knowing well the old Chinese proverb that when power is concentrated high office is always dangerous, he insisted on cross-examining prosecution witnesses, including his wife, whose video testimony was played in court. Bo claimed she was "insane" and that, in any case, she had confessed to her crime under pressure. He vigorously denied her assertion that he had openly discussed with her on the telephone the embezzlement of state funds. "The most amateur of the corrupt," he insisted, would never attempt such a thing. Bo arguably had a point, but for that revealed truth he was rudely rewarded: condemned to life imprisonment for bribery, embezzlement, and abuse of power, and packed off to the same prison in which his Communist-stalwart father once spent time. "The facts of the first instance verdict are clear," the high court said in its final ruling, posted on its website. "The evidence is reliable, sufficient, and the sentence is appropriate." Hard-nosed scholars of law present in the courtroom might have whispered *dura lex sed lex* (the law is hard, but it is the law), but the last loud word actually went to Bo's principal enemy, the president of China and the general secretary of the Communist Party, Xi Jinping. Convinced that Bo was plotting to protect himself with the security services at his command, to disrupt a leadership transition, and to rip the Party apart, Xi was unforgiving. The lesson of the whole affair, he said, is that since China is a socialist country ruled by law that does not trample on the dignity and authority of the people, the courts and the police must be reformed so that hereafter "the handle of the knife [*dāo bà zi*] is firmly in the hands of the Party and the people."[50]

Why Despotism?

Rethinking Despotism

The callous contract killing of a Russian businessman by unnamed thugs and the life sentence handed down to a powerful Chinese poligarch in a well-rehearsed show trial are rasping reminders of how the new despotisms try to disguise their power to ruin and destroy the lives of their troublesome subjects. The cunning also makes clear that scholarly efforts to probe and prick the backside of these despotisms are fraught. They are risky and can be dangerous. It is no easy task to unmask the mechanics of despotic power. Even to speak and write about them is equivalent to their betrayal. Blocked access to sources and trying to periscope around ninety-degree corners are constant frustrations. Fieldwork has its personally touch-and-go moments; as Simon Wiesenthal once noted, probing arbitrary power often resembles studying disease in a swamp. Equally formidable is the intellectual challenge of crafting a plausible narrative by means of comparisons that draw together and make intelligible so many disparate dynamics operating in such a wide variety of different contexts structured by different languages. The burden of comparison is compounded by the difficulty of choosing particular materials so as to lend them a wider significance. The choices are inescapably arbitrary, in that they never come blessed with veracity by a pre-given reality. Deciding the significance of characters, events, and institutions requires choosing an interpretative framework that helps us make plausible sense of things. But that equally requires harnessing concepts that offer to bring clarity and persuasion to the table. Hence the special challenge of this book: to enrich the field of despotology (let's call it) by crafting a convincing case for reviving and rethinking the out-of-fashion and mostly forgotten idea of despotism.

It is worth pausing briefly, for this is the right moment to see the point of plumbing the depths of past political thinking in search of a precious old term whose recovery and creative reworking arguably help us to understand better the significance of the times in which we are living and what might be done to prevent future political damage to the lives of millions of people. The term "despotism" has a breathtakingly complex history. With roots in ancient Greece, the word *despotēs* (perhaps from the Mycenaean Linear B word *do-po-ta*) originally referred to the supposed benevolent rule of a husband over his wife, children, and slaves within the household. The word was kept alive during the Byzantine Empire, when it was mainly a court title bestowed on the sons or sons-in-law of reigning emperors, and then revived with gusto in early modern Europe.

"Despotism" was used at first as a term to differentiate Christian Europe from Eastern powers. It was an Orientalist signifier of abuse, a fighting word in the European imaginary, a key term that served as the heir to Christian disparagement of the world of Islam. From the sixteenth century, fed by casual anecdotes and formal reports about the behavior of Grand Seigneur sultans provided by European embassies in Constantinople, Ottoman Turkey came to

THE NEW DESPOTISM

be seen as the perfect embodiment of the seductively dark powers of despotism.[1] For many observers, it was a byword for the destruction of individual property, the widespread ignorance produced by the state ban on printing presses, sexual perversions, and arbitrary rule by fiendish sultans. Despotism was understood as a whole political order centered on the sultan's seraglio, a space of unimaginable luxury where the ruler administered power through subalterns, who were subject to strangulation if they fell from favor. The seraglio was a point of unrestrained power serviced by a strange cast: dwarfs, mutes, black and white eunuchs, hordes of captive women of Christian origin hand-picked to satisfy the lusts of a ruler more inclined to "unnatural" practices. Our old acquaintance Montesquieu thought in this way. The reports in his possession on Persians, Turks, Arabs, Tartars, Siamese, Japanese, Chinese, and the peoples of the Indian subcontinent convinced him that they were willing accomplices and victims of despotism. Many other observers agreed, among them Colonel Alexander Dow, an English employee of the East India Company, whose widely read work *The History of Hindostan* (1772) included "A Dissertation Concerning the Origin and Nature of Despotism in Hindostan." Dow was sure that "the faith of Mahommed is peculiarly calculated for despotism . . . it is one of the greatest causes which must fix for ever the duration of that species of government in the East." Other causes (said the colonel) included fear, the soporific effects of frequent bathing, and sweltering heat: "The languor occasioned by the hot climate of India, inclines the native to indolence and ease" and "the labour of being free." Prohibitions on drinking wine added to the torpor of subjects: "It prevents that free communication of sentiment which awakens mankind from a torpid indifference to their natural rights." He added that the victims of despotism "become cold, timid, cautious, reserved and interested [biased];

strangers to those warm passions, and that cheerful elevation of mind, which renders men in some measure honest and sincere."[2]

The Orientalist picture of pusillanimous Hindus falling victim to Muslim despotism was widely believed. But then along came a surprise: a remarkable change of meaning, and political function, of the word "despotism." During the eighteenth century, the "phantom of despotism" (the often-quoted phrase of Abraham-Hyacinthe Anquetil-Duperron, translator, writer, and scholar of the history, geography, religions, and laws of the Indian subcontinent) began to haunt the house of Europe, and beyond. For a variety of reasons, in the Atlantic region, despotism became a topic of intense public debate among the privileged literate classes, especially in France.

One far-reaching reason was the frontal challenge posed by better-informed writers who cast doubt on Montesquieu's assertion in his *De l'esprit des lois* that despotism was a "naturalized" feature of the major states of Asia. His work certainly proved influential among many Europeans who pondered Asian societies during the second half of the eighteenth century. Scholars, merchants, travelers, and empire-builders swallowed whole the thesis of Oriental despotism. But when Europeans began to receive a rush of fresh reports from the world beyond Europe, intellectual challenges were launched against the reigning orthodoxy. These provocations had the not-always-intended effect of loosening up the category: opening its mind and widening its horizons. The category became less predictable, more restless, and politically promiscuous.

Partly this happened because some writers dared cast doubt on the standard pictures of the East. Among the most influential masterpieces written by those who concentrated their attention on Asia, and who dissented from the orthodoxy, was Anquetil-Duperron's treatise *Législation orientale* (1778).[3] It accused Montesquieu and others of misdescribing governments and societies of the East. They had formulated "un système de despotisme qui n'existe réellement nulle part." The political orders of Turkey and the Mogul Empire were not instances of arbitrary and unchecked power wielded by abusive despots served by obsequious officials, Anquetil-Duperron urged. There were slaves in Asia, but not everybody there was enslaved. In reality, the rulers of these polities were mutually bound to their subjects by customs and written and unwritten laws. Their actions were constrained by the countervailing powers of notables and religious authorities, by petitioners seeking justice, the practice of court consultations *(durbars),* and widespread access to public gazettes containing details of government business. Power was similarly checked by the customary and legal protection of religious diversity, as in the early Mogul Empire of Akbar, and by rights of property in land and trade; Anquetil-Duperron even insisted that private property was better protected in Ottoman Turkey than in England.

Législation orientale masterfully noted how talk of despotism was connected to European imperial expansion by merchants and missionaries. Anquetil-Duperron questioned its "assertions sans preuves" and offered a more accurate account of Eastern polities. By portraying those polities as unstable systems of arbitrary power, discourses on despotism surmised that European colonization was a generous gift, bringing social stability and good and lawful government to peoples who had been suffering under the fear, violence, and inequities of despotism. Anquetil-Duperron thus accused his opponents of using the word "despotism" to excuse the oppression practiced by Europeans in Asia. Their conviction that the East enjoyed no private property, for instance, served as a justification of the colonial confiscation of native lands. Anquetil-Duperron predicted that by defaming the colonized as victims of despotism, imperial expansion would heap indignity and misery upon the peoples of the East.

The scholar-adventurer had a point, taken up by later distinguished scholars.[4] But in a strange twist of fate, in ways he most definitely didn't intend, his case was anticipated or extended by writers and public officials who argued that Eastern despotisms had attractive features that were worth bringing home to Europe. Pointing to the reforms promoted by tough eighteenth-century monarchs such as Frederick II of Prussia, they were sure despotism could be benevolent. Among the first thinkers who reasoned in this way was the famous opponent of torture and the death penalty, Milan-born author Cesare Beccaria, whose *Dei delitti e delle pene* (1764) made a case for a new species of benevolent monarchy in which "the despotism of many can be corrected only by the despotism of one man, and the cruelty of a despot is proportional not to his strength, but to the obstacles he has to contend with."[5] His plea for undivided power was read carefully and quoted by Catherine II of Russia; such were the times that the book landed Beccaria jobs with the reforming Habsburg rulers Maria Theresa and Joseph II. Without doubt, the most influential champions of despotic government were the French Physiocrats. During the last years of the long reign of Louis XV (1710–1774), they promoted a new type of absolute monarchy based on what they described as natural laws, such as free trade in grain. The job of government, they said, was to safeguard the free operation of these natural and necessary laws of government and society. They proudly called such government based on natural laws *despotisme légale* and "enlightened despotism." Along these lines, with examples of rulers like Catherine II and Leopold of Tuscany in mind, the Milanese aristocrat Giuseppe Gorani (1740–1819) similarly published a widely read case for a "true despotism" that would work to establish "natural order" by strengthening a monarchy actively committed to getting rid of cramping taxation schemes, rules, and regulations; the result would be to unleash market forces of trade and commerce against the caste privileges of such intermediary bodies as the church, magistrates, and local assemblies. François Quesnay's *Le despotisme de la Chine* (1767) put things even more sharply. He insisted that "the government of China" was impressive and certainly worth emulating exactly because it was a "legal despotism" in that "the sovereign of that empire takes into his own hands exclusively the supreme authority" and consistently applies "wise and irrevocable laws," which are "the laws of the Natural Order."[6]

Such reasoning stood at right angles to the old Orientalist disparaging of Eastern despotism. It was striking for a less positive reason as well: it proved there were moments when European intellectuals were easily seduced by fantasies of undivided sovereign power and the despotic patronage and employment it dangled under their noses.[7] The historical record nevertheless shows that the intellectual tango with despotism sparked furious public backlashes from those who figured despotism was a global phenomenon, and a global menace. The semantic shift had deeper roots: in the second half of the seventeenth century, the phrase "arbitrary and despotic power" had first been used by pamphleteers to attack the absolutism of the Sun King, Louis XIV.[8] But—in part thanks to Gorani, Quesnay, and the hellishly good intentions of Anquetil-Duperron—during the eighteenth century trouble erupted, with great political consequences. The newfangled word "despotism" pushed its way into the English language in 1727, from the older French *despotisme*. It quickly joined the forces of revolution. The shift was fueled by a combination of several forces, including general alarm at talk of the advantages of despotism, mounting evidence of the territorial ambitions of monarchies in Austria, Prussia, and Russia, and dramatic political events such as Louis XV's coup d'état (1771) and the first partition of the Polish-Lithuanian Commonwealth (1772). With the help of honest confessions by reigning monarchs ("There are and always will be monsters among princes," wrote Frederick II), political radicals began to say that European monarchies were beginning to resemble despotisms elsewhere—for instance, in their aggressive taxation policies, suppression of religious minorities, and wooing of public opinion by uncontrolled, arbitrary power.[9] Denis Diderot, famous coeditor of the *Encyclopédie*, the great Enlightenment reference work for the arts and sciences, was among those leading the charge. "A despot," he wrote, "even if he were the best of men, by governing in accordance with his good pleasure, commits a crime." He added: "A first despot, just, steady, and enlightened, is a great calamity; a second despot, just, steady, and enlightened, would be a still greater one; but a third, who should succeed with all these great qualities, would be the most terrible scourge with which a nation could be afflicted."[10] His compatriot Jean-Louis Carra, a journalist, parliamentarian, and librarian, called upon his fellow citizens to resist despotism because it threatened to "enslave" his native France "under the ruins of her *moeurs,* her fortune, and her liberty." Moved by "honesty and rage," this resistance would finally bring to an end the despotism that had oppressed the French people for centuries. He added: "What a triumph!"[11] For his efforts, Carra was guillotined in October 1793 by local bloodthirsty Jacobin revolutionaries, but his sentiments were echoed across the Channel by the English writer and Anglican priest Vicesimus Knox, who caused a great stir by attacking the British monarchy in the name of the principles of the French Revolution. "The grand adversary of human virtue and happiness is DESPOTISM," he thundered, in upper case. "Look over the surface of the whole earth, and behold man, the glory and deputed lord of the creation, withering under the influence of despotism, like the plant of temperate climes scorched by the sun of a torrid zone." He added: "Despotism is indeed an Asiatic plant; but brought over by those who have long lived in Asia, and nursed in a hot-house with indefatigable care, it is found to vegetate, bloom, and bear fruit, even in our cold, ungenial climate."[12] The idea that despotism had little to do with climatic conditions and so could travel and threaten liberty everywhere found its greatest popularizer in Thomas Paine. His publishing sensation *Rights of Man* (the explosive first part was published in London in March 1791) railed against the arbitrary power of despotic governments everywhere. "Government with insolence is despotism," he wrote, "but when contempt is added it becomes worse; and to pay for contempt is the excess of slavery." He added a memory from the time when he actively contributed to the military struggle of the American colonists against British imperial troops and their German allies: "This species of government . . . reminds me of what one of the Brunswick soldiers told me who was taken prisoner by the Americans in the late war: 'Ah!' said he, 'America is a fine free country, it is worth the people's fighting for; I know the difference by knowing my own: in my country, if the prince says eat straw, we eat straw.' God help that country, thought I, be it England or elsewhere, whose liberties are to be protected by German principles of government, and Princes of Brunswick!"[13]

Intended to be read aloud to not-yet-literate peoples who gathered in gin parlors, coffeehouses, and public squares, this kind of rhetoric proved powerful. It showed how a term with a deeply prejudiced past had turned politically aggressive, and progressive, in support of government based on power-sharing and democratic representation. The term "despotism" became what German scholars call a basic concept *(Grundbegriff)*; the word attracted great attention, stirred up public controversy in the world of newspapers, books, and pamphlets, and, most dramatically, ignited political upheavals that helped bring down monarchies in the American colonies, Haiti, and France. By the last quarter of the eighteenth century, throughout the Atlantic region the language of despotism and talk of its fickle bossiness had become a deadly weapon in the resistance to the arbitrary power of monarchs, whether they were charming, benevolent, or cruel. The figure of the despot as a "monster" became central in the politics of defending society against "criminal" rulers gripped by whim and wildness.[14] The semantic shift was later recorded in the shared reminiscences of the aging Thomas Jefferson and John Adams. Adams confided that "the fundamental Article of my political Creed is, that Despotism, or unlimited Sovereignty, or absolute Power is the Same in a Majority of a popular Assembly, an Aristocratical Counsel, an Oligarchical Junto and a Single Emperor. Equally arbitrary cruel bloody and in every respect, diabolical." Jefferson agreed: "I shall not die without a hope that light and liberty are on steady advance . . . even should the cloud of barbarism and despotism again obscure the science and liberties of Europe, this country remains to preserve and restore light and liberty to them. In short, the flames kindled on the 4th. of July 1776 have spread over too much of the globe to be extinguished by the feeble engines of despotism. On the contrary they will consume these engines, and all who work them."[15]

Abusive Power

Following the late eighteenth-century American and French revolutionary upheavals, the idea of despotism lived on for a while.

Adams and Jefferson were not alone when speaking the language of despotism. Scotsman James Mill (in his three-volume *The History of British India*, first published in 1818) argued that despotism was not just a product of exotic Asia but a "semi-barbarous" form of government that exists in all nations in their formative stages. In Mill's treatment, despotism was the product of desire and imagination unrestrained by knowledge and discipline. Its most extreme variant was "the Hindu form of government" and its "degrading and pernicious system of subordination." His son, John Stuart Mill, elaborated the point, saying that there is "no spring of spontaneous improvement in the people themselves," and the absence of private property and "good despots" are the hallmarks of Asian societies, their improvement in matters of government and property required help from colonial powers and "intermediate" bodies such as the East India Company. "Despotism is a legitimate mode of government in dealing with barbarians," he wrote, "provided their end be improvement." What was needed, he concluded, was a "ruler full of the spirit of improvement," a "vigorous despotism" that prepared the way for its own supersession, into representative government.[16]

The father's and son's embrace of the term proved to be its swan song. For a variety of reasons that have much to do with optimism about the coming of laissez-faire and representative government in its Atlantic heartlands, the concept of despotism gradually faded from political life. Nobody could foresee what was around the corner: two global wars, aerial bombardment, concentration camps, chemical weapons, totalitarianism, and the atomic bomb, followed by the rise in the early years of our century of a new type of despotism that globally threatened power-sharing democracy. During the course of the nineteenth century, dictionaries still trotted out stale definitions, as if they were saddled with the obligation to record things past, and there were periodic splutters of interest in the subject of despotism by scholars, though they tended to regard it either dismissively or with mere antiquarian interest. A late nineteenth-century dictionary, for example, defined a despot as a ruler "who exercises or possesses absolute power over another" and despotism as "absolute control over others."[17] There was nothing new there. There was only antiquarian fatigue at the thought of an outdated mode of rule outperformed by liberal, parliamentary government.

On the scholarly front, Emile Durkheim's study of Montesquieu's writings was symptomatic of the shift in perception. It accused the master of misleadingly making a fetish of sovereignty and forms of state. Durkheim helped bury the whole idea of despotism. He said monarchy and despotism should be treated as epiphenomena, as political symptoms of underlying social orders that required a genuinely sociological explanation of their peculiar dynamics. The bad habit of treating state forms "at first sight" as the "most important" dynamic produces a misunderstanding, Durkheim said. "Since the ruler stands . . . at the 'summit' of society and is often, quite understandably, called the 'head' of the political system, everything is thought dependent on him." In reality, argued Durkheim, political forms are expressions of underlying social dynamics. Monarchy is an expression of social factors: differentiation, particularity of interests, and competition for honor. Despotism is different. It is a kind of "monarchy in which social orders have all been abolished and there is no division of labor, or a democracy in which everyone, except the ruler, is equal, but in servitude. It is like a monster in which only the head is alive, having absorbed all the energies of the body."[18]

Such treatments ensured that during the early years of the twentieth century, "despotism" became a zombie term that belonged to the political language of yesteryear. There were stray political scientists, lawyers, and journalists who continued to use the term, but despite their best intentions their wise counsel was dispatched to hell.[19] Terms like "dictatorship," "corporatism," "autocracy," "total state," and "totalitarianism" prevailed.

The unhappy fate that befell the word "despotism" naturally raises a challenging question: Why, more than two centuries after its remarkable public efflorescence, should we bother attempting to revive a notion that has such a checkered history, and that seemingly belongs to a bygone era? Why continue to use a term that faded from fashion decades ago? Here are the short answers, the compelling reasons why the subject of despotism is very much alive.

Most obviously, the word "despotism" still has a powerful ethical sting in its tail. It should bring shivers to spines. Its practical effect is to underscore the universal dangers of arbitrary power. Consistent with its usage during most of the early modern period (and throughout this book), despotism is a foghorn concept, an early warning detector, a normative category in the arsenal of the critics of publicly reckless power. Philosophers might say it implies a counterfactual thought experiment: it helps us to understand more deeply both the risks of publicly unaccountable rule and the advantages of power-sharing democracy. Put differently, despotism is a precautionary concept: it enables us to figure out where arbitrary power could lead us, pokes and prods us to imagine the disappearance of power-restraining democracy, and warns us of what would be lost if the practice of public monitoring and restraint of arbitrary power were politically defeated. The new despotism, these pages have tried at length to show, is a world shaped and defined by forms of power that protect concentrations of wealth, manipulate communications media, and encourage people to behave like pusillanimous subjects of rulers who are both deeply corrupted and hostile to the ideals of a power-sharing democracy based on the dignity, freedom, and equality of citizens.

Authoritarianism?

In this ethical sense, the term "despotism" stands against the glib and ethically questionable category "authoritarianism." That word has enjoyed much recent popularity, which arguably stems from its imprecision and hence from its malleability in the hands of a wide range of scholars, journalists, politicians, and pundits, often to suit their own scholarly and political standpoints and concerns. The term "authoritarianism" suffers from a bundle of incorrigible weaknesses. For a start, it is descriptively misleading. Simply put, the language of authoritarianism wrongly supposes that the new despotisms are devoid of democracy, which is the supposed opposite of an authoritarian regime. Authoritarian regimes are said to be the antithesis of democracies. As we have seen during the course of this book, the reality is different. The term "authoritarianism" fails to grasp the kaleidoscopic quality of despotisms such as Saudi Arabia, China, and Russia, including the locally produced "democratic" techniques of government used by their despots to shape and control their subjects. The new despotisms certainly fall well short of the public-accountability standards of monitory democracy. Their rulers may claim they are shining examples of "managed democracy" or "people's democracy," as Russian and Chinese officials and intellectuals do. But the tricky empirical fact is that the new despotisms are not the simple opposites of democracy. The descriptor "authoritarianism" gravely underestimates their phantom-democratic qualities: the ongoing skittishness of rulers; the fear of losing power that stokes their willingness to experiment with the governing arts of consultation; and their engagement in constant self-examination, self-justification, and experimentation with what they call democratic practices. These locally produced forms of consultation are not of marginal significance; rather, they are important features of the new despotisms, which are not straightforwardly systems of haughty "authoritarian" power ruled by leaders who narcissistically suppose their unquestionable superiority.

The term "authoritarianism" is suspect for a more telling reason, to do with a built-in bias of its political ethics. Most people who use the word seem unaware that it is a recent invention, an Atlantic-region neologism with liberal and Anglo-American biases.[20] It divides the world into "bad" authoritarian regimes and "good" democracies. It makes the mistake of supposing that the Atlantic region is the world. The refusal of the term "authoritarianism" that runs through these pages thus has another basis, this time to do with normative objections to the presumption that Atlantic-style liberal democracy is the standard by which the rest of the world is to be measured and adjudged. Supposing that democracy can be reduced to free and fair elections and that electorally governed polities such as the United States, Britain, and France are the alpha and omega of democracy is a category mistake. It wildly exaggerates the health and strength of these ailing democracies. It ethnocentrically supposes that places such as Taiwan, India, South Africa, and Indonesia are carbon copies of Atlantic-style liberal democracy and its norms. And it carelessly understates the problem of how to tame the devils of arbitrary power, a problem that is not just a liberal democratic specialty but a worldwide problem that the idea of despotism seeks squarely to address.[21]

Symptomatic of the ethical narrowness of the term "authoritarianism" is the way political scientists and others use it to refer to a type of regime in which a powerful ruling group supposes without further question that it has authority, an absolute right to assert itself against its actual or potential opponents. The fishy thing about the term is the way it bowdlerizes or destroys outright the precious meaning and rich political significance of the root word "authority." It does so by mistakenly collapsing the vital difference between authority and power, which are not the same thing, as the neologism "authoritarianism" carelessly implies. In practically every culture on our planet, there's a well-documented history of treating authority as the originally derived or explicitly delegated entitlement to act on behalf of others.[22] In this way of thinking, to enjoy authority in any given situation is to be empowered by the authorization of others who count—for instance, ancestors, or a constitution, or the people. "Authority" is a word with rich connotations of "legitimate," "justifiable," "right," and "reasonable." It serves as an independent measure of the legitimacy of those who rule. To speak of authority is to imply that the use of might is not necessarily right. By contrast, power, the ability to act, to get things done—for instance, in concert with supporters or in opposition to opponents—operates according to its own self-ascribed standards. Power can quite readily be exercised in unauthorized ways, using intimidation, blackmail, and force, especially when the chips are down and push comes to shove. That is why, contrary to blithe usages of the term "authoritarianism," the vital distinction between authority and power needs to be preserved, which is what the term despotism most certainly does and has always done. The coeditor of the *Encyclopédie*, Diderot, made this point forcefully clear in his entry on the subject. "Power that is acquired by violence is only usurpation," he said, whereas "*authority* comes from another origin . . . the consent of those who have submitted to it by a contract made or assumed between them and the individual on whom they have bestowed *authority*."[23]

Voluntary Servitude

If a cardinal reason for rescuing and refurbishing the category of "despotism" is that doing so helps to crystallize opposition to publicly unaccountable and abusive power, then there is a second and equally compelling reason: despotism brings to mind the problem of voluntary servitude. Especially during its eighteenth-century heyday, the theory of despotism spotlighted a strange paradox that surely remains important today: those who exercise power arbitrarily over others are quite capable of developing techniques of rule that fabricate subjects who willfully offer up their "consent," upon which the despotism happily nourishes itself. The paradox of voluntary servitude is absent in such terms as "autocracy," "tyranny," and "authoritarianism," all of which have strong connotations of rule through heavy-handed force. By contrast, and put simply, despotism is a hard government in soft velvet form. It lures subjects into subjection. The "'perfect subject' in a despotism demands to be dominated without being consulted."[24] Despotism seduces its subjects, invites them to collaborate; it persuades them of its necessity. It offers them chances, only to teach them that resistance is pointless. The slave licenses the master. More than that: the slave likes or perhaps loves the master. The dynamic is one in which the prey prevaricates and then yields to the predator. Despotism is a form of power that transforms subjects into willing instruments of rulers. The eighteenth-century French writer Nicolas-Antoine Boulanger feared the way despotism nourished and nurtured subjects who "kiss their chains" and "numb themselves to their own existence." A century later, the Irish dramatist and poet Oscar Wilde similarly warned that despots feed upon the "body and soul" of a "People" who adore them.[25] Contemporary satires of despotism similarly probe the political anesthetics of arbitrary power, as the Azeri government of President Ilham Aliyev found in 2009 after falling afoul of a sly viral video of a mock press conference featuring fawning journalists asking questions of a donkey (youth activist Adnan Hajizada dressed in a donkey suit) that was heaping warm praise on Azerbaijan for its world-class treatment of donkeys. Much the same sentiment is captured by the bitter joke told by Egyptian satirists who oppose military rule led by President Abdel Fattah el-Sisi. "O Pharaoh, who turned you into a despot?" asks a loyal subject. The ruler's sardonic reply: "No one stood in my way." A Saudi dinner table jest has the same flavor. To test the true depth of his subjects' loyalty, the king orders a checkpoint to be set up on busy Highway 40 linking Riyadh with the largest cities of the country. Despite the inconvenience, there is no outcry among motorists, so the king orders identity checks, then the imposition of fines on all drivers passing through the clogged crossing. Traffic jams become huge, but cheerful compliance reigns supreme, without so much as a whimper of resistance from drivers. So the ruler orders the checkpoint officers to slap the face of each driver who has been stopped, checked, and fined. Eventually one driver blows a fuse. The king is interested in the exception and summons the angry driver to one of his sumptuous palaces to explain his disloyalty. "I waited patiently in the queue all morning, Your Highness," confesses the subject. "But then I thought: surely at least two officers should be assigned to slap us so the line moves twice as fast!"

The facts of voluntary servitude are old; the phrase itself is comparatively new, traceable to an astonishing essay written more than four centuries ago by a twenty-two-year-old Catholic student of law and classics who hailed from the provincial nobility of southwestern France, Étienne de La Boétie. His *Discours de la servitude volontaire* (unpublished in his lifetime, probably written in 1552–1553) supposes that God-given natural law predisposes each living individual to liberty in the company of others.[26] But if "freedom is our natural state," then the problem is to account for why people are "delighted and charmed" by rulers who rob them of their liberty. La Boétie's surprising answer is that since people are not "naturally" lacking in reason or the courage to live freely, their subordination to despots has to be understood as self-subordination. Subjects are the proximate cause of their own subjection. Servitude is chosen. People do not lose their liberty; rather, they win their enslavement. So how does this happen?

La Boétie proposed that servitude feeds upon habit and custom. Just as the ancient King Mithridates trained himself to drink poison, so subjects "learn to swallow, and not find bitter, the venom of servitude." Their habits of subordination are reinforced by the arts of "reverence and admiration" deployed by rulers. The cleverest of rulers act as if they are magicians, performing tricks like those of Pyrrhus, king of Epirus, whose big toe was believed to have curative powers, or the earliest kings of Egypt, who reportedly appeared before their subjects only when carrying cats or wearing firesticks on their heads. Bondage is equally bolstered by selectively distributed rewards: "Through big and small favors . . . there are found almost as many people for whom tyranny is profitable as those to whom liberty would seem desirable."

La Boétie's solution to the problem of voluntary servitude was simple but demanding. He called upon his readers to remember that the power of rulers is derived from their subjects. They have no power over their subjects except by means of them. "Resolve to serve no more, and you are at once freed," he wrote. He added: "Then you will behold the ruler, like a great Colossus whose pedestal has been pulled away, fall of his own weight and break into pieces." These words of counsel would eventually inspire millions of people who feared and despised despotism. The whole idea of voluntary servitude incited great refusals. It offered a solution to the problem of how to rid the world of despots. Especially during the eighteenth century, the Atlantic region's preoccupation with the strange mechanics of voluntary servitude ran through the writings of many thinkers, poets, and essayists, all of whom pointed out that despotism is a puzzling form of rule because "despotists" who "despotize" to nurture popular support in effect by signing a "silent contract" with their trusting and obedient subjects. Diderot expressed the point succinctly. "The arbitrary rule of a just and enlightened prince is always bad," he wrote. "His virtues are the most dangerous and the surest form of seduction: they lull a people imperceptibly into the habit of loving, respecting, and serving his successor, whoever that successor may be, no matter how wicked or stupid."[27]

The reference here to the political dangers of seduction by rulers had deep Eastern taproots, traceable back through the classical Greek *despótēs* (from *dómos,* "house," and *pósis,* "husband, spouse") to its earliest cognates in such languages as Avestan (*də̄ng patoiš,* "lord of the house") and Sanskrit *(dámpati-s).* Note the originally positive connotations of the word, describing the master responsible for taking good care of his household; this is why, as we have seen already, some early modern observers praised the benevolent quality of despotism.[28] Most others despised and feared its grip. Voluntary servitude was soon seen as the gelling agent of despotism by a wide range of Atlantic-region political thinkers and writers, including aristocrats (François Fé-

THE NEW DESPOTISM

nelon and Montesquieu among them) and radical republicans (such as Thomas Gordon and John Trenchard) who feared the possibility of a durable alliance of kings and the common people based on a combination of favors, pensions, manipulation, and vote buying.[29] Those who put their fingers on the problem of voluntary servitude often said that despotism was much more than the rule of one for the sake of one, or a plague on the lands of the East. The really worrying feature of modern despotism, they maintained, is the way it seduces and enslaves its subjects. It does so by infecting and degrading language, family life, ethics and social customs and rituals. It destroys equality and friendship among citizens. Despotism showers its subjects with patronage that induces "the lethargy of the people . . . . kept up by acts of kindness," noted Abbé Raynal.[30] Despotism breeds despots. It trains its subjects to become creepers and crawlers, lickspittles and toadies.

Diderot's coeditor of the *Encyclopédie*, French mathematician, musicologist, and philosopher Jean-Baptiste le Rond d'Alembert, chipped in by recommending further research into the topic of the "despotisme des bien-faiteurs" (despotism based on patronage, favoritism, and benefactors). The really worrying thing about despotism, he said, is the manner in which it paralyzes its public critics. Despotic rule corrupts the republic of letters by rendering writers dependent on their patrons, thereby crushing their capacity for clearheaded thought, public eloquence, and courageous censure of unbridled power.[31] The Anglo-Irish politician and formidable scribbler Edmund Burke issued a similar warning about the dangers of despotism. Describing it as a type of government "where all the inferior orbs of power are moved merely by the will of the Supreme," he warned of its spread: "Scarcely any part of the world is exempted from its power. And in those few places where men enjoy what they call liberty, it is continually in a tottering situation." While Burke vigorously denounced despotism as a type of rule that is capricious, foolish, and violent, he noted its strangely attractive and imperishable quality: "The truth is," he wrote, "this unnatural power corrupts both the heart and the understanding. And to prevent the least hope of amendment, a king is ever surrounded by a crowd of infamous flatterers, who find their account in keeping him from the least light of reason, till all ideas of rectitude and justice are utterly erased from his mind."[32]

Several major mid-nineteenth-century thinkers anxious about the spread of modern despotism tried to give a novel twist to the idea of voluntary servitude. We have already seen that the liberal philosopher and parliamentarian John Stuart Mill worried that citizens living under conditions of representative government could be swallowed alive by state bureaucracies in which "all the collective interests of the people are managed for them, all the thinking that has relation to collective interests done for them, and in which their minds are formed by, and consenting to, this abdication of their own energies." Citizens would then leave "things to the Government, like leaving them to Providence." Their subservience to government policies would be "synonymous with caring nothing about them, and accepting their results, when disagreeable, as visitations of Nature."[33] Mill's thoughts on "naturalized" servitude were inspired by his acquaintance Alexis de Tocqueville, who had earlier linked the corrupting effects of despotism to the dynamics of representative democracy.[34] Especially worrying, he argued, is the advent of a gentler but highly invasive form of servitude bound up with the growth of democratic entitlements. "I think the type of oppression threatening democratic peoples is unlike anything ever known," he wrote. He had in mind a new form of popular domination fostered by the growth of impersonal but invasive centralized state power. In a wide range of matters, from supplying bread to the hungry and jobs for the unemployed to caring for the sick and educating the young, government becomes ever more meddlesome in the daily lives of people. In the name of democratic equality and talk of the people, government becomes regulator, inspector, advisor, educator, and punisher. The trend is undisturbed by the "rare and brief exercise of free choice" in the ritual of periodic elections. It is reinforced by the rise of capitalist manufacturing industry. The new industrial class (unlike Marx, Tocqueville lumps together capital and labor and labels them an "aristocracy") calls on government to regulate the lives of workers and to provide the harbors, canals, roads, and other large-scale infrastructural projects deemed necessary for wealth creation. States themselves become directly involved in manufacturing, employing large numbers of engineers, architects, mechanics, and skilled workers. The consequent spread of state administration is more invasive, more controlling, than any previous species of despotism, Tocqueville asserted: "Day by day citizens fall under the control of the public administration, to which they insensibly surrender ever greater portions of their individual independence. These very same citizens, who periodically upset a throne and trampled on the feet of kings, more and more submit themselves, without resistance, to the smallest dictate of a clerk." This modern form of despotism prides itself on its gentleness. It claims to do away with *autos-da-fé,* fetters and executioners. Its mission is to "civilize" its subjects. It sets out to build all-embracing techniques of control that feel benevolent, mild, and life-enhancing. This despotism dispenses with identifiable despots. It brings to perfection the governing arts of voluntary servitude. It cultivates a form of disciplinary power that treats its citizens as subjects, yet wins their support and robs them of their wish to participate in government or take an interest in the public good. "Over these [citizens] is elevated an immense, tutelary power, which takes sole charge of assuring their enjoyment and of watching over their fate. It is absolute, attentive to detail, regular, provident, and gentle." Tocqueville added: "It works willingly for their happiness, but it wishes to be the only agent and the sole arbiter of that happiness. It provides for their security, foresees and supplies their needs, guides them in their principal affairs, directs their testaments, divides their inheritances." In the name of expanding democratic equality, the new despotism "renders the employment of free will less useful and more rare; it confines the action of the will within a smaller space and bit by bit it steals from each citizen the use of that which is his own. Equality has prepared men for all of these things: it has disposed them to put up with them and often even to regard them as a benefit."

Democracy's Future

Dalliances

Helped by hindsight, it's easy to spot that Tocqueville mostly misjudged the future. Europeans scrambling for colonies, the rise of populist and fascist political parties, the catastrophes of two global wars, concentration camps, and genocide in Europe and Asia were among the coming events beyond his ken. He certainly miscalculated the long-term effects of what widely came to be called "the social question": the refusal of nineteenth-century workers to identify with the group he labeled the industrial "aristocracy." The analysis of the "despotism of capital" provided by his contemporary Karl Marx better explained the resulting nineteenth-century class conflict, the early resistance of workers to what he dubbed the despotism of the workshop.[1] Marx also correctly noted how the contradictions of modern capitalism and the organized resistance of workers to its ruinous effects helped trigger the growth of friendly societies, cooperatives, trades unions, and social democratic parties, as well as calls for building socialism or communism either through political reforms backed by strikes and boycotts, demands for a universal franchise, and government intervention or through revolutionary violence.

Tocqueville can be excused for getting these and other important future developments wrong, but surely he was right to be concerned about the cancerous growth of voluntary servitude inside the body politic of modern representative democracy. His broad observation that in the name of "the people" this degeneration could ultimately result in the death of a democracy proved prescient, especially during the decades of the 1920s and 1930s, when the long grave dug by the Great War of 1914–1918 was filled with the bones of the big majority of fledgling parliamentary democracies.[2] Tocqueville's insight remains relevant. His way of thinking undoubtedly helps us understand why more than a few despotisms of our time (Hungary, Russia, China, Turkey, and Kazakhstan are on a lengthening list) have roots in failed local efforts by citizens and their elites to craft durably democratic power-sharing arrangements and ways of life.

Classical Greek thinkers were interested in this dynamic. They commonly noted that assembly democracy and tyranny were twins, and that the power struggles and disorder produced by democracy would result in tyranny, the singular rule of a cruel boss. Plato was sure that "tyranny naturally arises out of democracy." His contemporaries even used the now obsolete verb *demokrateo* *(δημοκρατέω)* to describe how through time democracy contradicts its commitment to equality by stirring up attempts to grab power and to exercise control over others.[3]

Tocqueville reasoned differently. Writing in the age of representative democracy, he was the first modern observer to say that in practice democracy and despotism are not simple opposites, because the gravest danger facing modern representative democracy is not cruel tyranny but a type of popularly attractive arbitrary power unknown to the ancient Greek world. The idea was brilliant, and helps us better comprehend the despotism described in this book:

a brand-new type of voluntary servitude that flourishes globally in the shape of despotic states that snuggle together, strike deals and strategic partnerships, and spread their tentacles well beyond their own borders into the heartlands of monitory democracy on a scale unknown to previous ages.

This global entanglement of the new despotism and the old monitory democracy is a distinctive feature of our times, and it highlights why despotism is not an exclusively Eurasian phenomenon and why the word itself is not a synonym for sovereign state power. It is more accurate to say that while despotism is a type of territorial state, it is much more than a state. Despotism is a mode of power. It is a way of fashioning voluntary servitude in a wide range of settings, a set of methods of handling people and things, a political means of forcefully deciding in the name of the people who gets how much, when, and how. Despotism has tessellated and tenticular features. Housed and nurtured by territorial states, it stretches across borders into a variety of regional and global settings. It has definite contagious effects. No continent or country enjoys immunity. In sub-Saharan Africa, for instance, more than a few states are plagued by bullish attempts by governments to rig elections, cuddle up to the military and security forces, and "encroach onto the judiciary and legislature." Disfigured by "clientelistic networks," corruption, and heartbreaking gaps between rich and poor, they frustrate "freedom of speech, assembly, and association" and efforts by civil society and the media "to play a watchdog role."[4] The case of South Africa, once considered a textbook candidate for a successful transition to power-sharing democracy, shows that among the most unsettling features of the new despotism is the way its spirit, language, and institutional dynamics are taking root *within* the democratic world. Tocqueville was on the right trail: descriptively speaking, democracies are not straightforwardly the pure opposite of an impure despotism. Those who piously suppose we are living in a world where the heavenly angel of "democracy" must be protected at home against the earthly devil of despotism abroad are profoundly mistaken. Equally mistaken are political scientists who say that geopolitical proximity to democratic regimes greatly increases the chances of successful democratization of an "authoritarian regime."[5] Just like Hamlet trapped in difficult circumstances, they fail to know a hawk from a handsaw. They suffer a measure of self-deceit, an inability to journey beyond themselves, an unwillingness to see that the inequality, lawlessness, corruption, and voluntary servitude they spot and denounce in others elsewhere are gaining ground and reshaping life within their home territories.

The evidence for the dalliance between democracy and despotism is everywhere piling up. The entanglement often comes in small but significant installments. Benjamin Netanyahu operates Twitter accounts in Arabic and Farsi. The American fast-food giant KFC has planted its flag on the soil of Uzbekistan, reassuring customers that its signature dishes serve halal meat only. With the backing of the Saudi government, Google markets an app named Absher that enables "guardian" men to track the real-time movements of wives and daughters. Turkey's military pension fund, Oyak, rescued British Steel from shutting down. The despotisms of our age reciprocate by spending a lot of cash to lobby lawmakers and by employing public relations firms to raise their visibility in countries such as the United Kingdom, Germany, France, Japan, Italy, India, and the United States. Despots are extended red-carpet welcomes decorated with guards of honor, wreath-laying ceremonies, speeches about brotherhood among nations, ceremonies to sign and seal bilateral trade and investment agreements, and sumptuous state dinners. Cities such as London and New York are awash with despots' intelligence gatherers ("The entire city is a nest of spies," a British intelligence source told journalists in 2017, referring to London).[6] Chinese capital buys the company that manufactures London's black cabs. Chunks of dark money are moved around by exiled oligarchs who own homes in favored city districts, dine in posh restaurants, and use local law firms, private investigators, and PR companies to service their interests. The new despotisms meanwhile deploy trolls (human-created fake accounts) and bots (automated accounts) to transform Facebook, Google, Twitter, and other social media platforms into antisocial media that fund and distort electoral campaigns, mobilize bigotry, and spread gossip and fake news to millions of unsuspecting citizens. The General Staff Department of the People's Liberation Army in China calls this espionage, hacking, spam bombing, and virus infection of foreign databanks and websites "technical reconnaissance" (jì shù zhēn chá). In the 2014 Ukraine elections, Russian hackers even made their way inside the country's central election commission, deleted core files, and planted a virus designed to swing the final result in favor of Right Sector, an ultranationalist political party that fortunately received less than 1 percent of the final vote. With Russian state media already reporting fake results, Ukrainian government cybersecurity experts, working round the clock, managed to block the vote-swinging malware just an hour before the final outcome was due to be announced.[7] Despotisms work toward the construction of a new digital ecosystem dominated by proxy media accounts, business organizations, intelligence agencies, and cybercriminals. Working behind the scenes, they oppose or collude with democratic political parties and try to tip the balance of results in otherwise free and fair elections. There are freakish moments, as when the Chinese government, the enemy of general elections, outshined the European Union and the United States by providing Cambodia with computers, printers, voting booths, ballot boxes, and election monitors in support of its corrupted mid-2018 general election.

All this ought to be obvious, but equally disconcerting is the flip-side trend: in a perverse twist of fate, the powerful forces of democracy aid and abet despots well beyond the borders of their own states. In matters of investment, infrastructure projects, and trade, and in such basic fields as electricity generation and water supply, democracies help despotisms plan, fund, and operate megaprojects. The giant Central Asia–South Asia power project CASA-1000, which exports surplus hydroelectricity from Tajikistan and Kyrgyzstan to Pakistan and Afghanistan, has been funded by the European Investment Bank and the World Bank. In such dalliances, democracies are no angels. Consider the way democracies such as Britain pioneered methods of data-driven, intelligence-led policing that were partly copied by outfits like the China Electronics Technology Group Corporation and later applied to the mass surveillance of Uighur Muslims in China's Xinjiang region. Or look at the way more than a few democracies aid and abet the new despotisms militarily. US weapons manufacturers extract huge profits from the vile wars of West Asia. Lucre is the driving force behind the massive arms sales delivered by the US government to Israel ($38 billion over ten years); in effect, Israel draws upon US taxpayers' money to buy weaponry produced by US arms manufacturers. During the Obama administration, the federal government gave the green light for US arms manufacturers to sell over $115 billion of weaponry to Saudi Arabia. The Trump administration signed letters of intent quadrupling these figures. Arms sales to the United Arab Emirates and Qatar have also helped fatten the bottom line of arms manufacturers like Lockheed Martin, Raytheon, Boeing, and General Dynamics. None of these arms merchants would like to see their market share decline. They thrive on war and threats of war, and hence they are normally offered bipartisan support in the US political spectrum. The general point here is that these arms sales are instances of a wider pattern whereby all democracies make bags of money and buy influence by selling huge quantities of state-of-the-art F-18 and Typhoon fighter jets, cluster bombs, remote-controlled tanks, handheld lasers ("dazzlers") that temporarily blind their victims, cybersecurity widgets, silent weapon systems powered by electrical energy instead of gunpowder, and drones capable of climbing to ten miles, swooping down to read license plates from nearly two miles away, and unloading five-hundred-pound bombs.

The new despotisms are also engaged in despotism promotion. These countries expand beyond their own borders by entering into legally binding trade deals, joint business ventures, and partnerships, including tourism. They are entangled through various regional bodies. Their effects radiate well beyond borders. Despotism hunts in packs. The finest place to stay in Minsk, Belarus, is the deluxe Beijing Hotel, owned by a Chinese hotel management company. Chinese companies led by Huawei and the state-owned investment company CITIC are leading investors in multibillion-dollar "safe city" and "smart city" projects in Uzbekistan. States such as Tajikistan and Russia do deals to share military bases. Since the 2013 coup d'état in Egypt, Saudi Arabia, the United Arab Emirates, and Kuwait have pumped an estimated $12 billion into that country. In early 2014, the governments of Oman and Iran concluded an agreement to build a $1 billion gas pipeline across the Gulf of Oman to provide Iranian gas to Oman for twenty-five years. For its part, the Omani regime has declined political union with other Gulf monarchies, yet it has supported the building of a security alliance designed for mutual protection when public trouble erupts, as happened in Bahrain in 2011, when troops from Saudi Arabia helped rescue the regime from collapse. Since the enforcement of US-inspired economic sanctions, Putin's Russia has concentrated on expanding its "eastern vector." Several flagship deals with China have been signed, including a $400 billion contract for the supply of gas for thirty years, and negotiations are under way to establish an alternative banking payment system shared by both countries.

China's global reach, meanwhile, is spreading fast. It is rapidly becoming an empire, if by empire we mean a jumbo-sized state that exercises political, economic, and symbolic power over millions of people at great distances from its own heartland, without much regard or respect for the niceties of sovereignty. Unusually, its new empire is for the moment deeply entangled with the United States and its partners. China is the US government's largest foreign creditor, holding more than $1 trillion of its debt known as Treasurys. But there are signs of decoupling—for instance, in the field of digital payments systems, where the global rise of Alipay, UnionPay, and WeChat Pay is matched by the partial blocking inside China of European- and American-issued credit cards. Elsewhere, Beijing-financed megaprojects are reordering the lives of many millions of people, from South Africa, Nigeria, and Sri Lanka to Cambodia, Chile, and Hungary. The Party-state economy has outflanked the United States as the world's largest trader. It is now Africa's biggest trading partner and rivals the United States in Latin America, where Chinese investment, extraction of resources, and trade jumped tenfold in the first decade of this century. China signs megadeals with such countries as Saudi Arabia; though Saudi Arabia was the last country officially to recognize the People's Republic of China, in 1990, Sino-Saudi relations are now flourishing. The China National United Oil Company, a joint subsidiary of China National Petroleum Corporation and Sinochem Corporation, is Saudi Arabia's biggest oil customer. China is its overall largest trading partner. The "comprehensive strategic partnership" extends to mining, housing, finance, infrastructure projects, and joint counterterrorism exercises. Saudi Arabia is among the world's biggest importer of weapons, including DF-5 (CSS-5) and DF-21 intercontinental ballistic missiles; jointly produced Chinese-Pakistani JF-17 fighter jets; and intelligence, surveillance, and reconnaissance drones. In the Central Asian despotisms (Kazakhstan, Kyrgyzstan, Tajikistan, Turkmenistan, and Uzbekistan), which stretch from the Caspian Sea in the west to China in the east, and from Afghanistan in the south to Russia in the north, department stores and bazaars are stuffed full of Chinese goods. In 2009, China was connected to Turkmenistan by a 1,200-mile gas pipeline. Chinese military expenditure is mushrooming (its army has enjoyed two decades of double-digit budget growth), and global military and diplomatic operations are under way. A new naval base has been built in Djibouti, and there have been rescue missions in Libya and Yemen, extensive military involvement with global organizations such as the United Nations, and first-time policing experiments in cities such as Dubrovnik. There is active support for the building of cross-border institutions like the African Continental Free Trade Agreement and the Asian Infrastructure Investment Bank. And China now leads more than twenty new multilateral institutions founded on pragmatic consent, not formal treaty alliances.[8]

Despotism and Democracy

The spreading power of the new despotisms well beyond their own borders and their bewildering patterns of entanglement with actually existing democracies are striking—so striking, in fact, that when historians a generation from now look back on these dalliances, crooked dealings, military adventures, and the new despotisms' "soft power" and "sharp power" self-promotion, they may be in a position to record with certainty what today we can only imagine: that despite their many local variants, despotic forms of power managed to join together to alter the balance of forces in strategically significant parts of our planet and radically weaken power-sharing forms of democracy, to the point where despotism became the only game in town. Nobody yet knows whether this can or will happen. In this dark scenario, democracy might well be pushed aside, or perhaps forcibly suppressed and compulsorily forgotten. It would be replaced by cunning new ways of ruling arbitrarily over people by winning their loyalty and governing in their name, along the way displaying great resilience—the ability to withstand resistance and recover from internal and external shocks over long cycles of time.

The future is of course forbidden fruit, a tenebrous figure, a fickle guardian of secrets small and large. It forbids us knowledge of the months, years, and decades to come. Yet although the future is by definition beyond our grasp, the subject of despotism demands that we think with a wise sense of precaution about what is to come. Despotism is a grave matter. It requires us to pay attention to its contemporary growth and to its possible future triumph. As Tocqueville saw, modern despotism dictates that blind or willful ignorance of future possible ills is foolish, even inexcusable, and certainly more perilous than botched musings about the world to come.

Pressured by global events, precautionary ways of thinking about possible darker political outcomes have for some time been fashionable. They have motivated the saturnine speculations and fictions of a wide range of political thinkers and writers whose sense of direction strived to be far in advance of the world around them. A century ago, for instance, Atlantic-region literature began to move well ahead of politics, and in opposition to the stale orthodoxies of political thinkers and analysts weighed down by bureaucratic minds. Jack London's *Iron Heel* (1908) was among the first dystopian novels to catapult readers into a future where a state is run by a cruel oligarchy of robber barons contemptuous of democracy but supported by loyal unionized workers and a caste of armed mercenaries. A glass-walled One State that conquers the world by scientifically managing its uniformed and numbered subjects with the help of secret police known as the Bureau of Guardians is the theme of Yevgeny Zamyatin's *We* (1924). Kafka's *The Trial* (1925) plunges readers into a world of faceless bureaucracy that torments its subjects with feelings of guilt and dooms them to powerlessness. There is Aldous Huxley's *Brave New World* (1932), a portrayal of a totalitarian world infantilized by drugs and pleasure. The violence of dismal systems of arbitrary power against nonconformist individuals motivates the tale told in Vladimir Nabokov's *Invitation to a Beheading* (1935–1936). George Orwell's *1984* (1949) kicks off with the shock of a clock striking thirteen on an unpromising cold spring morning. And there is Margaret Atwood's premonitory novel *The Handmaid's Tale* (1985), an anatomy of a totalitarian Republic of Gilead in which women are the chattels of husbands, fathers, heads of household, and a ruling theocracy, the black-clad Commanders of the Faithful.

Each of these novels was preoccupied with examining the way power comes to be exercised arbitrarily by a few at the expense of the many. Each dystopia imagined spine-chilling futures by using the method of creatively extrapolating from actual present-day trends. The fictional imaginings of these novels were rightly praised for their novelty. Their efforts to dethrone totalitarian power using words were compelling because the repulsion they induced in readers was so utterly credible. They showed by means of mocking satire how harsh realities could twist and tangle the real lives of people into haunting unreality. Their authors are still today cited as guides and prophets who are said to have understood what was to come. But they did not. Writing during the last century, these brave authors cannot be blamed for getting things wrong. What is certain, however, as this book has shown at some length, is that their imagined futures of total state control with minimal resistance actually missed the mark in several important ways.

The new despotism of our time is different from the totalitarian domination that preoccupied the thoughts of these writers. It is less spectacular, more complex, and much cleverer, a shape-shifting form of power whose protean qualities are harder to summarize, yet much more sophisticated in their ability to dissolve the spirit of democracy in the acids of voluntary servitude and popular acquiescence to arbitrary power. The foghorn concept of despotism forces us to sit up and pay attention to these dangers, as they are manifested in countries otherwise as different as Turkey, Belarus, Russia, Vietnam, Brunei, and Singapore. In our times, despotic power is much more than the rule of faceless clerks and the bossing of factory owners, as Tocqueville and Marx supposed. The new despotism is not the old fat-cat, cigar-puffing plutocracy. It is not understandable through images of castles or cruel violence or vast assembly lines that transform humans into mere cogs, or in terms of subjects drugged into submission by hallucinatory pleasures, total media surveillance, or religious misogyny.

The key point here is that the new despotism is a form of extractive power with no historical precedent. It is a strangely resilient type of domination with recombinant qualities. We have seen how it feeds upon sweet talk by rulers of the people and experiments with governing procedures that they claim are democratic. These despotisms are phantom democracies. They thrive on top-to-bottom favoritism, which in effect draws everyone into a cat's cradle of corruption, with the result that despotisms harbor inside their borders a multiplicity of petty despotisms. Everybody is contaminated by information others have on them—what Russians call *kompromat.*

The new despotisms are plutocracies, but their extreme concentrations of wealth are camouflaged by the deployment of scrambled political languages that have the tactical effect of enabling rulers to gaslight their subjects by being different things to different people at different times. The new despotism is a new form of state-regulated surveillance capitalism. It musters the latest tools of artificial intelligence and robotics to hack and spy on their subjects. It also functionally depends on loyal middle classes who are prepared to trade some liberties for comfortable peace and quiet. Periodic elections and digital media storms offer a voice to subjects, whose quiet subservience is reinforced by handouts, official talk of the need for legality and order, and the public camouflaging and privatization of violence.

This overview of the leading features of the new despotism brings us to the most surprising but perhaps least palatable reason the old term "despotism" is indispensable for making new sense of our times. It has to do with a double-sided irony: just as today's despotisms (think of Hungary, Turkey, Vietnam, and especially China) display more than a few phantom democratic qualities that mask and legitimate their arbitrary power, so the democracies of our age are plagued by despotic forms of unaccountable power that threaten to destroy the spirit and substance of their egalitarian openness and fairness, and to replace them with voluntary servitude to arbitrary power. Remarkable are the many ways the new despotisms and the old democracies enjoy friendly relations. They find themselves bound together by companies like Goldman Sachs, a "great vampire squid wrapped around the face of humanity," and McKinsey, which for many years has provided active support for large state-owned and state-guided corporations in despotisms such as Saudi Arabia, Turkey, China and Russia (including, in defiance of foreign governments' sanctions, Russia's VEB Bank, which is an arm of the Russian state and entangled with Russian intelligence).[9] Press releases say that "McKinsey has sought to make a positive difference to the businesses and communities in which our people live and work. Tens of thousands of jobs have been created, lives improved and education provided thanks to the work we have done with our clients." The company adds: "Like many other major corporations, including our competitors, we seek to navigate a changing geopolitical environment, but we do not support or engage in political activities."[10]

Competitor terms such as "tyranny," "autocracy," and "authoritarianism" cannot easily grasp the significance of these sugary words, nor the despotic power dynamics with which they are entangled. When used today by intellectuals, journalists, and politicians, these orthodox terms suppose misleadingly that in theory and practice democracy is their opposite. Tyranny is not democracy, which is the antagonist of autocracy and authoritarianism, and so on. In striking contrast, the word "despotism" discourages us from thinking in black-and-white terms. It instead urges those who speak of despotism to spot its inner connections with democracy, to see not only that in the real world the two political forms are disturbingly entangled and share more than a few elective affinities but also that there is plenty of despotism *inside* states that consider themselves democracies.

Among the first to speak in this way, to suggest that the concept of despotism could rebound on those who used it by drawing their attention to its dangers within their own societies, was a traveling aristocrat, the comte de Ségur, who fought as a colonel on the side of the American colonies against the British and who served for five years as French ambassador to Catherine the Great. "All foreigners, in their recitals," Ségur wrote, thinking of the French prison system symbolized by the Bastille, "have painted with vivid colors the sad effects of the despotic government of the Russians, and yet it is fair to admit that in this epoch we do not completely have the right to declaim thus against arbitrary power."[11] Our mentor and friend Tocqueville later developed this idea. He was probably the first political writer to see and say that in a descriptive sense modern despotisms lie on the same continuum as modern representative democracies. Just as his account of "gentle despotism" highlighted the vulnerability of modern democracy to voluntary servitude, so these pages have suggested more than a few ways in which the new despotisms mirror and mimic and taunt actually existing democracies. This is the biggest and most troubling thought inspired by the word "despotism": the new despotisms of our century are disturbing simulacra of so-called democracies now bogged down in various dysfunctions and pathologies. Despotism is not a foreign reality outside and beyond these democracies. It is *inside* them, merely an extreme and better-functioning form of these democracies at their weakest and worst.

Within the world of actually existing democracy, in countries such as India, Britain, France, Japan, and the United States, the style and substance of despotic power are evidently alive and well. These so-named democracies are in the grip of many decadent trends that bear a definite resemblance to the main features of the despotisms they supposedly abhor. With just a touch of exaggeration we could say that democracies are beginning to resemble proto-despotisms. Consider how in the United States, India, and other democracies elected populist governments, nourished by citizen indignation and dollops of dark money, steel the hand of despotism by doing all they can to undermine independent courts, discredit expertise, and boost executive state power. Or ponder the power of big business. In practically every democracy, millions of people spend substantial periods of their daily lives working dutifully inside the air-conditioned command-and-control hierarchies of rich and powerful global corporations such as Goldman Sachs, Royal Dutch Shell, Siemens AG, Toyota, and Mitsubishi. Like their corporate counterparts in Turkey, China, Iran, and Singapore, companies such as Tüpraş, Alibaba, Setad, and DBS Bank, these conglomerates can be thought of as houses of voluntary servitude—Marx would have analyzed them as examples of the "despotism of capital"—whose substantial power to manipulate and annul taxation arrangements, shape whole economies, and bully democratically elected governments strengthens the hand of a fabulously wealthy class of people connected to the inner circles of government. With plutarchy comes the growth of a vulnerable precariat of people, especially young people, scuffling and scraping to make ends meet. Despite their stated official commitments to equal life chances for citizens, these democracies function as grazing grounds for big-business despotism and its damaging and disfiguring social effects: widening gaps between rich and poor and, at the highest levels of government, flourishing top-down webs of dark money, organized lobbying, patronage, and revolving doors between government and the corporate world. Little wonder that there are swelling numbers of disaffected citizens who feel themselves to be subjects and survivors compelled to tread the waters of life, or that most democracies

THE NEW DESPOTISM

are today in the political grip of populist rhetoric fed by focus groups, opinion polling, and permanent big-data campaigning by parties specializing in the slick cultivation of media conspiracies and confabulations.[12] The drift toward despotism is compounded by the advent of a new kind of "surveillance capitalism" driven by giant state-backed data-harvesting corporations that colonize, manipulate, and reshape the personal lives of many millions of people for the sake of profit and power.[13]

The spirit and substance of democracy are further corroded by the militarization of police tactics at public protests and the criminalization of asylum-seekers, refugees, religious minorities, and other groups. Not even constitutional courts and their rulings are fail-safe barriers against despotism. An unlovely example of how democracies are incubators of despotism is the Israeli democracy's use of law to spread lawlessness in the city of Jerusalem, where nearly four hundred thousand Palestinians are daily subject to constitutional arrangements and court decisions over which they have little or no control. Most Palestinians living in the city (95 percent) are not Israeli citizens and are therefore not eligible to vote in Knesset parliamentary elections. Palestinians are the targets of legally approved evictions, the building of Jewish-only settlement roads, and a parliament-approved mammoth concrete wall that severely hampers their daily movements. Their applications for municipal building permits are typically rejected or left unprocessed. Palestinians are subject to the imposition of often-unpayable taxes, such as the national insurance tax and municipal taxes for water, sewerage, and other services they rarely receive. But these and other arrangements, in accordance with the principle of *dura lex sed lex,* are said by the Israeli authorities to be legitimate and perfectly in accordance with the prevailing laws.

Resistance

Corporate surveillance and domination of the working lives and daily routines of citizens; the entanglement of their elected governments in webs of dark money, organized lobbying, revolving doors, and patronage; the drift toward plutocracy and generally worsening social inequality; and creeping lawlessness camouflaged by talk of rule of law: these are only a few of the worrying trends inside today's democracies. They should encourage thinking citizens to wonder where these democracies are heading. Might these currents be forewarnings, danger signals, harbingers of the tortoise-paced transformation of actually existing democracies into phantom democracies that look and feel like the despotisms they supposedly stand against? And if that is so, if the old democracies are tacitly joining forces with the new despotisms, what can be done to reverse this convergence? *Can* anything be done?

The concept despotism has the advantage of inducing a sense of political urgency about the growing dangers of publicly unaccountable power in various parts of our world. Mindful of both the charms of despotism and the connections it enjoys with power-sharing democracy, the term has strategic value. It is a disruptor, a fighting word. It challenges the complacency of those who are convinced that the problem of dangerously unaccountable power will vanish if it is ignored. The term warns that there are publicly important things at stake. It is designed to stir up political interest by raising questions about how to deal politically with forms of power deemed threatening to the promise of a decent, open, and just life for all. It asks whether and to what extent the new despotism and its mechanics of voluntary servitude are vulnerable to economic, social, and geopolitical shocks, to political disruption and resistance. It touches on a very basic problem facing democrats and so-named democracies in these early years of the twenty-first century: Are there effective ways of loosening the grip of despotism on people's lives so that democratic ideals and institutions and ways of life are everywhere given a better chance to survive, even to flourish?

There are plenty of observers who decline to acknowledge or address these questions, as if the real threats to freedom and equality and self-government posed by the new despotism will somehow just go away, spontaneously vanish into thin air, or fall like rotting fruit to the ground, courtesy of the passing of time. They simply don't care. Their antipolitical motto is that trouble should never be troubled unless trouble troubles. Others find themselves deeply perplexed about what these despotisms represent and where they are leading the world. They do not know what to think. Still others are so worried by the trend that they draw the conclusion that policies of getting tough with Russia, Iran, and China are urgently needed, even that force will be required to weaken and undo their grip on our world. The priority, comments an opinionated Irish-American celebrity whose gimcrack book on despotism gives the precious word a bad name, is to confront "the number-one state sponsor of terror" (Iran) and "the despotic regimes that aid and abet the terrorists."[14]

The new warriors sound old trumpets. Another man of Ireland, nineteenth-century poet Michael Joseph Barry, who served time in prison for his commitments to the Young Ireland movement, was certain that physical violence was the only sure way to bring down despots and their despotisms. "What rights the brave? The sword! / What frees the slave? The sword! / What cleaves in twain / The despot's chain, / And makes his gyves [fetters] and dungeons vain? / The sword!"[15] Barry later recanted his widely reported views on violence (he became a police magistrate in Dublin) for understandable reasons that have since been widely rehearsed. War and other forms of violence are at odds with the life-loving and life-enhancing ethics of democracy.[16] Violence also begets violence; those who use violence can certainly be devoured by its devils. There is as well the harsh fact that most despotic states have formidably large standing armies and police forces, and that despotic rulers, armed like Jove with thunderbolts, are competent at hunting down their domestic opponents and crushing street protests using water cannons, pepper spray, beanbag guns, stun guns, rubber bullets, armored cars, and tanks. And there is the point that violence, even when used in self-defense, lacks guarantees of success. It can backfire badly on those who deploy it. The principle of unintended consequences undoubtedly applies to acts of military intervention in the name of democracy. When things grow rough for the local opponents of despotic regimes, there is an understandable temptation to dispatch advisors, ship over technical equipment, smuggle in weapons, or even send troops backed by drones and bombers. But war always has unintended consequences and poisonous effects. Aside from its astonishing ecological and human destructiveness, contemporary war brings heartbreak, breeds armed enemies, and most often wrecks the prospects for democratic reconstruction.[17] The harsh principle of unintended consequences will undoubtedly apply to future wars guided by artificial intelligence and robotic weapons. Despots like to boast of their prowess, as if they are invincible warhorses with golden shoes and four white fetlocks. At carefully staged press conferences, Xi Jinping and his top commanders, dressed in military fatigues, proudly show off their latest high-tech weapons, among them underwater missiles, miniature robotic tanks, and sleek black military drones. They boast that China is now too big to fail. They are sure that, with such sophisticated arms, they can deter any conflict with the United States and thereby win without fighting. In military matters, Putin, that prince of payback, oozes self-confidence that in future confrontations fortune will continue to come the way of his Russia, thanks to technical prowess, hard-nosed diplomacy, battle-readiness, and determination. This outlook is energized by simple folk wisdoms, such as the story (apparently one of Putin's favorites) of a father who passes a prized sword to his son, who in turn sells it for a fancy watch. "I understand style, son," says the father, "but when thieves come to our house what good will that watch be?"

It is unclear what value the prized sword might have under conditions of cyberwarfare that targets electricity grids, airports, banks, and hospitals, or in so-called hybrid wars featuring robots fighting robots, hypersonic missiles, and lightning-fast swarms of drones guided by deep learning. Also unclear is whether the new despotisms, for the sake of their own survival and flourishing, are ineluctably drawn to making war on their neighbors or on faraway enemies. What is clear is that the perils and drawbacks of using violence against states such as China, Russia, Saudi Arabia, and Iran help explain why the political opponents of despotism are, for the time being, more attracted to nonviolent methods such as backroom diplomacy, public calls for independently monitored free elections, technological blockades, tariffs and trade embargos, investment sanctions, investment deals, human rights protests, aid withdrawals, and consumer boycotts. Whether and to what extent these methods, alone or combined, can be successful in motivating the subjects of despotism to refuse to serve their despots, as La Boétie recommended, strongly depends on circumstances and pesky factors like good timing and luck, which are often the same.

But in each and every case, as we have seen throughout this book, the resilience of the new despotisms should not be underestimated. It is a well-documented fact that no twentieth-century totalitarian system collapsed because of internal crises. Its Italian, German, Japanese, and Khmer variants were overthrown only by outside military force. The same rule may apply to the new despotisms, whose breakdown, if and when it happens, might well lead not to a vibrant monitory democracy but to a new and more resilient version of despotism.

Among the most remarkable features of despotic regimes is their ability to cope with crises, sometimes through surprising reforms. Their rulers know well that leaky ships are vulnerable to the smallest gusts of wind. It is true that despotisms experience storms of political disorder, when everything seems lost and the bell rings time against their rulers. They can indeed run aground, or collapse into a heap of ruins. They cannot last forever. No power regime is blessed with eternal life. Even in the short term, digital mutinies that trigger popular revolutions against despotic states such as Iran cannot be ruled out. Yet more likely in the foreseeable distance is the victory of their shock-absorbing institutions and their tools of crisis management against the threats and dangers of implosion. Helped along by outside military and economic support and rescued by a realignment of domestic forces within the governing arrangements, despotisms have a knack for turning what seem to be their miserable end games into survival and renewed strength.

Even when it comes to rising unemployment, growth stagnation, capital disinvestment, stock market shocks, and high-level financial corruption, despotisms display a definite resilience. Their staying power defies most predictions of the kind first made by a principal contributor to the Scottish Enlightenment, Adam

Ferguson. "National poverty . . . and the suppression of commerce," he wrote in 1767, "are the means by which despotism comes to accomplish its own destruction. Where there are no longer any profits to corrupt, or fears to deter, the charm of dominion is broken, and the naked slave, as awake from a dream, is astonished to find he is free."[18] More astonishing is the contemporary survival of the thought that "authoritarian" regimes are dogged by sluggish growth and stagnation, and that democratic openings are typically triggered by economic crises, slowdowns, or stagnation. The expectation of journalists, market analysts, and politicians that countries such as China, Turkey, and Iran cannot easily stay afloat during economic doldrums is grounded in this presumption; so is the strategy of imposing economic sanctions against despotic regimes.

Supporting evidence for both perspectives is in short supply, not least because they seriously underestimate the stock of shock-absorbing and crisis management tools available to these regimes. Consider the determined efforts of the Chinese government to ban rogue finance firms and to bring greater transparency to the massive private fund management industry by co-locating risk-proofed "sunshine investors" and legal, tax, and regulatory expertise in the newly built Beijing Fund Town. The tough methods used by the regime to deal with the 2015–2016 Shanghai stock market crisis—banning initial public offerings, limiting short selling under threat of arrest, clamping down on stock sales by large stockholders, encouraging large pensions and mutual funds to buy more stocks, funneling central bank cash into the purchase of shares—reflect the determination of the new despotisms, which are modes of state capitalism that manage to defy the simple forces-and-relations-of-production analyses found in theoretically reductionist versions of historical materialism.[19] Many despotisms already outperform economically the Atlantic-region democracies. The case of the single-party despotism of Vietnam is instructive. An anticorruption push in 2018 by the government of Nguyen Phu Trong chilled spines in the top-level Party-state apparatus, with many arrests of high officials and business tycoons. The Party is skilled at enforcing clampdowns on "deviations," which range from "opportunism" to loose talk of multiparty pluralist democracy. Online surveillance and offline policing of dissenters are tight. A government "advanced persistent threat unit" routinely punishes blogs and websites accused of publishing uncensored commentary and news. Cybersecurity laws require YouTube and Facebook to store all traffic generated by their Vietnamese users, for examination by the police. The rulers of Vietnam meanwhile pride themselves on fostering official annual growth rates of around 6–7 percent and exports valued in excess of GDP, including products such as Samsung smartphones and Nike sports gear. The local communist leaders are champions of domestic deregulation and reducing the costs of doing business. Encouraging foreign investment in manufacturing and high-tech industry are priorities. So is countering trade liberalization through the country's membership in the Association of Southeast Asian Nations, the World Trade Organization, and the Regional Comprehensive Economic Partnership.

Despotisms like Vietnam show in practice there is no necessary affinity between capitalism and power-sharing democracy. To the contrary, these years of the twenty-first century suggest that despotism has a special fancy for the risk-taking and profiteering of capitalism. There is surely a wider parable about state capitalism and despotism lurking near the beginning of the film *Crazy Rich Asians* (2018), when the New York University economics professor and American-born Chinese character Rachel Chu says, minutes after landing for the first time at Singapore's Changi Airport, "I can't believe this place has a cinema and a butterfly garden. JFK is just salmonella and despair." The comment captures the remarkable innovation and growth patterns in the Asia Pacific region, led by state capitalist regimes that include Singapore, Cambodia, Vietnam, and Laos. The mention of opulence also grasps something of the swagger of these new despotisms, their ability to bounce back from weakness and to impress and win the loyalty of their subjects at home, even to portray themselves as the saviors of decadent forms of democratic capitalism.

So is the rise of the new despotisms an unbreakable trend? Is the spread of despotic power unstoppable? Many despots think so. Puffed with pride, they are certain the future belongs to them. Convinced the days of lily-livered Western domination and its democracy are numbered, the new despots in Luanda, Istanbul, Shanghai, and Budapest swank and skite about their homegrown systems of "governance" and "democracy." They brag that their governing structures are more effective because they enjoy the legitimacy of the "sovereign" people whom they rule arbitrarily. Nowhere is such talk so sonorous than in the most formidable state despotism, the People's Republic of China. Facing boycotts led by the US government, Huawei Technologies founder Ren Zhengfei defiantly explains that "America doesn't represent the world. America only represents a portion of the world," so if "the lights go out in the West, the East will still shine. And if the North goes dark, there is still the South." According to Xi Jinping, his regime is now well on its way to building "a moderately prosperous society" shaped by "greater democracy, more advanced science and education, thriving culture, greater social harmony, and a better quality of life."[20] This is a grand vision. The material effects of China's power, already felt on every continent, just may hold the keys to the global future of despotism. One thing is now certain: just as the Soviet Union was once the great hope for socialism, so China is now the global torch-bearer of despotism.

We have seen that China is more than just one despotic state among others. It is a strident big power that is fast becoming a global empire *(dìguó)* deeply entangled economically, culturally, and politically not just with other despotisms but also with the United States and its closest partners. Whether or to what extent the emergent Chinese global empire can be managed effectively by its rulers using despotic methods, liberated from the well-known contradictions between center and periphery that plagued all previous empires, is a matter that will occupy future research and reflection and politics. For now it is safe to say that all despotisms of our age, notwithstanding their remarkable survival and growth capacity, are shadowed by particular tensions and troubles. Turkey is besieged by neighborhood tensions and military rivals. Oman is stalked by its overdependence on carbon and the death of its childless ruler Sultan Qaboos, whose favored successor, a cousin, was confirmed on national television by a council of relatives who consulted a sheet of paper tucked in a sealed secret envelope stored in the royal palaces of Muscat and Salalah. The leaders of Vietnam have not yet delivered on their promises of reducing endemic rural poverty and providing high-quality universal health care and free primary and secondary school education. It is unclear whether Saudi Arabia can transition from a petro-despotism to a postcarbon political economy based on mixed sources of investment. The rulers of Singapore are facing the deep challenge of governing a population that is both declining (its fertility rate is currently around 1.2 children per woman) and aging so rapidly (the average life expectancy was 83.1 years in 2017) that the ratio of employed people to retired seniors is expected to halve (from 4.7 workers per retiree in 2016 to only 2.3 in 2030).

Such challenges should serve as reminders to despots everywhere that politics, the priceless art of publicly defining and dealing with complex problems and determining in practice which people get how much, how, and when, cannot be eliminated from human affairs. The reminders double as a warning about the ultimate vulnerability of the new despotisms: the political slips and stumbles potentially produced by their refusal to open themselves up to public scrutiny and public control of the power they exercise arbitrarily over their subjects in a wide range of fields. The early modern critics of arbitrary power we have already met were arguably on the right track when emphasizing the propensity of despotisms to overstep the limits of effective and authoritative power. True, their warnings often overstated the recklessness of despotism. Yet their cardinal point was that despotism tends to overextend its reach and so destroy its own omnipotence. Diderot's peppery remark that "all arbitrary power rushes toward its own destruction" pushed in this direction.[21] He wanted to warn his readers that a special place in hell is reserved for despotism. Plagued by foolish arrogance, the twin of hubris, it has the unintended effect of spreading doubts in the minds of its subjects and teaching its opponents by poor example to shield themselves as citizens from its foolishly brazen power.

But how can citizens and their representatives practically defend themselves against folly and hubris? Tocqueville's answer: through constitutional refusals of concentrated state power; citizen struggles for a free press and public assembly and local self-government; and the defense of a civil society of freely acting associations operating at a distance from government, in accordance with the principle that "strength is born of association."[22] Like a bottled message from a bygone era, the general point about the strategic importance of defending power-sharing institutions and civil society associations remains pertinent today but needs theoretical refinement and political expansion. The times have changed. The new despotisms are different. Yet their resilience must not be exaggerated. With wide gaps between rich and poor, a squeezed middle class, and top-to-bottom corruption laced with lawlessness and camouflaged violence, despotisms are everywhere haunted by the specter of Hong Kong–style public resistance. They are vulnerable to surprise disruptions, digital mutinies, and media storms. Founded on digital communication networks, despotisms are forced to recognize the potential power of the powerless, in the shape of media-enabled disturbances whose counternarratives disrupt everyday life and potentially threaten to disintegrate the whole political order, especially through the clever use of such insurgent tactics as street theater, laughter, skywriting, sing-ins and pray-ins, electoral mobilization, consumer boycotts, and wildcat strikes.[23]

The defense of civil society institutions and citizen efforts to build new democratic ways of living and handling power remain of basic importance in the rejection of despotism, at home and abroad.[24] Such resistance can have wider effects, especially if it takes aim at the fundamental design flaw of despotism. When measured on a scale of vulnerability, the dangers posed by the hubris of arbitrary power rank highest. The new despotisms are not demiurges and deities on earth. Blind arrogance and foolish pride are easily their most poisonous fruits. They are a form of power marked by a shortage of institutions that call to account the powerful for their actions, inactions, and wrongdoings. We have seen throughout this book that there are indeed experiments by despots with opinion polling, e-consultation exercises, and public forums. However, on balance, despotism blocks and chokes public scrutiny and independent restraint of the powerful. It shields them from internal probes and public sanctions of their indiscretions and unwillingness to admit personal responsibility for failures to respond to the expressed wishes and concerns of their subjects. Despotism seduces its rulers into imagining they do not have to learn from their mistakes. It tricks them into thinking they can ignore the costs of failure, or postpone dealing with them or simply let others suffer the consequences.

Despots suppose, wrongly, that power exercised arbitrarily is power ennobled. Monitory democracy, the radical vision of public scrutiny and restraint of unaccountable power through check-and-balance institutions, citizen participation, and cultures of voting in a wide range of domains, is thus not just a clear political alternative to the new despotism. The lack of monitory democracy is the greatest weakness of despotic power. Despotism thrives on popular beliefs in good queens and benign kings, skilled managers and shrewd technicians of power. But the harsh truth is that despotism unleashes vaulting ambition and lusts for power that frustrate its own search for eternality. The powerful find that the unexpected is especially untamable. Well-functioning monitory democracies nurture institutional practices and watchdog bodies (such as public inquiries, judicial review, and futures commissions) that serve as early warning systems and risk-reduction mechanisms designed to deal with uncertainty and surprises. The new despotisms try to mimic these methods of mastering uncertainty, surprises, and unintended consequences.[25] Yet unplanned events such as the large-scale death of nonhuman species, a freak nuclear explosion, a big bank collapse, poisoned food chains, or unexpected defeat on the battlefield can rock despotic power to its foundations. Unintended consequences may quickly follow. Despots can quarrel and fight openly; splits at the top may trigger public resistance. Judges speak against the rulers. Investigative journalists risk everything, including their lives. Police and military commanders may grow restless. Digital mutinies and nonviolent strikes by organized groups can give birth to a rebellious civil society. Established institutions may show signs of crumbling. Rigged elections can be lost. Like an unsteady colossus, rulers can be made to stumble, or to come crashing to the ground. Big dramas can grow from small beginnings. Democratic openings can happen. Backed by demands for public accountability and supported by networked civil society actions and citizen organizations, the push for monitory democracy can spread, even across borders, into the heartlands of despotic states.

This kind of scenario may be a fiction or fantasy, a mistaken and uncomprehending picture of how things might develop in the coming decades of our century. Perhaps those who govern the new despotisms are much too clever and too well-resourced to allow any of this to happen. Perhaps they will enjoy more than their fair share of luck. Let us imagine no tanks rumble through their streets. Suppose the American empire, in the grip of successive populist governments that trash the ideals and institutions of power-sharing democracy, fails to keep abreast of the new Chinese empire and its global allies. Consider the possibility that the citizens and representatives of actually existing democracies ignore the warning signals and turn blind eyes to the trends sketched in these pages. Imagine that the spread of despotism outside and inside democracies sparks little or no resistance, or that nobody listens to public thinkers and writers and activists brandishing burning sticks, keeping watch, being there on the spot, eyes wide open, sounding the political alarm. Suppose as well, for a variety of understandable but inexcusable reasons, the friends of democracy just don't get around to dealing with the demons and scrubbing clean the soiled Augean stables inside their own dysfunctional systems of government. Presume state-backed surveillance capitalism and dark money elections gain ground, the power of the rich is unchallenged, and arbitrary exercises of power become the shameless norm in practically all walks of life. Imagine the friends of democracy nevertheless cling to their mistaken belief that history still stands on the side of American-style liberalism. Assume they succumb to innocent self-deception, fail to open their minds, and refuse to dissect their own ignorance about the new despotism. Dare to imagine that in the end most people fail to realize they are being marched inch by inch toward the scaffold. Might we then draw the conclusion that despotism is fated to play the lead role at center stage in the daily lives of many hundreds of millions of people in the coming years of this century? Or perhaps even that despotism is the future of democracy?

Further Reading

The global literature on the history of the idea and practice of despotism, both past and present, is extensive. Readers wishing to venture beyond the list of materials cited in this book's endnotes may choose to consult the following short selection of highly relevant essays, pamphlets, books, and online resources:

Art, David. "What Do We Know about Authoritarianism after Ten Years?" *Comparative Politics* 44, no. 3 (April 2012): 351–373.

Bobbio, Norberto. "Dispotismo." In *Dizionario di politica*, edited by Norberto Bobbio et al., pp. 276–283. Turin, 2004.

Boesche, Roger. *Theories of Tyranny from Plato to Arendt*. University Park, PA, 1996.

Boulanger, Nicolas-Antoine. *Recherches sur l'origine du despotisme oriental*. London, 1762.

Brown, Wendy, Peter E. Gordon, and Max Pensky. *Authoritarianism: Three Inquiries in Critical Theory*. Chicago, 2018.

Curtis, Michael. *Orientalism and Islam: European Thinkers on Oriental Despotism in the Middle East and India*. Cambridge, 2009.

Derathé, Robert. "Les philosophes et le despotisme." In *Utopie et pragmatisme au XVIIIe siècle: Le pragmatisme des Lumières*, edited by Pierre Francastel, pp. 57–75. Paris, 1963.

Dobson, William J. *The Dictator's Learning Curve: Inside the Global Battle for Democracy.* New York, 2012.

Felice, Domenico, ed. *Dispotismo: Genesi e sviluppi di un concetto filosofico-politico.* 2 vols. Naples, 2001–2002.

Geddes, Barbara, Joseph Wright, and Erica Frantz. *How Dictatorships Work: Power, Personalization, and Collapse.* New York, 2018.

Gessen, Masha. *The Man without a Face: The Unlikely Rise of Vladimir Putin.* London, 2012.

Internet Archive. "Despotism" (contains nearly 400,000 entries). Available at https://archive.org/search.php?query=despotism&sin=TXT.

Kaiser, Thomas. "The Evil Empire? The Debate on Turkish Despotism in Eighteenth-Century French Political Culture." *Journal of Modern History* 72, no. 1 (2000): 6–34.

Kelsen, Hans. "Foundations of Democracy." *Ethics* 66, no. 1, part 2 (October 1955): 1–101.

Kurfirst, Robert. "J. S. Mill on Oriental Despotism, Including Its British Variant." *Utilitas* 8, no. 1 (March 1996): 73–87.

Latour, Bruno, and Peter Weibel, eds. *Making Things Public: Atmospheres of Democracy.* Cambridge, MA, 2005.

Linz, Juan J. *The Breakdown of Democratic Regimes: Crisis, Breakdown, and Reequilibration.* Baltimore, MD, 1978.

Magyar, Bálint, and Julia Vásárhelyi, eds. *Twenty-Five Sides of a Post-Communist Mafia State.* Budapest, 2017.

Mandt, Hella. "Tyrannie, Despotie." In *Geschichtliche Grundbegriffe,* vol. 6, edited by Otto Brunner, Werner Conze, and Reinhart Koselleck, pp. 651–706. Stuttgart, 1972–1997.

Marx, Karl. "The British Rule in India." In *Karl Marx / Friedrich Engels: Collected Works,* vol. 12, pp. 125–133. New York, 1975–2004.

Marx, Karl. "The Future Results of British Rule in India." In *Karl Marx / Friedrich Engels: Collected Works,* vol. 12, pp. 217–222. New York, 1975–2004.

McInerney, D. J. *James Mill and the Despotism of Philosophy: Reading "The History of British India."* New York, 2009.

Meierhenrich, Jens. *The Remnants of the Rechtsstaat: An Ethnography of Nazi Law.* Oxford, 2018.

Minuti, Rolando. "Mito e realtà del dispotismo ottomano: Note in margine ad una discussione settecentesca." *Studi settecenteschi* 1 (1981): 35–59.

Moradi, Hassan Ghazi. *Despotism in Iran.* Pittsburgh, PA, 2017.

Mujanović, Jasmin. *Hunger and Fury: The Crisis of Democracy in the Balkans.* London, 2018.

Quesnay, François. "Despotisme de la Chine." In François Quesnay, *Œuvres économiques complètes et autres textes,* vol. 2, edited by Christine Théré, Loïc Charles, and Jean-Claude Perrot, pp. 1005–1114. Paris, 2005.

Ranum, Orest. "D'Alembert, Tacitus, and the Political Sociology of Despotism." *Studies on Voltaire and the Eighteenth Century* 191, in *Transactions of the Fifth International Congress on the Enlightenment,* pp. 547–558. Oxford, 1980.

Richter, Melvin. "The Concept of Despotism and l'Abus des Mots." *Contributions to the History of Concepts* 3 (2007): 5–22.

Richter, Melvin. "Despotism." In *Dictionary of the History of Ideas: Studies of Selected Pivotal Ideas,* vol. 2, edited by Philip P. Wiener, pp. 1–18. New York, 1973.

Rosanvallon, Pierre. *Democratic Legitimacy: Impartiality, Reflexivity, Proximity.* Princeton, NJ, 2011.

Rubiés, Joan-Pau. "Oriental Despotism and European Orientalism: Botero to Montesquieu." *Journal of Early Modern History* 9, nos. 1–2 (2005): 109–180.

Saïd, Edward. *Orientalism.* New York, 1978.

Schabert, Tilo. *Boston Politics: The Creativity of Power.* Berlin, 1989.

Scheppele, Kim. "Autocratic Legalism." *University of Chicago Law Review* 85, no. 2 (2018): 545–583.

Snyder, Timothy. *On Tyranny: Twenty Lessons from the Twentieth Century.* London, 2017.

Urbinati, Nadia. *Me the People: How Populism Transforms Democracy.* Cambridge, MA, 2019.

Valensi, Lucette. *Venise et la Sublime Porte: La naissance du despote.* Paris, 1987.

Xuetong, Yan. *Leadership and the Rise of Great Powers.* Princeton, NJ, 2019.

Notes

Dark Times, Again

1. A survey from twenty-seven countries found that 51 percent of interviewees were "not satisfied with the way democracy is working," while 45 percent were "satisfied." Richard Wike, Laura Silver, and Alexandra Castillo, "Many across the Globe Are Dissatisfied with How Democracy Is Working," Pew Research Center, April 29, 2019, https://www.pewresearch.org/global/2019/04/29/many-across-the-globe-are-dissatisfied-with-how-democracy-is-working. Similar findings with different emphases were reported by researchers at the Economist Intelligence Unit, whose 2019 report *Democracy Index 2018: Me Too?* (https://www.eiu.com/public/topical_report.aspx?campaignid=Democracy2018) documented a steady ten-year rise in citizens' concerns about "transparency, accountability and corruption." The report noted that other research bodies "such as the World Values Survey (WVS), Eurobarometer, Latinobarometro and Afrobarometer" had "demonstrated that confidence in democracy is on the wane" (p. 5). The V-Dem *Annual Democracy Report 2018* (Gothenburg, 2018) noted that "the aspects of democracy that make elections truly meaningful are in decline. Media autonomy, freedom of expression and alternative sources of information, and the rule of law have undergone the greatest declines among democracy metrics in recent years" (p. 1). Freedom House's *Freedom in the World 2018* (Washington, DC, 2018) survey concluded, "Democracy is in crisis. The values it embodies—particularly

the right to choose leaders in free and fair elections, freedom of the press, and the rule of law—are under assault and in retreat globally" (p. 1).

2. Larry Diamond, "Democracy after Trump: Can a Populist Stop Democratic Decline?," *Foreign Affairs,* November 14, 2016; see also "Democracy Demotion: How the Freedom Agenda Fell Apart," *Foreign Affairs,* July / August 2019.

3. The quotations are from Diamond, "Democracy after Trump"; Yascha Mounk, *The People vs. Democracy: Why Our Freedom Is in Danger and How to Save It* (Cambridge, MA, 2018), p. 20. See also Steven Levitsky and Daniel Ziblatt, *How Democracies Die* (New York, 2018), pp. 1–10.

4. Kim Parker, Rich Morin, and Juliana Menasce Horowitz, Pew Research Center, *Looking to the Future, Public Sees an America in Decline on Many Fronts,* March 2019, https://www.pewsocialtrends.org/2019/03/21/public-sees -an-america-in-decline-on-many-fronts.

5. The word "fracasomania"—the propensity to see failures everywhere—was coined by Albert O. Hirschman and discussed in his *Rival Views of Market Society and Other Recent Essays* (Cambridge, MA), p. 12. The biological metaphor appears throughout David Runciman, *How Democracy Ends* (London, 2018); compare the quite different treatment in John Keane, *Power and Humility: The Future of Monitory Democracy* (Cambridge, 2018).

6. Prime Minister Mark Rutte, "The EU: From the Power of Principles towards Principles and Power," Churchill Lecture, Europa Institut at the University of Zurich, February 13, 2019, https://www.government.nl/documents /speeches/2019/02/13/churchill-lecture-by-prime-minister-mark-rutte -europa-institut-at-the-university-of-zurich.

7. John Keane, "Mexico: The Cactus Democracy," *The Conversation,* July 18, 2017, https://theconversation.com/mexico-the-cactus-democracy-81025.

8. *Informe Latinobarómetro 2018* (Santiago de Chile, 2018), pp. 34–35; Debasish Roy Chowdhury and John Keane, *How to Kill a Democracy . . . the Indian Way* (Oxford, 2020).

9. Siva Vaidhyanathan, *Anti-Social Media: How Facebook Disconnects Us and Undermines Democracy* (New York, 2018); Russell Muirhead and Nancy L. Rosenblum, *A Lot of People Are Saying: The New Conspiracism and the Assault on Democracy* (Princeton, NJ, 2019); and John Keane, *Democracy and Media Decadence* (Cambridge, 2013).

10. Thorstein Veblen, *The Vested Interests and the Common Man* (New York, 1919), p. 125.

11. David Van Reybrouck, *Against Elections* (London, 2018); Jason Brennan, *Against Democracy* (Princeton, NJ, 2016); Christopher H. Achen and Larry Bartels, *Democracy for Realists: Why Elections Do Not Produce Responsive Government* (Princeton, NJ, 2016); Shawn W. Rosenberg, "Democracy Devouring Itself: The Rise of the Incompetent Citizen and the Appeal of Right Wing Populism," University of California, Irvine, 2019, https://escholarship.org/uc/item/8806z01m.

12. P. Diamond, *The End of Whitehall? Government by Permanent Campaign* (London, 2019).

13. Ajay Gudavarthy, *India after Modi: Populism and the Right* (New Delhi, 2018).

14. "'At War with Russia': EU Parliament Approves Resolution to Counter Russian Media 'Propaganda,'" *Russia Today*, November 23, 2016, https://www.rt.com/news/367922-eu-resolution-russian-media.

15. "No One Can Lecture Turkey about Human Rights: Turkey's Erdoğan," *Hürriyet*, December 10, 2018, http://www.hurriyetdailynews.com/no-one-can-lecture-turkey-about-human-rights-turkeys-erdogan-139609; Mohammad bin Rashid Al Maktoum, *Flashes of Thought* (Dubai, 2013), 16; "Democracy Deep-Rooted in Our Society: Sheikh Mohammed," *Khaleej Times*, October 4, 2015, https://www.khaleejtimes.com/nation/government/democracy-deep-rooted-in-our-society-shaikh-mohammed.

16. Su Changhe, "需将西方民主从普世知识降级为地方理论" [Western democracy must be demoted from a universal idea to a local theory], *Guangming Daily*, May 28, 2016, http://news.sina.com.cn/c/2013-05-28/092127244512.shtml.

17. The remark by Liu Cixin is cited in Jiayang Fan, "The War of the Worlds," *New Yorker*, June 24, 2019, p. 34; the internment is described in Liu Cixin, "Post-Deterrence Era, Year 2 Australia," in *Death's End* (New York, 2016), http://santiw.com/DeathsEnd/536.html.

18. Seva Gunitsky, *Aftershocks: Great Powers and Domestic Reforms in the Twentieth Century* (Princeton, NJ, 2017).

19. Perhaps along the lines of Ignazio Silone's *The School for Dictators* (New York, 1938), a satirical instruction manual for budding fascist dictators. The book is written in the form of a fictional trialogue that features

Mr. W., the future dictatorial ruler of the United States; Professor Pickup, his secret advisor; and Thomas the Cynic, whom the two Americans meet during their European travels. Thomas undertakes to instruct them about the workings of the fascist mind and how best to apply the techniques of fascist rule in America.

20. A generation ago these were Franz Neumann's objections to the term "despotism" in "Notes on the Theory of Dictatorship," in *The Democratic and the Authoritarian State: Essays in Political and Legal Theory*, ed. Herbert Marcuse (London, 1957), p. 235.

21. "Cash Found in Shoeboxes at Halkbank Ex-Manager's Home Not Bank's Money: Turkish PM," *Hürriyet Daily News*, February 11, 2014, http://www.hurriyetdailynews.com/cash-found-in-shoeboxes-at-halkbank -ex-managers-home-not-banks-money-turkish-pm-62314.

22. George Soros, as quoted in Michael Steinberger, "George Soros: Bet Big on Liberal Democracy," *New York Times*, July 17, 2018.

23. Niccolò Machiavelli, *The Prince*, in *The Prince and The Discourses*, ed. Max Lerner (New York, 1950), chapter XIV, pp. 53–56.

24. Leszek Kolakowski, "In Stalin's Countries: Theses on Hope and Despair," *Politique Aujourd'hui*, July–August 1971, typescript.

25. Montesquieu, "Voyage de Gratz à la Haye: Hollande" and "Notes sur l'Angleterre," in *Oeuvres complètes*, ed. Daniel Oster (Paris, 1964), pp. 326–331 and 331–334.

26. Runciman, *How Democracy Ends*, pp. 168–178.

27. Samuel P. Huntington and Clement H. Moore, eds., *Authoritarian Politics in Modern Society: The Dynamics of Established One-Party Systems* (New York, 1970), p. 509.

28. John Keane, *When Trees Fall, Monkeys Scatter: Rethinking Democracy in China* (London, 2017).

29. Friedrich Nietzsche, *Götzen-Dämmerung, oder Wie mann mit den Hammer philosophiert* (Berlin, 2016 [1889]), p. 32.

30. The inexact and (crypto-) teleological character of the phrase are on display in Alina Rocha Menocal, Verena Fritz with Lise Rakner, "Hybrid Regimes and the Challenges of Deepening and Sustaining Democracy in Developing Countries," *South African Journal of International Affairs* 15, no. 1 (June 2008): 29–40.

31. These labels can be sampled in Guillermo A. O'Donnell, "Delegative Democracy," in *Counterpoints: Selected Essays on Authoritarianism and Democratization* (Notre Dame, IN, 1999); Fareed Zakaria, *The Future of Freedom: Illiberal Democracy at Home and Abroad* (New York, 2007); Francis Fukuyama, *The End of History and the Last Man* (London, 1992); Steven Levitsky and Lucan A. Way, *Competitive Authoritarianism: Hybrid Regimes after the Cold War* (New York, 2012), p. 5; and David Collier and Steven Levitsky, "Democracy with Adjectives: Conceptual Innovation in Comparative Research," *World Politics* 49, no. 3 (1997): 430–451.

32. Franz Neumann, "Notes on the Theory of Dictatorship," in *The Democratic and the Authoritarian State: Essays in Political and Legal Theory*, ed. Herbert Marcuse (Glencoe, IL, 1957), pp. 233–256.

33. *The Republic of Plato*, ed. Benjamin Jowett (Oxford, 1888), books 1 and 8.

34. Montesquieu, *De l'esprit des lois* (Paris, 1979 [1748]), book 5, chapter 13, p. 185, and book 2, chapter 5, p. 141.

35. Montesquieu, *Lettres Persanes*, vol. 1 (Paris, 1873 [1721]), letters 148, 146, 102, and vol. 2, letters 59 and 37. Compare Montesquieu's remark in *Considerations on the Causes of the Greatness of the Romans and Their Decline* (New York, 1965 [1748]). Under conditions of despotism, he wrote, "there is always real dissension. The worker, the soldier, the lawyer, the magistrate, the noble are joined only inasmuch as some oppress the others without resistance. And, if we see any union there, it is not citizens who are united but dead bodies buried one next to the other" (chapter 9, p. 94).

36. The word "totalitarianism" is often overused and underdefined when describing the new despotisms, as in Madawi al-Rasheed, "Why the U.S. Can't Control MBS: Reining in the Rogue Prince," *Foreign Affairs*, November 5, 2018: "Saudi Arabia has effectively transformed into a totalitarian regime in which all of the power of the state is concentrated in one person's hands."

37. Michael Bratton, *Power Politics in Zimbabwe* (Boulder, CO, 2014). Among the most astute literary treatments of Mugabe-style dictatorships is Ngugi wa Thiong'o's *Wizard of the Crow* (London, 2007), a fearless satire in which the fictional Free Republic of Aburiria is dominated by a kleptocratic ruler. Dressed in dark pinstriped suits bearing the words "Might Is Right," the ruler loves every "eating, shitting, sneezing, or blowing his nose" moment

on television. He is "the sole voice of the people" and is convinced that his reign "would end only after the world has ended."

38. Peta Thornycroft, "'Hitler' Mugabe Launches Revenge Terror Attacks," *Daily Telegraph*, March 26, 2003; background developments are well analyzed in Stuart Doran, *Kingdom, Power, Glory: Mugabe, Zanu and the Quest for Supremacy 1960–1987* (Gauteng, 2017).

39. Karl Marx, *Capital: A Critical Analysis of Capitalist Production*, vol. 1 (Moscow, 1970), p. 338. In the face of much contrary evidence, Karl A. Wittfogel's *Oriental Despotism* (New Haven, CT, 1957) similarly argued that irrigation societies of ancient Mesopotamia, Egypt, and elsewhere were highly centralized, state-sponsored despotisms.

40. Simeon Kerr, "Tales of Broken Men and 'Ritz Detox' Emerge from Gilded Cage," *Financial Times Weekend*, February 17 / 18, 2018, p. 4.

41. Henry Hale, *Patronal Politics: Eurasian Regime Dynamics in Comparative Perspective* (New York, 2015).

42. Jonathan Joseph, *Varieties of Resilience: Studies in Governmentality* (Cambridge, 2018).

43. David Sherfinski, "McCain: 'Russia Is a Gas Station Masquerading as a Country,'" *Washington Times,* March 16, 2014.

44. Ernst Cassirer, *The Myth of the State* (London, 1975 [1946], pp. 277–296.

45. Sebastian Strangio, *Hun Sen's Cambodia* (New Haven, CT, 2014), 116; "Erdoğan: A New Turkish Era?," *Inside Story,* August 12, 2014, https://www.aljazeera.com/programmes/insidestory/2014/08/erdogan-new-turkish-era-201481116514700344.html; Sebastian Whale, "Mikhail Gorbachev Says Vladimir Putin Views Himself as 'Second Only to God,'" *Telegraph,* November 21, 2014.

46. Paul Theroux, "The Golden Man: Sapamurat Niyazov's Reign of Insanity," *New Yorker,* May 28, 2007, pp. 56–65.

Wealth, Money, Power

1. See Thomas Paine, *Rights of Man, Part the First* (London, 1791), p. 21: "When despotism has established itself for ages in a country, as in France, it is not in the person of the King only that it resides. It has the appearance of being so in show, and in nominal authority; but it is not so in practice and in

fact. It has its standard everywhere. Every office and department has its despotism, founded upon custom and usage. Every place has its Bastille, and every Bastille its despot. The original hereditary despotism resident in the person of the King, divides and sub-divides itself into a thousand shapes and forms, till at last the whole of it is acted by deputation."

2. Montesquieu, *The Persian Letters* (Indianapolis, IN, 1976), letter 37.

3. John Stuart Mill, "That the Ideally Best Form of Government Is Representative Government," in *Considerations on Representative Government*, chapter 3, in Mill, *Essays on Politics and Society*, ed. J. M. Robson (Toronto, 1977), p. 403.

4. Thucydides, *History of the Peloponnesian Wars* 1:17. A brief account of sultanism is found in Max Weber's *Economy and Society: An Outline of Interpretive Sociology*, vol. 1, ed. Guenther Roth and Claus Wittich (Berkeley, CA, 1978), pp. 231–232.

5. Alexei Mukhin, *Pharaoh* (Alexandria, VA, 2018), especially chapter 3. Insofar as top-dog despots are constantly surrounded by clusters of well-organized courtier associates and potential rivals, their inner circles are not understandable in the honeyed terms outlined in the classic work *Il libro del cortegiano* (1528) by the Renaissance writer Baldassare Castiglione, for whom the ideal courtier is "quick-witted and charming, prudent and scholarly" and committed to the task of making the "prince realize the honor and advantage accrue to him and his family from justice, liberality, magnanimity, gentleness and all other virtues befitting a ruler."

6. Paul Lendvai, *Orbán: Hungary's Strongman* (Oxford, 2018), p. 167. See also Bálint Magyar, *Post-Communist Mafia State: The Case of Hungary* (Budapest, 2016), pp. 90–91, and, more generally, Alena V. Ledeneva, *How Russia Really Works: The Informal Practices That Shaped Post-Soviet Politics and Business* (Ithaca, NY, 2006).

7. Franz Neumann, "Notes on the Theory of Dictatorship," in *The Democratic and the Authoritarian State: Essay in Political and Legal Theory*, ed. Herbert Marcuse (Glencoe, IL, 1957), p. 245; see also his *Behemoth: The Structure and Practice of National Socialism, 1933–1944*, 2nd ed. (New York, 1944), p. 430 and (quoting Hitler) p. 439: "The mass meeting is necessary if only for the reason that in it the individual, who . . . feels lonely and is easily seized with the fear of being alone, receives for the first time the picture of a greater

community, something that has a strengthening and an encouraging effect on most people."

8. Marc Valeri, *Oman: Politics and Society in the Qaboos State* (New York, 2009), p. 198.

9. Rano Turaeva, "Tanish-bilish," in *The Global Encyclopaedia of Informality,* vol. 1, ed. Alena Ledenova (London, 2018), pp. 71–73.

10. Zygmunt Bauman and Leonidas Donskis, *Moral Blindness: The Loss of Sensitivity in Liquid Modernity* (Cambridge, 2013).

11. *The Gulistan of Sadi; or, The Rose Garden of Shekh Muslihu'd-din Sadi of Shiraz,* translated by Edward Backhouse Eastwick (Delhi, 2018 [1852]), chapter 1, story 1; cf. Ramita Navai, *City of Lies: Love, Sex, Death, and the Search for Truth in Tehran* (New York, 2014).

12. Dávid Jancsics, "'A Friend Gave Me a Phone Number'—Brokerage in Low-Level Corruption," *International Journal of Law, Crime and Justice* 43, no. 1 (2014): 68–87. The scale of protection rackets is often vast, as in Russia, where according to some estimates 70–80 percent of business firms pay on average 10–20 percent of their profits for protection service. See Mark Galeotti, "The Russian 'Mafiya': Consolidation and Globalisation," in *Global Crime Today: The Changing Face of Organised Crime,* ed. Mark Galeotti (New York, 2005), p. 57; and Dina Siegel, "Vory v Zakone: Russian Organized Crime," in *Traditional Organized Crime in the Modern World: Responses to Socioeconomic Change,* ed. Dina Siegel and Henk van der Bunt (New York, 2012), pp. 27–49.

13. Bálint Magyar, *Post-Communist Mafia State: The Case of Hungary* (Budapest, 2016), p. 75; cf. Eric J. Hobsbawm, *Primitive Rebels* (Manchester, 1959), p. 40. The term "poligarch" is first used in Tamás Frei, *2015—A káosz éve és a Magyar elit háborúja* (Budapest, 2013).

14. E. J. Hobsbawm, *Primitive Rebels: Studies in Archaic Forms of Social Movement in the 19th and 20th Centuries* (Manchester, 1971), p. 40.

15. Miklós Haraszti, "Orbán Will Now Create a System Where There Is No More Need to Win an Election," *The Slovak Spectator,* April 11, 2018, https:// spectator.sme.sk/c/20800649/hungary-election-orban-victory-aftermath -haraszti.html.

16. GAN Integrity, *Macedonia Corruption Report,* January 2018, https:// www.business-anti-corruption.com/country-profiles/macedonia.

17. Phorn Bopha, "Hun Sen Encourages Cambodians to Emulate Chinese-Style Wealth," *Cambodia Daily,* December 30, 2012. The broader practical consequences of this rhetoric are probed in Sebastian Strangio, *Hun Sen's Cambodia* (New Haven, CT, 2014).

18. Strangio, *Hun Sen's Cambodia.*

19. Marc Valeri, *Oman: Politics and Society in the Qaboos State* (New York, 2009), pp. 100–117.

20. Ignacy Krasicki, "The Drunk," in *Polish Fables: Bilingual Edition,* trans. Gerard T. Kapolka (New York, 1997), p. 65: "After living on the bottle day and night / The sick drunk smashed his glasses in his fright / He cursed mead, called wine, beer a thug / Then he got well . . . and drank straight from the jug."

21. Joachim Ahrens, Herman W. Hoen, and Martin C. Spechler, "State Capitalism in Eurasia: A Dual-Economy Approach to Central Asia," in *Politics and Legitimacy in Post-Soviet Eurasia,* ed. Martin Brusis, Joachim Ahrens, and Martin Schulze Wessel (Houndmills, UK, 2016), pp. 47–71.

22. Cui Jia, "Verdict Called Reassuring to Businesses," *China Daily,* April 11, 2019.

23. Andrei Vernikov, "The Impact of State-Controlled Banks on the Russian Banking Sector," *Eurasian Geography and Economics* 53, no. 2 (2012): 250–266.

24. Anders Åslund, *How Capitalism Was Built: The Transformation of Central and Eastern Europe, Russia, and Central Asia* (Cambridge, 2007), pp. 47–53; Minxin Pei, *China's Crony Capitalism: The Dynamics of Regime Decay* (Cambridge, MA, 2016).

25. See James S. Henry, *The Price of Offshore Revisited* (London, 2012).

26. See the UBC and PWC report, *New Visionaries and the Chinese Century: Billionaires Insights* (2018), https://www.pwc.com.au/financial-services/pdf/ubs-billionaires-2018.pdf.

27. Details are drawn from the Shanghai-based Hurun Report and the Washington-based Center for Responsive Politics, as reported in Michael Forsythe, "Billionaire Lawmakers Ensure the Rich Are Represented in China's Legislature," *New York Times,* March 2, 2015. See also my *When Trees Fall, Monkeys Scatter: Rethinking Democracy in China* (London, 2017).

28. Daniel Kimmage, "Russia: Selective Capitalism and Kleptocracy," in Freedom House, Radio Free Europe / Radio Liberty, and Radio Free Asia,

Undermining Democracy: 21st Century Authoritarians (New York, 2009), pp. 49–64.

29. P. Lilley, *Dirty Dealing: The Untold Truth about Global Money Laundering* (London, 2000), p. 27; Serguey Braguinsky, "Postcommunist Oligarchs in Russia. Quantitative Analysis," *Journal of Law and Economics* 52, no. 2 (2009): 307–349.

30. Paul Klebnikov, *Godfather of the Kremlin: Boris Berezovsky and the Looting of Russia* (New York, 2000), pp. 5, 320; see also Chrystia Freeland, *Sale of the Century: Russia's Wild Ride from Communism to Capitalism* (New York, 2000), and David E. Hoffman, *The Oligarchs: Wealth and Power in the New Russia* (New York, 2011). The spread of criminal violence during this period is well analyzed in Vadim Volkov, *Violent Entrepreneurs: The Use of Force in the Making of Russian Capitalism* (New York, 2002).

31. Karen Dawisha, *Putin's Kleptocracy: Who Owns Russia?* (New York, 2014); Katherine Hirschfeld, *Gangster States: Organized Crime, Kleptocracy and Political Collapse* (New York, 2015); Larry Diamond, "Democracy Demotion: How the Freedom Agenda Fell Apart," *Foreign Affairs,* July / August 2019; and Richard Sakwa's important critique, "Is Russia Really a Kleptocracy?," *Times Literary Supplement,* February 4, 2015.

32. Niccolò Machiavelli, *The Prince,* in *The Prince and The Discourses,* ed. Max Lerner (New York, 1950), chapter xvii, p. 62, and chapter xxi, p. 81.

33. Claus Offe, *Contradictions of the Welfare State,* ed. John Keane (London, 1984). In what follows, compare the classic descriptions of the vassalage system by F. L. Ganshof, "Benefice and Vassalage in the Age of Charlemagne," *Cambridge Historical Journal* 6, no. 2 (1939): 147–175, and Charles Edwin Odegaard, *Vassi and Fidelis in the Carolingian Empire* (New York, 1972).

34. Sean L. Yom, "Understanding the Resilience of Monarchy during the Arab Spring—Analysis," *Eurasia Review,* April 6, 2012.

35. National Bureau of Statistics of China, "Main Items of General Public Budget Expenditure of the Central and Local Governments (2017)," http://www.stats.gov.cn/tjsj/ndsj/2018/html/EN0703.jpg.

36. "Fifth Generation Star Li Keqiang Discusses Domestic Challenges, Trade Relations with Ambassador," WikiLeaks, March 15, 2007, https://wikileaks.org/plusd/cables/07BEIJING1760_a.html.

37. Stein Ringen, *The Perfect Dictatorship: China in the 21st Century* (Hong Kong, 2016), p. 164. Cf. Bruce Dickson, *The Dictator's Dilemma: The Chinese Communist Party's Strategy for Survival* (New York: 2016); Douglas Besharov and Karen Baehler, eds., *Chinese Social Policy in a Time of Transition* (Oxford, 2013); Zheng Yongnian, "Between the State and the Market: The Political Logic of Social Policy Reform in China," in *Social Development and Social Policy: International Experiences and China's Reform*, ed. Qi Dongtao and Yang Lijun (Singapore, 2016).

38. Aristotle, *The Politics of Aristotle*, ed. Ernest Barker (London, 1968), IV, xi, 1295b–1296b.

39. Jürgen Kocka, "The Middle Classes in Europe," *Journal of Modern History* 67, no. 4 (December 1995): 783–806.

40. Francis Fukuyama, *Political Order and Political Decay: From the Industrial Revolution to the Globalisation of Democracy* (London, 2014), pp. 403–408, 440–445. See my debate with Fukuyama in "Can Democracy Survive a Shrinking Middle Class?," *The Conversation*, September 4, 2013, https://theconversation.com/can-democracy-survive-a-shrinking-middle-class-17813. Compare the counterevidence from countries such as Thailand and the Philippines in Joshua Kurlantzick, *Democracy in Retreat: The Revolt of the Middle Class and the Worldwide Decline of Representative Government* (New Haven, CT, 2014).

41. Karen Stenner, "Three Kinds of 'Conservatism,'" *Psychological Inquiry* 20 (2009): 157; compare her remarks in Tom Jacobs, "Authoritarianism: The Terrifying Trait That Trump Triggers," *Pacific Standard*, March 27, 2018.

42. Hannah Arendt, *The Origins of Totalitarianism* (New York, 1973 [1951]), p. 338.

43. Alexis de Tocqueville, "Quelle espèce de despotisme les nations démocratiques ont à craindre" [What kind of despotism democratic nations have to fear], in *De la démocratie en Amérique*, ed. François Furet (Paris, 1981), part 4, chapter 6, pp. 383–388; and *Correspondance d'Alexis de Tocqueville et de Gustave de Beaumont*, in *Oeuvres completes*, ed. J. P. Mayer (Paris, 1967), book 8, part 1, p. 421.

44. Czeslaw Milosz, *The Captive Mind* (New York, 1990 [1951]), p. 66. The mistaken presumption that modern despotism would have ruinous economic consequences is spelled out by Montesquieu, who was sure that in despotic

states economic initiative would be crushed so that "nothing is repaired, nothing improved . . . all is deserted" (*Spirit of the Laws,* vol. 14, p. 61).

A Phantom People

1. Montesquieu, *Considerations on the Causes of the Greatness of the Romans and Their Decline* (New York, 1965 [1734]), p. 210.

2. Karl Deutsch, *The Nerves of Government: Models of Political Communication and Control* (New York, 1963), p. 21.

3. See John Keane, "Understanding the Chinese Communist Party: A Conversation with Yu Keping," OpenDemocracy, April 15, 2014, https://www.opendemocracy.net/john-keane/understanding-chinese-communist-party-conversation-with-yu-keping; see also Matthew Frear, "An Anatomy of Adaptive Authoritarianism: Belarus under Aleksandr Lukashenka" (PhD diss., University of Birmingham, 2011).

4. Niccolò Machiavelli, *The Prince and the Discourses* (New York, 1950), chapter 9, p. 39.

5. John M. Letiche and Basil Dmytryshyn, eds., *Russian Statecraft: The Politika of Iurii Krizhanich* (Oxford, 1985), pp. 188, 205.

6. Sebastian Heilmann and Elizabeth J. Perry, eds., *Mao's Invisible Hand: The Political Foundations of Adaptive Governance in China* (Cambridge, MA, 2011), pp. 8–10 and 62–103; see also Sebastian Heilmann, "From Local Experiments to National Policy: The Origins of China's Distinctive Policy Process," *China Journal* 59 (2008): 1–30.

7. Cited in Evan Osnos, "Born Red," *New Yorker,* June 4, 2015.

8. Quoted in the dispatch released by WikiLeaks, "Budapest Daily June 26 [2007] D) Budapest 992," https://wikileaks.org/plusd/cables/07BUDAPEST1043_a.html.

9. Xenophon, *Hiero, or The Tyrant: A Discourse on Despotic Rule,* trans. H. G. Dakyns (Project Gutenberg, 2013), https://www.gutenberg.org/files/1175/1175-h/1175-h.htm.

10. Sheena Chestnut Greitens, *Dictators and Their Secret Police: Coercive Institutions and State Violence* (Cambridge, 2016).

11. See Marina Walker Guevara et al., "Leaked Records Reveal Offshore Holdings of China's Elite," *International Consortium of Investigative Jour-*

nalists, January 21, 2014, http://www.icij.org/offshore/leaked-records-reveal-offshore-holdings-chinas-elite.

12. Václav Havel, *Leaving* (London, 2008), p. 70.

13. From the untitled sonnet known as "Natur und Kunst" (1802?), in *Johann Wolfgang von Goethe: Selected Poetry*, ed. David Luke (London, 2005), pp. 125–126.

14. Angus McIntyre, ed., *Aging and Political Leadership* (South Melbourne, 1988), p. 299n10.

15. Augusto Roa Bastos, *I, the Supreme* (London, 1987), p. 409.

16. *Memoirs of the Prince de Talleyrand*, ed. Duc de Broglie (London, 1891), p. 119.

17. Hua Yu, *China in Ten Words* (London, 2013), p. 3.

18. Ain Bandial, "Your Gilded Chariot Awaits: Brunei Sultan Celebrates 50 Years in Power," Reuters, October 5, 2017, https://www.reuters.com/article/us-brunei-royals/your-gilded-chariot-awaits-brunei-sultan-celebrates-50-years-in-power-idUSKBN1CA0NA.

19. Yunshan Liu, "Five Dimensions in Understanding the CPC," *China Insight*, July 7, 2014; Xuequan Mu, "Facts & Figures: CPC's 'Mass Line' Campaign Wraps up with Achievements," Xinhuanet, October 7, 2014, http://news.xinhuanet.com/english/china/2014-10/07/c_127069864.htm. Xi Jinping's appearance at CCTV is recorded at http://news.xinhuanet.com/politics/2016-02/19/c_1118102868.htm.

20. Huaguang Huang and Jianzhang Luan, *The Roadmap of the 18th CPC National Congress and the Chinese Dream* (Beijing, 2013), p. 2.

21. John Keane, *Democracy and Media Decadence* (Cambridge, 2013), p. 207.

22. Yu Keping, "Democracy or Populism: The Politics of Public Opinion in China," in *Human Rights and Good Governance*, ed. Zhang Wei (Leiden, 2016), p. 303; John Fitzgerald, *Awakening China: Politics, Culture, and Class in the Nationalist Revolution* (Stanford, CA, 1996), p. 118.

23. The whole idea of nurturing governmentality among the subjects of power is discussed by Michel Foucault, "The Subject and Power," in *Michel Foucault: Beyond Structuralism and Hermeneutics,* ed. H. Dreyfus and P. Rabinow (London, 1982), p. 790.

24. Gustave Le Bon, "The Sentiments and Morality of Crowds," in *The Crowd: A Study of the Popular Mind* (Dunwoody, GA, 1897), p. 39.

25. Carlos Fuentes, *The Eagle's Throne* (New York, 2006).

26. T. W. Adorno et al., *The Authoritarian Personality* (New York, 1950), p. 971.

27. Czeslaw Milosz, *The Captive Mind* (London, 1953), chapter 3.

28. Sigmund Freud, "Group Psychology and the Analysis of the Ego," in *The Standard Edition of the Complete Psychological Works of Sigmund Freud*, vol. 18, ed. James Strachey (London, 1955), pp. 121, 65–68; Freud, "Moses and Monotheism," in *The Standard Edition of the Complete Psychological Works of Sigmund Freud*, vol. 23, ed. James Strachey (London, 1964), p. 109.

29. Pippa Norris and Ronald Inglehart, *Cultural Backlash: Trump, Brexit, and the Rise of Authoritarian Populism* (Cambridge, 2018), p. 7.

30. Heinrich Popitz, *Phenomena of Power: Authority, Domination, and Violence* (New York, 2017), pp. 14–15. Popitz refers to this type of subordination as "authoritative power": "recognizing the superiority of others as standard-setters, and striving to be ourselves recognized, to receive from those standard-setters signs to the effect that one has proven himself" (p. 15).

31. Diedrich Westermann, *Geschichte Afrikas: Staatenbildung südlich der Sahara* (Cologne, 1952).

32. Tacitus, *The Histories* (New York 1975 [100–110 BCE]), book 1, section 36.

33. During Xi's first visit to Trinidad and Tobago, it was his "very beautiful" and "very warm" glamorous wife, Peng Liyuan, who turned the trip into a media sensation. Throughout the visit, "the Chinese first lady," reported *China Daily,* "impressed the Caribbean country not just with her music, but also her kindness and language capability." Zhao Yanrong, "First Lady Turns on the Charm, Impresses Hosts," *China Daily,* June 4, 2013; Matt Sheehan, "Michelle Obama's Visit to China Sparks 'Fashion Showdown' with China's First Lady," *Huffington Post,* March 22, 2014, https://www.huffpost.com/entry/michelle-obama-china-visit_n_5006027.

34. Tim Arango, "Oprah, Rupert Murdoch, Harvard: Saudi Prince's U.S. Tour," *New York Times,* April 6, 2018.

35. See the *Tajikistan Young Leaders Program Final Report* (Arlington, VA, 2015).

36. "Happiness," UAE Government, https://government.ae/en/about-the-uae/the-uae-government/government-of-future/happiness, accessed November 30, 2019.

37. Amy Khor, "Feedback Unit's 21st Anniversary Dinner Speech," Pan Pacific Hotel, Singapore, October 12, 2006; Singapore Ministry of Community Development and Sports, *Building Bridges: The Story of Feedback Unit* (Singapore, 2004); OSC (Our Singapore Conversation) Committee, *Reflections of Our Singapore Conversation: What Future Do We Want? How Do We Get There?* (Singapore, 2013); and Garry Rodan, *Participation without Democracy: Containing Conflict in Southeast Asia* (Ithaca, NY, 2018), chapter 5.

38. Giovanni Gentile, *Che cosa é il fascismo. Discorsi e polemiche* (Florence, 1925), p. 98; similar contemporary observations about "the coming of the masses" are made by José Ortega y Gasset, *The Revolt of the Masses* (New York, 1932).

39. Vladimir Nabokov, "Tyrants Destroyed," in *The Stories of Vladimir Nabokov* (New York, 1997 [1938]), p. 455.

40. Cited in Daniel Bell, "Notes on Authoritarian and Democratic Leadership," in *Studies in Leadership: Leadership and Democratic Action*, ed. Alvin W. Gouldner (New York, 1965), p. 402. Compare the remark of Gáspár Miklós Tamás: "This is not like old fascism, with its marches, dreams of conquest and global triumph. This is a very uneventful glide toward the precipice, without resistance. We are past the point of danger. It has already happened" (quoted in the Al Jazeera video documentary by Theopi Skarlatos, *Prejudice and Pride in Hungary,* November 21, 2018, https://www.aljazeera.com/programmes/radicalised-youth/2018/10/prejudice-pride-hungary-181029060026570.html).

41. As reported by Robert Ley and quoted in Hannah Arendt, *The Origins of Totalitarianism* (New York, 1973 [1951]), p. 339.

42. *The Gulf Today* (Sharjah, UAE), May 10, 2014, p. 2.

43. John Quincy Adams, "Inaugural Address" (March 4, 1825), in *The Addresses and Messages of the Presidents of the United States, Inaugural, Annual, and Special, from 1789 to 1846*, vol. 1, ed. Edwin Williams (New York, 1846), p. 577.

44. Kerry Brown, *Ballot Box China—Grassroots Democracy in the Final Major One-Party State* (London, 2011); Lianjiang Li and Kevin J. O'Brien, "The Struggle over Village Elections," in *The Paradox of China's Post-Mao Reforms,* ed. Merle Goldman and Roderick MacFarquhar (Cambridge, MA, 1999), pp. 129–144; Baogang He, *Rural Democracy in China: The Role of Village Elections* (New York, 2007); Youtian Liu, 村民自治: 中国基层民主建设的实践与探索

[Villager self-government: Practice and exploration of grassroots democracy building in China] (Beijing, 2010).

45. "避免‘钉子户’北京首由居民投票表决拆迁" [Avoid "nail households": Beijing residents voted to decide demolition], Sohu.com, April 6, 2007, http://news.sohu.com/20070604/n250388337.shtml; and John Keane, *When Trees Fall, Monkeys Scatter: Rethinking Democracy in China* (London, 2017). A wit with a sharp tongue described the election as a "demolition by ballot"; see "开发商多倾向分步拆迁听取民意是进步" [Developers' multistep demolition programs show progress in listening to public opinion], August 6, 2007, http://bj.house.sina.com.cn/scan/2007-06-08/1459195471.html.

46. The term is used in "习近平在庆祝人民政协成立65周年大会上作重要讲话" [Xi Jinping's keynote speech to celebrate the 65th anniversary of the Chinese People's Political Consultative Conference], September 22, 2014, http://www.cppcc.gov.cn/zxww/2014/09/22/ARTI1411347580249386.shtml.

47. The following details are drawn from Keane, *When Trees Fall, Monkeys Scatter,* pp. 103–104.

48. "阿里巴巴选举"公益合伙人" [Alibaba selected public interest committee], Xinhuanet, November 5, 2015, http://www.ah.xinhuanet.com/2015-05/11/c_1115243017.htm.

49. The principles and practices of representative democracy are examined in my *Breve Historia del Futuro de las Elecciones* (Mexico City, 2018), and Sonia Alonso, John Keane, and Wolfgang Merkel, eds., *The Future of Representative Democracy* (Cambridge, 2011).

50. See the study (covering the period from 1982 to 2005) by Monica Martinez-Bravo et al., "Political Reform in China: Elections, Public Goods and Income Distribution," National Bureau of Economic Research, 2012, http://www.nber.org/papers/w18101; and Lianjiang Li, "The Empowering Effect of Village Elections in China," *Asian Survey* 43, no. 4 (August 1, 2003): 648–662.

51. Ronald Wintrobe, *The Political Economy of Dictatorship* (New York, 1998), p. 20; Edmund Malesky and Paul Schuler, "The Single-Party Dictator's Dilemma: Information in Elections without Opposition," *Legislative Studies Quarterly* 36, no. 4 (November 2011): 491–530.

52. See the Inter-Parliamentary Union figures published at http://www.ipu.org/parline-e/reports/2309_E.htm.

53. Yahya Kamalipour, *Media, Power and Politics in the Digital Age: The 2009 Presidential Election Uprising in Iran* (Lanham, MD, 2010); Tao Dong-feng, "乌坎事件与中国特色的维权" [Wukan incident and rights defense with Chinese characteristics], 21ccom.net, November 1, 2012, http://www.21ccom.net/articles/zgyj/gqmq/2012/0112/51888.html; Rahul Jacob and Zhou Ping, "Wukan's Young Activists Embrace New Role," *Financial Times*, December 2, 2012. See also Scott Greene, "All Eyes on Wukan as Polls Open," *China Digital Times*, March 3, 2014, http://chinadigitaltimes.net/2012/03/all-eyes-on-wukan-as-polls-open; and the four-part Al Jazeera documentary series by Lynn Lee and James Leong, "Wukan: After the Uprising," June 26, 2013, http://www.aljazeera.com/programmes/specialseries/2013/06/2013626153044866869.html.

Media Power

1. The contours of the revolution of communicative abundance are examined in John Keane, *Democracy and Media Decadence* (Cambridge, 2013); see also my "The Unfinished Robots Revolution: Ten Tips for Humans," in *Digitizing Democracy*, ed. Aljosha Karim Schapals, Axel Bruns, and Brian McNair (New York, 2019), pp. 214–224.

2. Adam Ferguson, *An Essay on the History of Civil Society* (Dublin, 1767), pt. VI, sec. VI, p. 410.

3. See the background details in Christopher M. Davidson, "The United Arab Emirates: Economy First, Politics Second," in *Political Liberalization in the Persian Gulf*, ed. Joshua Teitelbaum (New York, 2009), pp. 223–248.

4. A point captured in the lengthy report by Johann Hari, "The Dark Side of Dubai," *Independent* (London), April 7, 2009: "When I ask the British expats how they feel to not be in a democracy, their reaction is always the same. First, they look bemused. Then they look affronted. 'It's the Arab way!' an Essex boy shouts at me in response, as he tries to put a pair of comedy antlers on his head while pouring some beer into the mouth of his friend, who is lying on his back on the floor, gurning [pulling a grotesque face]."

5. Niccolò Machiavelli, *The Prince and the Discourses* (New York, 1950), ch. 18; Machiavelli, *Life of Castruccio Castracani* (London, 2003 [1520]), p. 20. The dazzling late medieval "spectacles of state" promulgated by European rulers intent on shrouding their power in courtly magnificence and fantasy

representations of themselves as political lords blessed by the Lord Jesus Christ are well analyzed in Ernst H. Kantorowicz, "The 'King's Advent' and the Enigmatic Panels in the Doors of Santa Sabina," *Art Bulletin* 26 (1944): 207–231; and Gordon Kipling, *Enter the King: Theatre, Liturgy, and Ritual in the Medieval Civic Triumph* (Oxford, 1998). The matter of state rituals as forms of collective "metaphysical theater" that materially shape the sense of reality of subjects is insightfully analyzed by the anthropologist Clifford Geertz in *Negara: The Theatre State in Nineteenth-Century Bali* (Princeton, NJ, 1980).

6. Among the most influential examples is the work by the Nobel Prize-nominated Guglielmo Ferrero, *The Principles of Power: The Great Political Crises of History* (New York, 1942).

7. Hannah Arendt, "Ideology and Terror: A Novel Form of Government," in *The Origins of Totalitarianism* (New York, 1973 [1951]), p. 469.

8. Ma Jian, *China Dream* (London, 2018).

9. Javad Karamī-Rād Mīlānī, *Iqtisād-e siyāsī intikhābāt* (Tehran, 2017); Shireen Hunter, *Iran Divided: The Historical Roots of Iranian Debates on Identity, Culture and Governance in the Twenty-First Century* (Lanham, MD, 2014); Mahmoud Pargoo, "Paradoxes of Secularisation and Islamisation in Post-Revolutionary Iran" (doctoral dissertation, Australian Catholic University, Sydney, September 2018).

10. "Turkmenistan: Election Spectacle Hides Disturbing Economic Decline," Eurasianet, February 8, 2017, http://www.eurasianet.org/node/82311.

11. The despotic fantasy of abolishing all forms of language is spelled out in the classic "dictator novel" by Jorge Zalamea, *El gran Burundún Burundá ha muerto* (Buenos Aires, 1952), where strong-arm rule reduces citizens to grunting and squeaking beasts stripped of any intelligible language. The inverse fantasy of replacing language with an artificial language that grants rulers total control of their subjects is the theme of Václav Havel's satire *The Memorandum* (New York, 2012 [1965]).

12. Victor Klemperer, *Language of the Third Reich: LTI—Lingua Tertii Imperii* (London, 2013).

13. From the 2006 interview with Viktor Orbán cited in Bálint Magyar, *Post-Communist Mafia State: The Case of Hungary* (Budapest, 2016), 231, where he emphasizes that his governing party, Fidesz, "is not an organization based on one single coherent system of principles or an ideology—such an

organization is incapable of expanding beyond a certain point." Lee Hsien Loong's comment is drawn from his interview with *Fortune* magazine, April 3, 2000; the obituary of Lee Kuan Yew is the source of the remark by Carlton Tan, "Lee Kuan Yew Leaves a Legacy of Authoritarian Pragmatism," *Guardian,* March 23, 2015.

14. Michael Walzer, "Totalitarian Tyranny," in *Totalitarian Democracy and After,* ed. Yehoshua Arieli and Nathan Rotenstreich (London, 2002), p. 191.

15. Daniel Boorstin, *The Image: A Guide to Pseudo-Events in America* (New York, 1964).

16. Hannah Arendt, "Lying in Politics: Reflections on the Pentagon Papers," in *Crises of the Republic* (New York, 1972), pp. 1–47.

17. Haig Patapan and Yi Wang, "The Hidden Ruler: Wang Huning and the Making of Contemporary China," *Journal of Contemporary China* 27, no. 109 (2018): 47–60.

18. See Vladislav Surkov, *Texts 1997–2010* (Moscow, 2010), pp. 36ff., and Peter Pomerantsev, "Putin's Rasputin," *London Review of Books* 33, no. 20 (October 20, 2011): 3–6.

19. Surkov, *Texts 1997–2010,* pp. 30–31, 49, 71, 101, 111, 27 (translation amended). See also his lengthy discussion of the weaknesses of "Western democracy" and the coming "glorious century" of Putinism in "Putin's Long State," *Nezavisimaya Gazeta,* February 2, 2019.

20. Ministry of Foreign Affairs of the Russian Federation, *Report on the Human Rights Situation in the European Union* (Moscow, 2013), pp. 8, 87; Timothy Snyder, *The Road to Unfreedom: Russia, Europe, America* (New York, 2018), p. 91.

21. Peter Pomerantsev, *Nothing Is True and Everything Is Possible: Adventures in Modern Russia* (London, 2015), p. 79.

22. Karen Elliott House, *On Saudi Arabia: Its People, Past, Religion, Fault Lines—and Future* (New York, 2013), p. 32.

23. Among the most insightful analyses of how self-censorship and willful conformism operate under these conditions are Cherian George, *Freedom from the Press: Journalism and State Power in Singapore* (Singapore, 2012) and *Singapore, Incomplete: Reflections on a First World Nation's Arrested Political Development* (Singapore, 2017), ch. 20.

24. Audrey L. Altstadt, *Frustrated Democracy in Post-Soviet Azerbaijan* (New York, 2017).

25. David Bandurski and Martin Hala, *Investigative Journalism in China: Eight Cases in Chinese Watchdog Journalism* (Hong Kong, 2010); more recent cases are analyzed in my "Phantom Democracy: A Puzzle at the Heart of Chinese Politics," *South China Morning Post,* September 28, 2018.

26. Yongming Zhou, *Historicizing Online Politics: Telegraphy, the Internet, and Political Participation in China* (Stanford, CA, 2006), pp. 135–138.

27. Cong Cao, Richard P. Suttmeier, and Dennis Fred Simon, "Success in State Directed Innovation? Perspectives on China's Medium and Long-Term Plan for the Development of Science and Technology," in *The New Asian Innovation Dynamics: China and India in Perspective,* ed. Govindan Parayil and Anthony P. D'Costa (Basingstoke, 2009), pp. 247–264; see also Scott Kennedy, Richard P. Suttmeier, and Jun Su, "Standards, Stakeholders, and Innovation: China's Evolving Role in the Global Knowledge Economy," National Bureau of Asian Research, Seattle, WA, 2008, http://csis.org/images/stories/china/Kennedy/080915_Standards_Stakeholders_English.pdf; and Josef Bichler and Christian Schmidkonz, "The Chinese Indigenous Innovation System and Its Impact on Foreign Enterprises," Munich Business School working paper, 2012, http://www.munich-business-school.de/fileadmin/mbs_daten/dateien/working_papers/mbs-wp-2012-01.pdf.

28. M. A. Qiang, "薛蛮子案警示网络名人: 做人不能靠微博—甘肃频道—人民网" [The case of Xue Manzi sounds alarm for internet celebrities: self-discipline expressions on Weibo], People.cn, April 21, 2014, http://gs.people.com.cn/n/2014/0421/c188868-21043079.html.

29. The analogy is used by Fang Binxing, former president of Beijing University of Posts and Telecommunications and a key developer of the core technology behind the Great Firewall, during an interview with *Global Times,* February 18, 2011; see "Great Firewall Father Speaks out," Sina.com, 2011, http://english.sina.com/china/p/2011/0217/360410.html.

30. Further details are available in my *When Trees Fall, Monkeys Scatter: Rethinking Democracy in China* (London, 2017).

31. See, for example "Provisional Regulations for the Development and Management of Instant Messaging Tools and Public Information Services," China Copyright and Media, July 8, 2014, https://chinacopyrightandmedia

.wordpress.com/2014/08/07/provisional-regulations-for-the-development-and
-management-of-instant-messaging-tools-and-public-information-services.

32. Rebecca MacKinnon, *Consent of the Networked* (New York, 2013),
pp. 36–37, 133–139; and her *Race to the Bottom: Corporate Complicity in Chinese Internet Censorship* (New York, 2006), p. 12.

33. Nart Villeneuve, "Breaching Trust: An Analysis of Surveillance and Security Practices on China's TOM-Skype Platform," Information Warfare Monitor and ONI Asia, January 10, 2008; Jedidiah R. Crandall et al., "Chat Program Censorship and Surveillance in China: Tracking TOM-Skype and Sina UC," *First Monday* 18, no. 7 (June 30, 2013).

34. Tencent actively monitors WeChat's content, censoring blacklisted words, rumors, and speculations. Sina Corporation uses Weibo Credit, an unusual points system whose scale begins at 80; for each violation users are fined between 2 and 10 points. When they reach zero, their accounts are deleted. Prominent bloggers—the so-called Big V, verified Weibo account holders—have "assigned special editors." For estimates about the number of censors, see Gary King, Jennifer Pan, and Margaret E. Roberts, "Reverse-Engineering Censorship in China: Randomized Experimentation and Participant Observation," *Science* 345, no. 6199 (August 22, 2014): 1–10.

35. The phrase *fàn zuì*, or "getting rice drunk," is used to indicate a dinner gathering to discuss politics; the phrase is homonymous with "commit a crime." The mythical grass-mud horse, which began as an online video, soon featured in catchy songs, fake nature documentaries, cartoons, and everyday speech. It was originally created as an in-joke way of poking fun at government censorship of so-called vulgar content. Sounding nearly the same in Chinese as "f—k your mother" *(cào nǐ mā)*, it featured in a smash-hit online video depicting the grass-mud horse defending its habitat (successfully) against a "river crab" *(hé xiè)*, a homonym for "harmony," a favorite propaganda catchword of the regime. In verbal form, something can be said to have been "river-crabbed"—that is, censored or "harmonized." A "crab" also refers in Chinese to someone who is a bully. Since the Communist Party, the supposed guarantor of harmony, is often described officially as "the mother of the people," the phrase "mud-grass horse" or "f—k your mother" thus implies the need to "f—k the Party." It was not long before "grass-mud horse" also came to mean a web-savvy opponent of regime censorship.

36. See Jian Xu, *Media Events in Web 2.0 China: Interventions of Online Activism* (Brighton, UK, 2016).

37. "Freedom of Speech Does Not Protect Rumors," *Global Times*, December 4, 2012; see also Helen Gao, "Rumor, Lies, and Weibo: How Social Media Is Changing the Nature of Truth in China," *The Atlantic*, April 16, 2012.

38. Yao Li, *Playing by the Informal Rules—Why the Chinese Regime Remains Stable despite Rising Protests* (Cambridge, 2019).

39. See CCTV News post at http://www.weibo.com/2656274875/C12cdC5Xe?type=comment#_rnd1437812312429.

40. Dila Beisembayeva, Evangelia Papoutsaki, and Elena Kolesova, "Social Media and Online Activism in Kazakhstan: A New Challenge for Authoritarianism?," in *The Asian Conference on Media and Mass Communication, Official Conference Proceedings* (Osaka, 2013), pp. 1–15; Robert Mendick, "Tony Blair Gives Kazakhstan's Autocratic President Tips on How to Defend a Massacre," *The Telegraph* (London), August 24, 2014.

41. See my earlier account in "Phantom Democracy."

42. Shi Rong and Guo Jiu Hui, "Chinese Official Suspended for Asking 'People or Party?,'" Xinhua News Agency, June 22, 2009; my *When Trees Fall, Monkeys Scatter;* and my "A Canopy of Deadening Silence: The Beijing Media Assault on Hong Kong Citizens," *The Conversation*, October 15, 2014, http://theconversation.com/a-canopy-of-deadening-silence-the-beijing-media-assault-on-hong-kong-citizens-32543.

43. Steven Mufson, "This Documentary Went Viral in China. Then It Was Censored. It Won't Be Forgotten," *Washington Post*, March 16, 2015.

44. Harold Innis Adams, *The Bias of Communication* (Toronto, 1951); the point is further developed in Keane, *Democracy and Media Decadence*, pp. 1–76, 113.

45. Evgeny Morozov contrasts the "digital activist" with the "slacktivist," who is seen as the "more dangerous digital sibling, which all too often leads to civic promiscuity—usually the result of a mad shopping binge in the online identity supermarket." See Evgeny Morozov, *The Net Delusion: The Dark Side of Internet Freedom* (New York, 2012), pp. 70–71, 190–191.

46. The concept of a distributed network is first outlined in Paul Baran, *On Distributed Communications* (Santa Monica, CA, 1964); see also Janet Abbate, *Inventing the Internet* (Cambridge, MA, 2000), pp. 20–39, and the

analysis of distributed networks and power in W. Lance Bennett and Alexandra Segerberg, *The Logic of Connective Action: Digital Media and the Personalization of Contentious Politics* (Cambridge, 2013), p. 148.

47. Max Weber, *The Theory of Social and Economic Organization* (New York, 2010), p. 152.

48. Hannah Arendt, *On Violence* (Orlando, FL, 1970), p. 44.

49. "Public Opinion via Internet," *China Daily,* December 16, 2010.

50. Guohong Zhao, "提高执政党在新传播环境下的社会管理能力" [Enhance the Party's social management capability in new communication environment], *Study Times,* March 14, 2011.

51. "蔚蓝地图 (污染地图2.0版)" [Blue Map (pollution map 2.0 version)], March 19, 2015, http://mp.weixin.qq.com/s?__biz=MzA3NjM4MjcxNQ==&mid=204781789&idx=1&sn=60ac3993ec39e4e3cbdf0b3cef7c1d58&scene=18&scene=5#rd.

Velvet Fists

1. Montesquieu, *De l'esprit des lois* (Paris, 1979 [1748]), book 2, chapter 5, p. 141.

2. David Bandurski, "Propaganda Leaders Scurry off to Carry out the 'Spirit' of Hu Jintao's 'Important' Media Speech," China Media Project, June 25, 2008, http://cmp.hku.hk/2008/06/25/1079. On the parallel case of Vietnam, see Hai Hong Nguyen, *Political Dynamics of Grassroots Democracy in Vietnam* (London, 2016).

3. Nazanin Shahrokni, "The Politics of Polling: Polling and the Constitution of Counter-publics during 'Reform' in Iran," *Current Sociology* 60, no. 2 (March 2012): 202–221.

4. John Keane, *When Trees Fall, Monkeys Scatter: Rethinking Democracy in China* (London, 2017), 30–40. See also Suzanne Ogden, *Inklings of Democracy in China* (Cambridge, MA, 2002), pp. 385–386, and Wenfang Tang, *Populist Authoritarianism: Chinese Political Culture and Regime Sustainability* (Oxford, 2016), pp. 15–19.

5. John Keane, "Eine Partei Soll Smart Werden: Ein Gespräch mit Yu Keping über Die Zukunft der Kommunistischen Partei Chinas," *WZB-Mitteilungen* 144 (June 2014): 13–15.

6. Quotation sources and further details are provided in John Keane, "Tibet: Or, How to Ruin Democracy," *The Conversation,* March 30, 2013, https://theconversation.com/tibet-or-how-to-ruin-democracy-13075.

7. "Views of Chinese President—Global Indicators Database," Pew Research Center Global Attitudes Project, August 2015, http://www.pewglobal.org/database.

8. Frank Dikötter, *The Tragedy of Liberation: A History of the Chinese Revolution, 1945–57* (New York, 2013), pp. 100–103, 292–305; Dikötter, *Mao's Great Famine: The History of China's Most Devastating Catastrophe, 1958–62* (London, 2010).

9. Levada Center, "O tsentre" [About the center], https://www.levada.ru/nopisanie/o-tsentre.

10. All information about C-POR'S surveys can be found in its official website, http://www.c-por.org. Some details in this section are drawn from my lengthy interview with David Lao, a senior researcher at the Canton Public Opinion Research Center, Guangzhou, April 14, 2015.

11. "广州停车场涨价方案引争议 专业停车场或迎建设潮_扬子晚报网" [The proposal to increase parking fee in Guangzhou caused debate. More parking venues will be built], *Yangtze Evening News,* March 14, 2014, http://www.yangtse.com/system/2014/03/14/020523136.shtml; see also "广州停车费调整听证昨举行-中新网" [Public hearing on the increase of parking fee in Guangzhou was held yesterday], *Southern Daily,* March 29, 2014, http://finance.chinanews.com/auto/2014/03-29/6007919.shtml.

12. "市民多不赞成提高停车费, 质疑治堵效果" [Most citizens don't support the parking fee increase and challenge the effect of the proposal], Canton Public Opinion Research Center, March 12, 2014, http://www.c-por.org/index.php?c=news&a=ztdetail&id=2398&pid=55.

13. Li Gongming, "停车费有望降价,"涨价治堵论"还坚挺否?" [Parking fee is likely to drop. Can the proposal to manage traffic jam through increasing parking fee stand?], *New Express Daily,* July 5, 2015, http://news.163.com/15/0507/01/AOVNDV7F00014Q4P.html.

14. Walter Lippmann, *The Phantom Public* (New York, 1925).

15. Compare the oft-cited formulation of David Hume, "Of the First Principles of Government," in *Hume: Political Essays,* ed. Knud Haakonssen (Cambridge, 1994), p. 16: "Nothing appears more surprizing to those, who

consider human affairs with a philosophical eye, than the easiness with which the many are governed by the few; and the implicit submission, with which men resign their own sentiments and passions to those of their rulers. When we inquire by what means this wonder is effected, we shall find, that, as force is always on the side of the governed, the governors have nothing to support them but opinion. It is therefore, on opinion only that government is founded; and this maxim extends to the most despotic and most military governments, as well as to the most free and most popular."

16. Thomas Hobbes, *The Elements, etc.,* ed. Ferdinand Tönnies (Cambridge, 1928 [1650]), part I, chapter 19, section 11, p. 81. John Locke's *Two Treatises of Government* (1689) turned this understanding against Hobbes, to say that "despotical power" is "an absolute, arbitrary power one man has over another, to take away his life whenever he pleases" (in *The Works of John Locke* [London, 1823], Essay Two, section 15, p. 181).

17. Thomas Hobbes, *De Corpore Politico: Or, The Elements of Law, Moral and Politic* (London, 1655), part 2, chapter 3, in *The English Works of Thomas Hobbes of Malmesbury,* ed. Sir William Molesworth (London, 1840), pp. 149–150; Samuel Johnson, *A Dictionary of the English Language in Which the Words Are Deduced from Their Originals* (London, 1786 [1755]); see also Elias Canetti, "The Despot's Hostility to Survivors, Rulers and Their Successors," in *Crowds and Power* (Harmondsworth, UK, 1984), pp. 283–287.

18. Franz Neumann, "Notes on the Theory of Dictatorship," in *The Democratic and the Authoritarian State: Essays in Political and Legal Theory,* ed. Herbert Marcuse (London, 1957), p. 245.

19. John O. Koehler, *Stasi: The Untold Story of the East German Secret Police* (Boulder, CO, 2000); Jens Gieseke, *The History of the Stasi: East Germany's Secret Police 1945–1990* (New York, 2014).

20. Herodotus, *The Histories,* 5.92–5.93. According to the tale, a messenger sent by a far-distant ruler to the court of Thrasybulus, seventh-century BC tyrant of Miletus, seeks advice on how best to govern. Strolling through nearby fields, carefully watched by his guards, Thrasybulus falls silent, then suddenly answers by picking up a scythe and wading into a crop of ripening wheat to lop the tallest and best-formed ears of wheat; Aristotle narrates a different version of the same story in *Politics,* 5, 1311a. Compare Niccolò Machiavelli, *Life of Castruccio Castracani* (London, 2003 [1520]), pp. 13–14, 37.

21. Cherian George, "Consolidating Authoritarian Rule: Calibrated Coercion in Singapore," *Pacific Review* 20, no. 2 (2007): 127–145.

22. Chevalier de Jaucourt, "Despotisme," *Encyclopédie,* vol. 4 (Paris, 1754), p. 887: "In the despotic states . . . it happens that whoever ascends the throne first strangles his brothers, as in Turkey; or renders them blind, as in Persia; or turns them mad, as in the case of the Mogul: or, if these precautions are not taken, as in Morocco, each vacancy of the throne is followed by a frightful civil war" (my translation).

23. An ancient saying reportedly inspired by the surprise misfortune of the first king of Samos, Ancaeus. Defying a prophecy that he wouldn't live long enough to taste the wine produced from his own vineyards, Ancaeus staged a magnificent celebration of its first vintage. While raising the first goblet of the newly pressed wine to his lips, Ancaeus was suddenly interrupted. A courtier whispered in his ear that a wild boar had just begun to rampage through his vineyards. Startled, he rushed there to chase away the animal, only to be gored to death.

24. Lucian, "Phalaris," in *Phalaris, Hippias or The Bath and Other Works,* vol. 1 (Cambridge, MA, 1913).

25. Cited in Anne Quinney, "Excess and Identity: The Franco-Romanian Ionesco Combats Rhinoceritis," *South Central Review* 24, no. 3 (2007): 46–47; Eugène Ionesco, *Rhinoceros and Other Plays* (New York, 1960).

26. From the WikiLeaks cable, SECRET SECTION 01 OF 03 BAKU 000054 SIPDIS, January 27, 2010, 13:10, published at https://www.theguardian.com /world/us-embassy-cables-documents/245758.

27. Ian Traynor, "Hungary PM: Bring Back Death Penalty and Build Work Camps for Immigrants," *Guardian,* April 29, 2015.

28. Amnesty International UK, "Waleed Abu al-Khair, Imprisoned in Saudi Arabia for Defending Human Rights," January 12, 2018, https://www .amnesty.org.uk/saudi-arabia-free-human-rights-lawyer-waleed-abulkhair -abu-al-khair.

29. "Islam-Fearing Tajikistan Says Hijab Is for Prostitutes," Eurasianet, April 1, 2015, http://www.eurasianet.org/node/72816.

30. Darius Rejali, *Torture and Democracy* (Princeton, NJ, 2009).

31. Hannah Arendt, *The Origins of Totalitarianism* (New York, 1973 [1951]), p. 445.

32. See Mark Button and Peter Stiernstedt, "Comparing Private Security Regulation in the European Union," *Policing and Society* 28, no. 4 (2016): 398–414. See also European Parliament, Directorate-General for External Policies, *The Role of Private Security Companies (PSCs) in CSDP Missions and Operations* (Brussels, 2011): "This report demonstrates that potential negative effects range from decreased democratic accountability and governmental control to the perceptions of contractor impunity and insecurity among the civilian populations of host states. There is no catch-all solution to these problems, and for many governments the advantages of hiring private security contractors, such as the ability to fill urgent capability and personnel gaps, cost-efficiency and specialist expertise, outweigh the disadvantages" (p. 5).

33. Mehran Kamrava, *Qatar: Small State, Big Politics* (Ithaca, NY, 2015), pp. 135–139.

34. Consider the written constitution of the People's Republic of China. According to its second chapter, which covers the fundamental rights and duties of citizens, every citizen is equal before the law (Article 33). All citizens who have reached the age of eighteen enjoy the right to vote and to stand for election (Article 34). Every citizen is blessed with the freedoms of communication, civil association, and public assembly (Article 35). The generous entitlement to "enjoy freedom of religious belief" is granted, sensibly, on the condition that citizens don't engage in activities that "disrupt public order, impair the health of citizens or interfere with the educational system of the state" (Article 36). Citizens enjoy habeas corpus and personal dignity, and "insult, libel, false charge or frame-up" directed against them is strictly prohibited (Articles 37–38). Their rights to privacy are inviolable (Article 39), and all citizens of the People's Republic of China have the right to "criticize and make suggestions to any state organ or functionary" (Article 41).

35. See, for example, Manlio Bellomo, *The Common Legal Past of Europe: 1000–1800* (Washington, DC, 1995), and Richard Potz, "Islam and Islamic Law in European Legal History Islam and Islamic Law," European History Online, November 21, 2011, http://ieg-ego.eu/en/threads/models-and-stereotypes /from-the-turkish-menace-to-orientalism/richard-potz-islam-and-islamic -law-in-european-legal-history.

36. Yu Jiang, "近代中国法学语词的形成与发展" [Formation and development of modern Chinese legal language and terms], in 中西法律传统 [Chinese and western legal tradition], vol. 1 (Beijing, 2001).

37. The following section draws upon Martin Krygier, "The Rule of Law," in *The Oxford Handbook of Comparative Constitutional Law,* ed. Michel Rosenfeld and András Sajó (Oxford, 2012), 233–249, and Martin Krygier, "The Rule of Law: Legality, Teleology, Sociology," in *Relocating the Rule of Law,* ed. Gianluigi Palombella and Neil Walker (Oxford, 2009), pp. 45–69.

38. Chevalier de Jaucourt, "Despotisme," in *Encyclopédie,* vol. 4 (Paris, 1754), p. 888.

39. Randall Peerenboom, *China's Long March toward Rule of Law* (Cambridge, 2002), p. 7; cf. John Gillespie, "Understanding Legality in Vietnam," in *Vietnam's New Order,* ed. Stephanie Balme and Mark Sidel (New York, 2007).

40. An Baijie, "Xi Jinping Vows 'Power within Cage of Regulations,'" *China Daily,* January 23, 2013.

41. David L. Shambaugh, *China Goes Global: The Partial Power* (Oxford, 2013); Xi Jinping, "Working Together for a New Progress of Security and Development in Asia," speech in Dushanbe, June 15, 2019, https://www.fmprc.gov.cn/mfa_eng/zxxx_662805/t1673167.shtml.

42. Stephen Olson and Clyde Prestowitz, *The Evolving Role of China in International Institutions* (Washington, DC, 2011), p. 11, http://www.uscc.gov/research_archive.

43. Li Xiaojun, "Learning and Socialization in International Institutions: China's Experience with the WTO Dispute Settlement System," in *China Joins Global Governance,* ed. Mingjiang Li (Lanham, MD, 2012), pp. 75–94; Xiaojun Li, "Understanding China's Behavioral Change in the WTO Dispute Settlement System," *Asian Survey* 52, no. 6 (December 2012): 1111–1137.

44. "Firmly Safeguard Rule of Law in HK: People's Daily," *Xinhua News,* October 4, 2014, http://news.xinhuanet.com/english/china/2014–10/04/c_133691607.htm.

45. Along these lines, see the interesting introductory comments by Yan Fu on Chinese understandings of "law" in Montesquieu, 法意 [The spirit of the laws], trans. Yan Fu (Beijing, 1981), p. 2; Jothie Rajah, *Authoritarian Rule of Law: Legislation, Discourse and Legitimacy in Singapore* (New York, 2012); Karen Turner-Gottschang, James V. Feinerman, and R. Kent Guy, eds., *The*

Limits of the Rule of Law in China (Seattle, WA, 2015); Xiaobo Lu, *Cadres and Corruption: The Organizational Involution of the Chinese Communist Party* (Stanford, CA, 2000); Tom Ginsburg and Tamir Moustafa, eds., *Rule by Law: The Politics of Courts in Authoritarian Regimes* (New York, 2008); and Kim Lane Scheppele, "Autocratic Legalism," *University of Chicago Law Review* 85, no. 545 (2018): 545–583.

46. Kathryn Hendley, *Everyday Law in Russia* (Ithaca, NY, 2017).

47. Dan Washburn, *The Forbidden Game: Golf and the Chinese Dream* (London, 2014).

48. The famous "dual state" thesis, first outlined in Ernst Fraenkel's *The Dual State: A Contribution to the Theory of Dictatorship* (Oxford, 2017 [1941]), refers to a polity marked by a "line of division" between "a "normative state" that generally respects its own laws, and a "prerogative state" that violates the very same laws" (p. xiii).

49. See the contrasting interpretations by Rebecca Liao, "Why Bo Xilai's Trial Is a Victory for the Rule of Law in China," *The Atlantic,* August 7, 2013, and Donald Clarke, "The Bo Xilai Trial and China's 'Rule of Law': Same Old, Same Old," *The Atlantic,* August 21, 2013.

50. The original link to Xi's speech is no longer available, but it can be retrieved from the Internet Archive: "习近平重提 '刀把子' 论有什么深意?" [Why did Xi bring up again the "knife handle"?), People.cn, March 27, 2015, https://web.archive.org/web/20150327194201/http://politics.people.com.cn /n/2015/0120/c1001-26419531.html.

Why Despotism?

1. Franco Venturi, "Oriental Despotism," *Journal of the History of Ideas* 24 (1963): 133–142; R. Koebner, "Despot and Despotism: Vicissitudes of a Political Term," *Journal of the Warburg and Courtauld Institutes* 14 (1951): 293–296; Patricia Springborg, "The Contractual State: Reflections on Orientalism and Despotism," *History of Political Thought* 8, no. 3 (Winter 1987): 395–433; Alain Grosrichard, *Structure du sérail: La fiction du despotisme asiatique dans l'Occident classique* (Paris, 1979).

2. Alexander Dow, *The History of Hindostan,* vol. 3 (London, 1772), pp. vii–xxxvii.

3. The following quotations are drawn from Abraham-Hyacinthe Anquetil-Duperron, *Législation orientale* (Amsterdam, 1778), pp. 1–13.

4. Hanna Batatu, *The Old Social Classes and the Revolutionary Movements of Iraq* (Princeton, NJ, 1978) has shown that modern despotism in the world of Islam was typically the poisonous fruit of concerted efforts by European colonizers to destroy local civil society institutions, customs, and codes of law and to install and support mocked-up kings, shahs, and one-party rulers. Mikhail Rostovtzeff's classic *Caravan Cities* (Oxford, 1932) describes the long history of contractual legal codes that served in the same region to protect the property and rights of traders well before the European invasions and conquests.

5. Cesare Beccaria, *An Essay on Crimes and Punishments* (London, 1804), pp. 111–112. The positive defense of despotic power by name is usually credited to the French political writer Charles-Irénée Castel, abbé de Saint-Pierre, still well known today for his visionary proposals for international peace. Castel was sure that a strong, undivided monarchic state could benevolently protect its subjects from the mischief caused by petty tyrants, such that "when power is united to reason, it cannot be too great or too despotic for the greatest utility of society" ("Pour perfectioner le Gouvernement des Etats," in *Ouvrajes de politique,* vol. 3 [Rotterdam, 1733], p. 197).

6. Giuseppe Gorani, *Il vero dispotismo* (London, 1770); François Quesnay, "Foreword," *Le Despotisme de la Chine* (Paris, 1767), in Lewis A. Maverick, *China, a Model for Europe* (San Antonio, TX, 1946), pp. 141, 264. The ways of thinking and practical contributions of the Physiocrats are well captured by Georges Weulersse, *Le mouvement physiocratique en France* (Paris, 1910).

7. The eighteenth-century intellectual fascination with the vision of undivided state power as "an almighty pedagogue" is emphasized by Carl Schmitt, *Die Diktatur: Von den Anfängen des modernen Souveränitätsgedankens bis zum proletarischen Klassenkampf* (Berlin, 1978 [1928]), pp. 97–129.

8. The attack on "les triste effets de la puissance arbitraire et despotique de la cour de France" was led by the anonymously published series of "mémoires" or dissertations, *Les soupirs de la France esclave, qui aspire après la liberté* [The sighs of an enslaved France who yearns after liberty] (Amsterdam, 1689), part 3, September 15, p. 29. Often attributed to the French Calvinist pastor Pierre Jurieu (1637–1713), its attack on selfish and reckless uses of power caused a great stir despite its banning and burning by the royal censors.

9. Frederick of Prussia, *Refutation of Machiavelli's Prince: or, Anti-Machiavel,* ed. Paul Sonnino (Athens, OH, 1981), pp. 32–33: "Just as kings can do good when they want to do it, they can do evil whenever they please. . . . In every country there are honest and dishonest people just as in every family there are handsome persons along with one-eyed, hunchbacks, blind, and cripples. . . . [T]here are and always will be monsters among princes, unworthy of the character with which they are invested."

10. Denis Diderot, *Mémoires pour Catherine II,* ed. Paul Vernière (Paris, 1966), pp. 117–118. The follow-up remark is found in the best-selling anticolonial tract by Abbé Raynal, *A Philosophical and Political History of the Settlements and Trade of the Europeans in the West and East Indies,* vol. 8 (London, 1783), p. 32.

11. Jean-Louis Carra, *L'orateur des Etats-Généraux, pour 1789* (Paris, 1789), p. 12.

12. Vicesimus Knox, *The Spirit of Despotism* (London, 1795), pp. 3, 27. As the forces of Jacobinism seized the upper hand during the early phase of the French Revolution, Knox (unlike poor Jean-Louis Carra) saved his skin by recalling the work and thereafter refused publication until an anonymous edition appeared in 1821.

13. Thomas Paine, *Rights of Man, Being an Answer to Mr. Burke's Attack on the French Revolution* (London, 1791), p. 132; and see my *Tom Paine: A Political Life* (London, 1995).

14. Michel Foucault, *Abnormal: Lectures at the Collège de France 1974–1975* (London, 2003), pp. 94–95: "The despot can promote his will over the entire social body only through a permanent state of violence. . . . The despot is the permanent outlaw, the individual without social ties. The despot is the man alone. The despot is someone who . . . performs the greatest crime, the crime par excellence, of a total breach of the social pact by which the very body of society can exist and maintain itself. . . . The despot is the individual who promotes his violence, his whims, and his irrationality as the general law or *raison d'Etat.* . . . The first monster is the king. The king . . . is the general model from which, through successive historical shifts and transformations, the countless little monsters who people nineteenth-century psychiatry and legal psychiatry are historically derived. . . . All human monsters are descendants of Louis XVI."

15. John Adams to Thomas Jefferson (Quincy), November 13, 1815, and Thomas Jefferson to John Adams (Monticello), September 12, 1821, Founders Online, National Archives. The promiscuity of the language of despotism was evident in the well-known plea of Abigail Adams to her husband to "remember the Ladies, and be more generous and favorable to them than your ancestors" because all men "would be tyrants if they could" (March 31, 1776). John Adams replied, as men still do, that in practice men "have only the Name of Masters," so empowering women further would bring the "Despotism of the Peticoat" (April 14, 1776). Adams Family Papers, Massachusetts Historical Society, https://www.masshist.org/digitaladams/archive/doc?id=L17760414ja.

16. James Mill, *The History of British India*, 2nd ed., vol. 2 (London, 1820), pp. 166–167; John Stuart Mill, "Considerations on Representative Government," in *Collected Works of John Stuart Mill*, vol. 19, ed. John M. Robson (Toronto, 1977), p. 567; Mill, "On Liberty," in *Collected Works of John Stuart Mill*, vol. 18, ed. John M. Robson (Toronto, 1977), p. 224.

17. Webster's *Complete Dictionary of the English Language*, revised and improved by Chauncey A. Goodrich and Noah Porter (London, 1886), p. 363.

18. See Emile Durkheim, *Montesquieu: Quid secundatus politicae scientiae instituendae contulerit*, ed. W. Watts Willer (Oxford, 1997 [1892]), 29e, 31e, 39e–40e, 41e.

19. The few examples worth noting include the attack by Lord Hewart, lord chief justice of England, on the Westminster Parliament's surrender of its precious legislative powers to the "administrative lawlessness" of a bloated civil service bureaucracy in *The New Despotism* (London, 1929); the Tocqueville-style defense of the "old American 'horse and buggy' road of democracy with the Constitution as its foundation" against the worship of state power by the "Prophets of the New Deal" in Raoul E. Desvernine, *Democratic Despotism* (New York, 1936), pp. 231–243; the antifascist reflections of Charles E. Merriam, *The New Democracy and the New Despotism* (New York, 1939); Harold D. Lasswell, "Democracy, Despotism and Style [1949]," in *On Political Sociology* (Chicago, 1977), pp. 251–256 (Lasswell was the consultant for the short documentary *Despotism* [Encyclopaedia Britannica Films, 1946], https://www.youtube.com/watch?v=2L3N0StxYSw); and Robert Nisbet's account of the dangers posed to a "free society" by centralized "military, police, and bureaucratic power" in "The New Despotism," *Commentary*, June 1975, pp. 31–43.

20. See my detailed diagnosis of the term authoritarianism in *When Trees Fall, Monkeys Scatter: Rethinking Democracy in China* (London, 2017).

21. These key points are examined at length in my *Power and Humility: The Future of Monitory Democracy* (Cambridge, 2018), especially part 1.

22. See Carl Joachim Friedrich, *Authority* (Cambridge, MA, 1958); Chen Fengjun, "On the Conception and Contributing Factor of Authoritarianism," *Southeast Asian Studies* 4 (2000): 68–73; and Huang Wansheng, "A Dialogue on the Critiques of the New Authoritarianism," *Chinese Sociology and Anthropology* 23, no. 2 (1990): 77–93.

23. Denis Diderot, "Autorité Politique," in *Encyclopédie, ou dictionnaire raisonné des sciences, des arts et des métiers, etc.*, vol. 1, ed. Denis Diderot and Jean le Rond d'Alembert (Paris, 1751), p. 898.

24. Harold D. Lasswell, "Style in Political Communications," in *On Political Sociology* (Chicago, 1977), p. 251.

25. Nicolas-Antoine Boulanger, *Recherches sur l'origine du despotisme oriental* (1761), in *Oeuvres*, vol. 3 (Amsterdam, 1794), pp. 11–12; Oscar Wilde, *The Soul of Man under Socialism* (London, 1900), 73: "There are three kinds of despots. There is the despot who tyrannises over the body. There is the despot who tyrannises over the soul. There is the despot who tyrannises over the soul and body alike. The first is called the Prince. The second is called the Pope. The third is called the People."

26. The following quotations are my translations, drawn from Étienne de La Boétie *Le discours de la servitude volontaire*, ed. Pierre Léonard (Paris, 1976).

27. Denis Diderot, "Refutation of Helvétius," in *Diderot's Selected Writings*, ed. Lester G. Crocker (New York, 1966), pp. 297–298.

28. George B. Cheever, *The Hierarchical Despotism, Lectures on the Mixture of Civil and Ecclesiastical Power in the Governments of the Middle Ages etc.* (New York, 1844).

29. On Fénelon and Montesquieu, see Louis Althusser, *Montesquieu-Rousseau-Marx: Politics and History* (London, 1972), pp. 82–83. For the early attacks on despotism by Thomas Gordon, see *The Works of Tacitus . . . To Which Are Prefixed Political Discourses upon That Author* (London, 1728–1731) and (with John Trenchard) *Independent Whig: Or, A Defence of Primitive Christianity* (London, 1721), and *Cato's Letters* (London, 1724).

30. Abbé Raynal, *A Philosophical and Political History of the Settlements and Trade of the Europeans in the West and East Indies*, vol. 8 (London, 1783), p. 32.

31. Jean-Baptiste le Rond D'Alembert, "Essai sur la société des gens de lettres et des grands," in *Mélanges de littérature, d'histoire et de philosophie* (Berlin, 1753), especially pp. 384–386, 398.

32. Edmund Burke, "A Vindication of Natural Society" (1756), in *The Works of the Right Honourable Edmund Burke*, vol. 1 (London, 1899), pp. 80–82.

33. Mill, "Considerations on Representative Government," p. 401.

34. The following quotations are from Alexis de Tocqueville, *De la démocratie en Amérique*, vol. 2, preface by François Furet (Paris, 1981), pp. 385, 379. All translations are my own.

Democracy's Future

1. Karl Marx, *Capital: A Critique of Political Economy*, vol. 1 (New York, 1906), pp. 440 and (quoting Friedrich Engels) 446: "The slavery in which the bourgeoisie has bound the proletariat, comes nowhere more plainly into daylight than in the factory system. In it all freedom comes to an end both at law and in fact. The workman must be in the factory at half past five. If he comes a few minutes late, he is punished. . . . He must eat, drink and sleep at word of command. . . . The despotic bell calls him from his bed, calls him from breakfast and dinner. And how does he fare in the mill? There the master is the absolute law-giver. He makes what regulations he pleases; he alters and makes additions to his code at pleasure . . . [T]he courts say to the workman: Since you have entered into this contract voluntarily, you must now carry it out. . . . These workmen are condemned to live, from their ninth year till their death, under this mental and bodily torture."

2. John Keane, "The European Graveyard," in *The Life and Death of Democracy* (London, 2009), pp. 455–581.

3. Plato, "The Republic," in *The Dialogues of Plato*, ed. Benjamin Jowett (New York, 1897), book VIII, section 562, p. 392; on the use by Greek commentators and critics alike of the now obsolete verb *demokrateo (δημοκρατέω)* and its relation to other words like *aristokratia (ἀριστοκρατία, "aristocracy")*, *ploutokratia (πλουτοκρατία, "the rule of the rich")*, and *monokratoria (μονοκρατορία, "monocracy" or "the rule of a single person")*, see my *The Life and Death of Democracy*, pp. 58–60.

4. Aili Mari Tripp, *Museveni's Uganda: Paradoxes of Power in a Hybrid Regime* (Boulder, CO, 2010), pp. 193–194. The dynamics of corruption are bitingly satirised in Pepetela [Artur Carlos Maurício Pestana dos Santos], *The Return of the Water Spirit* (Oxford, 2002).

5. Steven Levitsky and Lucan A. Way, *Competitive Authoritarianism: Hybrid Regimes after the Cold War* (Cambridge, 2010), p. 5. Their survey of thirty-five cases of "competitive authoritarianism" in Africa, Asia, Latin America, and postcommunist Eurasia concludes that during the period from 1990 through 2008, "where linkage to the West was high, competitive authoritarian regimes democratized."

6. Carole Cadwalladr, "Brexit, the Ministers, the Professor and the Spy: How Russia Pulls Strings in UK," *Guardian*, November 5, 2017.

7. Siva Vaidhyanathan, *Antisocial Media: How Facebook Disconnects Us and Undermines Democracy* (New York, 2018); Alina Polyakova and Spencer P. Boyer, *The Future of Political Warfare: Russia, the West, and the Coming Age of Global Digital Competition* (Washington, DC, 2018); and Robert S. Mueller III, *Report on the Investigation into Russian Interference in the 2016 Presidential Election*, vol. 1 (Washington, DC, 2019).

8. Oliver Stuenkel, *Post-Western World: How Emerging Powers Are Remaking Global Order* (Cambridge, 2016); and John Keane, "The New Chinese Empire," *Focus* (Johannesburg) 85 (June 2019): 8–15.

9. Matt Taibbi, "The Great American Bubble Machine," *Rolling Stone*, April 5, 2010.

10. Cited in Walt Bogdanich and Michael Forsythe, "How McKinsey Has Helped Raise the Stature of Authoritarian Governments," *New York Times*, December 15, 2018.

11. Louis-Philippe, comte de Ségur, *Mémoires, souvenirs, et anecdotes, par le comte de Ségur*, vol. 1, in *Bibliothèque des mémoires: Relatif à l'histoire de France; Pendant le 18e siècle*, vol. 19, ed. F. Barrière (Paris, 1859), p. 345.

12. Many of these trends are diagnosed in my *Power and Humility: The Future of Monitory Democracy* (Cambridge, 2018). See also Jane Mayer, *Dark Money: The Hidden History of the Billionaires Behind the Rise of the Radical Right* (New York, 2016); Thomas Piketty, *Capital in the Twenty-First Century* (Cambridge, MA, 2014); and Nadia Urbinati and Arturo Zampaglione, *The Antiegalitarian Mutation: The Failure of Institutional Politics in Liberal Democracies* (New York, 2016).

13. John Keane, "Why Google Is a Political Matter: A Conversation with Julian Assange," *The Monthly,* June 2015, https://www.themonthly.com.au /issue/2015/june/1433080800/john-keane/why-google-political-matter; Shoshana Zuboff, *The Age of Surveillance Capitalism: The Fight for a Human Future at the New Frontier of Power* (New York, 2019).

14. Sean Hannity, *Deliver Us from Evil: Defeating Terrorism, Despotism, and Liberalism* (New York, 2004), p. 5; Sean Hannity, "Interview with Secretary of State Michael R. Pompeo," US Department of State, Washington, DC, November 2, 2018, https://www.state.gov/secretary/remarks/2018/11/287101 .htm.

15. Michael J. Barry, "The Sword," in *Benham's Book of Quotations* (London, 1948), p. 18a.

16. The points are discussed at length in my *Reflections on Violence* (London, 1996), *Violence and Democracy* (Cambridge, 2004), and *Power and Humility,* pp. 377–436.

17. See my "Does Democracy Have a Violent Heart?," in *Power and Humility,* pp. 379–409; and the remark by Bertrand Russell that "war is the chief promoter of despotism," in his *Power: A New Social Analysis* (London, 1938), p. 309.

18. Adam Ferguson, *An Essay on the History of Civil Society* (Edinburgh, 1966 [1767]), pp. 278–279.

19. Andreas Bieler and Adam David Morton, *Global Capitalism, Global War, Global Crisis* (Cambridge, 2018).

20. "United States Cannot Crush Us, Says Huawei Founder Ren Zhengfei," *Straits Times* (Singapore), February 19, 2019; Xi Jinping, *Secure a Decisive Victory in Building a Moderately Prosperous Society in All Respects and Strive for the Great Success of Socialism with Chinese Characteristics for a New Era,* report delivered at the 19th National Congress of the Communist Party of China, October 18, 2017, p. 23, http://www.xinhuanet.com/english/download /Xi_Jinping's_report_at_19th_CPC_National_Congress.pdf.

21. Denis Diderot, "Extracts from the Histoire des Deux Indes," in *Political Writings,* ed. John Hope Mason and Robert Wokler (Cambridge, 1992), p. 174. My *The Life and Death of Democracy* can fruitfully be read as an extended commentary on this remark, as a lengthy effort to redefine democracy as the most effective political weapon for dealing with the follies and catastrophes

that surely flow from the hubris produced by concentrations of arbitrary power.

22. See my "Despotism and Democracy: The Origins and Development of the Distinction between Civil Society and the State 1750–1850," in *Civil Society and the State: New European Perspectives,* ed. John Keane (London, 1988), pp. 35–71; and Leonard Krieger, *An Essay on the Theory of Enlightened Despotism* (Chicago, 1975), pp. 37–39. The remark about empowerment through group association is made in correspondence by Gustave de Beaumont to Tocqueville, cited in George Wilson Pierson, *Tocqueville and Beaumont in America* (New York, 1938), p. 101.

23. Zeynep Tufekci, *Twitter and Tear Gas: The Power and the Fragility of Networked Protest* (Princeton, NJ, 2017); Gene Sharp, *From Dictatorship to Democracy: A Conceptual Framework for Liberation* (London, 2011); Simon Tormey, *The End of Representative Politics* (Cambridge, 2015); Michael Walzer, *Political Action: A Practical Guide to Movement Politics* (New York, 2019). The strategic importance of laughter is analyzed in Li Mingtao, "Why They Say Autocratic Regimes Are Laughed to Death," *China Digital Times,* March 25, 2016, https://chinadigitaltimes.net/2016/03/translation-autocracies-laughed -death: "When someone dares to laugh, they remove a brick from the wall of despotism. When more and more people can't help but laugh, the wall is further dismantled. When everyone laughs together, the regime is basically at its end. Ceausescu's final speech, which began in strength and ended with flight, best reflects this change" (my translation).

24. Details of possible new democratic institutions and innovative strategies are discussed at length in my *Power and Humility.*

25. Andreas Schedler, *The Politics of Uncertainty: Sustaining and Subverting Electoral Authoritarianism* (Oxford, 2013).

Index

Index

Index   303

Index